T-Shirt
Swim Club

T-Shirt Swim Club

*Stories from Being Fat
in a World of Thin People*

IAN KARMEL
AND
ALISA KARMEL, PsyD, MScN

RODALE
NEW YORK

Published in the United States by Rodale Books, an imprint of
Random House, a division of Penguin Random House LLC, New York.

RODALE and the Plant colophon are registered trademarks of
Penguin Random House LLC.

LIBRARY OF CONGRESS CATALOGING-IN-PUBLICATION DATA
Names: Karmel, Ian, author. | Karmel, Alisa, author.
Title: T-shirt swim club : stories from being fat in a world of thin people /
Ian Karmel and Alisa Karmel, PsyD, MScN.
Description: New York : Rodale, [2024] | Includes bibliographical references.
Identifiers: LCCN 2023044393 (print) | LCCN 2023044394 (ebook) |
ISBN 9780593580929 (hardcover) | ISBN 9780593580936 (ebook)
Subjects: LCSH: Body image—Social aspects. | Fat-acceptance movement. |
Overweight persons—Social conditions. | Overweight persons—Public
opinion. | Overweight persons—Attitudes.
Classification: LCC BF697.5.B63 K37 2024 (print) | LCC BF697.5.B63
(ebook) | DDC 306.4/613—dc23/eng/20231017
LC record available at https://lccn.loc.gov/2023044393
LC ebook record available at https://lccn.loc.gov/2023044394

Printed in the United States of America on acid-free paper

rodalebooks.com
randomhousebooks.com

2 4 6 8 9 7 5 3 1

First Edition

Book design by Alexis Flynn

Dedicated to all the fat kids. It gets butter. Better!
Sorry. Better. It gets better.

CONTENTS

What Now?

INTRODUCTION

Welcome to the T-Shirt Swim Club. Some of you have been members for a long time and need no introduction. Some of you are new. Grab a chair. It's one of those good metal chairs, not one of the flimsy plastic ones you're worried about collapsing the entire time you're sitting in it. Some of you are wondering if you're in the right place, and the rest of you are just visiting, so let me get you up to speed. We're going to talk about being a fat person and how the world treats fat people. We're going to talk about how we (fat people) treat ourselves (terrible news—not well). The T-Shirt Swim Club is an open space where we can talk about how it feels to walk down the aisle of an airplane while the other passengers look at us with contempt in their eyes, as if we were holding three crying babies and a service donkey, praying we're not headed for that empty seat to their left. This club is about gym class and chafing. This club is about crying in the fitting room at Sears. This club is about sex and how fat people actually do have it. This club is about hating people for not loving you enough and hating yourself for the same reason.

This club isn't Weight Watchers. It's Lunchables and Gushers; Chinese buffets and chicken wings; pizza and beer. And then it's shame and kale smoothies for a month until it's time for chicken wings again.

Once you become a member of this club, you can never leave, because even when you stop wearing T-shirts in the pool, you'll always remember how it felt . . . the clingy, wet T-shirts and all the screwed-up feelings about being fat that made you think wearing one in the water was a good idea in the first place. Fat is forever. Even if you get less fat, fat is forever.

Quick side note—I'm going to use the term "fat." I'm going to call myself fat, I'm going to call other people fat, I'm going to refer to "fatness" as a general concept, and I'm going to use other phrases, too, but I didn't avoid "fat" for the first thirty-five years of my life and I'm not going to start now. It's a loaded word, but I don't think it's the word's fault that we treat fat people like garbage.

I'm Ian Karmel. In my life I've weighed 8 pounds and I've weighed 420 pounds, and right now I'm almost exactly in between the two. What I hope to do here, other than reminisce about discontinued snacks and Big Dogs T-shirts, is share how it feels to be fat and why it feels like that. I want to make an attempt at understanding myself, and I want to get as specific as possible while I'm doing that because I genuinely believe it's the only way to be relatable. I want to find other people like me out there, on every part of the journey. I want to find the kids stress-eating prosciutto, the grown-ups grimacing while they pull a third set of utensils out of the Chinese food delivery for one, the people disassociating while a doctor lectures them and when digging through a pile of shirts that almost fit to find the one that does. I want to find the person out there who is killing themselves with food because it's the most delicious way to kill yourself. Just like I was. I want to find you; I want to find me; I want us to know that we aren't alone. Unfortunately, I'm dumb as hell. Seriously, my spell-check is threatening to get a lawyer. I actually need to wrap this up to get to a time-share presentation. I'm dumb.

Thankfully, for all of us, the co-president of the club is my brilliant sister.

Alisa and I have been fat our whole lives—she dealt with it by becoming a doctor of psychology. I dealt with it by becoming a comedian, which is the opposite of a doctor. In the pages that follow, I'm going to talk about my life as a fat person and she's going to come in at the end in a brilliant "What Now?" section to explain some concepts, clear up some misconceptions, and generally call me on my bullshit.

It's impossible to write a comprehensive book about being fat. It's too personal. Everyone's experience is unique. A fat person's relationship to the world, to their family, to themselves, to their fat, is completely different from someone else's. Gender, race, sexual preference, physical ability, economic background, religious background, food deserts, food desserts, and ten million other things factor into it. So this is just our story, and please know that Alisa and I, as two fat people, understand as well as anyone that yours might not be the same. This club is the acknowledgment that we're all on our own journeys with fat. It is also a hope that it doesn't always have to feel quite so lonely.

T-Shirt
Swim Club

FAT.

Alternately, depending on the user, an adjective, an insult, an excuse, an anachronism, a term of endearment, a medical definition, a compliment, an alarm, an epidemic, an after-thought, and sometimes olive oil.

CHAPTER 1

T-Shirt Swim Club

Before all the pain, pancakes, and persecution, I was just a cute, fat little baby. Fat babies have a 100 percent approval rating. Admiring onlookers swoon, cooing over their biscuit dough legs and impossible little ham hands. People lose their minds around a fat baby. They speak in tongues. They melt into a puddle and recongeal just long enough to explode into a cloud of confetti. A fat baby is basically a human corgi. When they enter a room, that room is a happier place. People greet them by saying "Well, hello there" in a voice they didn't know they had until they saw the fat baby. People love fat babies, and lucky for them, most babies are fat, but I enjoyed it so much that I just kept on going into adulthood. Life gets more complicated for the babies who stay fat.

Being a fat toddler wasn't bad, though. Being fat lends itself beautifully to toddling. The world hasn't tried to make you feel bad about being fat. The world hasn't really tried to make you feel anything about being fat. Your life has a lot less shame and a lot more crayons; it's great. Plus, you're in preschool. I loved preschool. I attended the Mittleman Jewish Community Center in Portland, Oregon, and I might have peaked in those years, to be honest. Spending all morning learning about Purim and dinosaurs, spending all afternoon in the lap pool next to bobbing bubbes, and in between, lunch. There's a café at the Mittleman that, to this day, has yet to receive its proper respect from the Michelin Guide. I had hot dogs at this café. I had hamburgers. I discovered the knish at this café. I still can't wrap my mind around how the knish isn't a mainstay of American cuisine. It's so bad for you and it tastes like God's perfect potato. Along with psychotherapy and Mel Brooks, the knish should be counted among the Jewish people's greatest contributions to American culture. This café also had steak fries like you wouldn't believe. These things were sturdy. An honest man could build a home from these fries and raise five generations of strapping Scandinavian sons within its ketchup-soaked walls. I'm carrying on about this food now, but that was kind of my issue even then. I loved to eat.

Maybe I'm putting it the wrong way. Saying "I love to eat" is like saying "I'm a big fan of music." Let me be clear: I'm crazy about eating—figuratively, certainly, but also literally. I delighted in a good-quality steak fry, but you could put a pile of uncooked spaghetti in front of me and I'd eat it. I'd eat coffee beans. I'd chug maple syrup. I ate like Pac-Man. I ate for the same reason that people climb Mount Everest. Because it's there. When I was a toddler, I was caught standing in front of an open fridge with a brick of butter in my mouth. It's a cute story now, it was a cute story then, but there were a couple of decades in between where it felt like darkly comic foreshadowing.

I didn't realize it at the time, but I was eating for a whole bunch of reasons other than my own hunger. How could I realize it? I was a kid! I had just found out about pizza. We should remind kids about the moment they discovered pizza when they find out Santa is fake, by the way. Like, hey, I know we screwed you over on that whole Santa thing, but remember when we told you about pizza and that turned out to be real? It would soften the blow. (Also, yes, I'm a Jew who celebrated Christmas. We're allowed. We wrote all the best Christmas songs.) So there I was, blasting pizza, blasting knishes, blasting uncooked spaghetti, full of wonder. Adults didn't say a cross word about it because when it comes to boys and their diets, adults are mostly just bothered by that kid who only eats chicken fingers. Can't take him anywhere. He'll be at the sushi spot asking for dino nuggets. Don't get me wrong, I would have housed a dino nugget at the sushi restaurant, too, but I was also the toddler who once ate so much pickled ginger that I puked all over the inside of my dad's car.

It's kind of cute when you start packing on weight as a little kid anyway. You're a chubby little guy. It's the best kind of little guy. I kept packing the weight on, though. Bit by bit. Bite by bite. I'm not sure why it got less cute as I got older, but it was made clear, in no uncertain terms, that it was much less cute. I weighed 300 pounds by middle school. I was up to 350 pounds by high school. By the time I was in my thirties, I had tipped myself up over 420 pounds. That's for later, though. I'm not done telling you about why I was spending so much time at the Mittleman Jewish Community Center.

It was because I loved swimming and the Mittleman, for some reason, had two glorious pools. One of them was a warm-water pool that was always full of old people and it tasted like salt. This led me to believe that old Jewish people taste like salt, and nothing I've discovered in the decades since has given me a reason to think otherwise. Probably they were sweating off a lifetime of lox and pastrami, and anyway, it was none of my business if they tasted like salt. I did my time in that pool, but it wasn't my preferred destination. That honor belonged to the twenty-five-yard lap pool one room over. Crystal blue, shimmering, immaculate. Lane dividers that looked like floating strands of supersized Chanukah-themed novelty rigatoni. I jumped in that water so many times and from such an early age that I can't tell if it's my earliest memory or just my favorite one. I learned to swim in that pool. First, holding on to my mom. Then holding on to the side of the pool. Then holding on to a kickboard. Then holding on to nothing. We'd get patches to mark our progress, and we'd sew them onto our towels. My towel was heavy with patches. My towel looked like the sash of a Boy Scout who would go on to become either a great father or a politician who tries to ban oxygen because trans people also breathe it.

I was an amazing swimmer. To be clear, I wasn't a fast swimmer, but I was amazing at it. From my experience, speed is the wrong rubric with which to judge someone's ability in the water anyway. Where are you trying to go in such a hurry, to a different, wetter part of the lake? Don't be ridiculous. Speed is beside the point. Splashing around with an agenda just wears you out. I had some friends who played water polo in high school and they told me that they'd swim so hard that they'd get hot. In a pool, they'd get hot. Where do you go once you're hot in a pool? You go to hell, that's where you go. Psych—you're already there.

I wasn't fast in the water, but I was graceful. As I got older and bigger and fatter, my size made me a little clumsy on land, but in the water I was still extremely nice with it. I moved like a hairy dolphin, or a less hairy sea otter, or an equally hairy walrus. I was liberated from gravity. I could flip and somersault and twist my body in ways that, had I tried them on the ground, would have landed me *in* the hospital and *on America's Funniest Home Videos.* I experienced true euphoria when moving through the water. I felt like I belonged there, like I was meant to be aquatic. My body, so often the source of frustration on dry land, felt like it made sense in the water, which is a notion soaked in irony because the swimming pool might have been the first place I ever realized that I was fat, and it all started with a T-shirt.

At some point fat kids started wearing T-shirts in pools. I do not understand exactly when it began, where it came from, or who we thought we were fooling, but it happened when I was a kid and it happens now. The world is full of fat kids wearing

T-shirts while they're swimming. Every pool, pond, lake, river, and ocean worth a damn on this entire planet is a T-Shirt Swim Club. I can follow the logic of the shirts in the pool, to an extent. I was a fat kid, I had a fat belly, and I was embarrassed about being a fat kid with my fat little belly because . . . well, because I just was, I guess. While I was certainly self-conscious, that was never going to be enough to keep me entirely out of the water. Instead, I elected to conceal my unacceptable adolescent body with a disguise so inept that it's very nearly darling—a T-shirt. A T-shirt that would almost immediately become sopping wet. You can tell someone's fat when they're wearing a regular shirt, but when that thing becomes wet, it hugs the curves like crazy. It clings to the body like a baby that somebody is trying to hand to an uncle. A T-shirt in a pool does not obscure the fact that someone is fat. Instead, it accentuates everything, and it does so through a translucent cotton Big Dogs filter. The tragedy of the T-shirt is that it accomplishes the opposite of its goal—it broadcasts, "Of course this kid is fat; look at him wearing a shirt in the pool; only fat kids do that." It confirms the very thing you're trying to hide.

I've got a picture of me when I was seven or eight years old. I was at a friend's birthday party. We've got our arms over each other's shoulders. We'd just been in the pool and we're both shirtless, blissed out, and most likely hopped up on Gushers and Squeezits. This kid would go on to run cross-country in high school; I would go on to walk across food courts. Even at that young age you could already see our fates unfolding in our bodies. He was trim, blond, a lifetime of ski weekends hanging on his horizon. I looked like a tiny Seth Rogen. I had a gut, fun shorts, and a goofy smile. What I didn't have was a T-shirt, because I didn't give a damn, because I was eight. Within a year, I'd be wearing shirts in the pool, and I can't tell you exactly what changed in my brain, except that I must have figured out I was fat. I must have. I was wearing a T-shirt in the pool; only fat kids do that.

I'd like to take a moment to apologize to the very pale and to kids whose parents were overly concerned about skin cancer. I know some of you wore T-shirts in the pool, too, but go get your own book; this one is for fat kids.

I got older, which is pretty standard for kids. As I got older, the world got a little bit more cruel, which unfortunately is also pretty standard for fat kids. Every fat kid learns in a different way that it's wrong to be fat, but we all learn it. Sometimes it's a frightened parent trying to humiliate you into a more conventional body type; sometimes it's just some awful little kid named Adam saying "You're fat" on the playground in second grade. For me, it was Adam.

Adam didn't even say, "You're fat, and that's bad," or anything. It was a simple declaration—"You're fat"—but it was dripping with naked schoolyard contempt. Other kids laughed, agreeing that I was indeed fat. Your brain is a sponge at that age (you can learn Mandarin in, like, a week), and it certainly didn't take me long to realize that my body was bad. I know that kids are little shits, and they'll seize on whatever you've got and turn it into a weapon, but being fat is like a baseball bat covered in barbed wire. It doesn't take much creativity to make it hurt. That was that, I was *fat*.

I'm often tempted to apply a grim hindsight to my childhood. Now that I'm an adult, I can see all the terrible places I went, physically and mentally, because I was a fat kid. I can see the knock-on trajectory of certain experiences, and sometimes that trajectory took me down very dark paths. But it wouldn't be right to use the ink to paint a bleak picture of my childhood, because honestly, I was a happy little fat kid.

How could I not be a happy little fat kid? I had all the privilege of loving parents and a comfortable economic existence. I'm sure the adults worried about money from time to time, but it never made its way to me. It was safe and suburban. My parents were divorced, but what else is new? It was the 1990s: Getting divorced was the main thing that parents did back then. But the decade also came with plenty of benefits. My toys ruled. Weird Al was at the height of his power. The snacks were immaculate. Dunkaroos, Fruit by the Foot, and Lunchables roamed the earth. All kinds of Lunchables, by the way. They had pizza Lunchables, which stretched the definition of "pizza" like a chef tossing a disk of dough in the air. It was honestly more like "big soft-cracker Lunchables with chunky ketchup and salami," but that doesn't exactly leap off a supermarket shelf. It sure as hell leapt into my mouth, though. It was the last golden age of shameless snacks. The line between cereal and candy was smudged beyond all recognition. Reese's Peanut Butter Cups had a cereal. Rice Krispies Treats had a cereal. Not Rice Krispies, Rice Krispies Treats. A confectionary nepo baby. We've still got sugary cereals, but at least we make an effort to take them at face value. When I was growing up, we thought of foods brazenly named Cocoa Pebbles and Cinnamon Toast Crunch as part of a complete healthy breakfast. Eating a bowl of Cap'n Crunch was like having a slice of birthday cake for breakfast, but in the advertisements it was posed next to half a grapefruit and some whole wheat toast, so who the hell were we to argue with that?

Even the food that was meant to be healthy was just absolutely circus clown ridiculous. Exhibit A: SnackWell's—true pioneers in the health-food field. They invented an innovative food-preparation technique called "making the box green." They put out "healthy" cookies. The Devil's Food SnackWell's cookie was aptly named because Satan was, without question, involved on some level. Their texture was so unreal it felt like biting a cartoon tire. They tasted like an AI rendering of heaven. They were low-calorie and fat-free, then they just kind of mumbled through the rest of the ingredients. These little disks seemed like a miracle, but the only miracle was that we didn't really pay attention to sugar or carbohydrates in the 1990s. Our parents were raised on *The Jetsons*. Every American was steeped in the promise of hoverboards and flying cars. The idea that there could be a cookie that was, basically, good for you didn't seem all that far-fetched. It all felt of a piece with the promise of the decade. It was a time of unlimited progress and consumption fueled by science and capitalism working in close tandem, sometimes indistinguishable from each other. Compared to the benefits, the consequences felt inconsequential, if they were even considered at all. It was a time of more, faster, cheaper. It's easy to look back now and think we were naïve, but we'd all just found out about the internet, so was it really a stretch to think that SoBe was good for us? It was juice! Juice is good for you! Sure, it looked like neon milk. It tasted like licking a tropical battery. It resembled nothing that had ever existed in nature, but there was a lizard on the bottle, and I've never seen a fat lizard before, so there you go. It was health food. Never mind that when I drank a bottle my adolescent insulin would spike so hard the picture on the TV wobbled—it was juice, okay?

We now understand that we were in denial, but when you're chasing down your ninth SnackWell's of the night with a big gulp of SoBe, you want to believe in the future you grew up thinking you were owed. As the garbage patch floating in the Pacific and the cholesterol lining my arteries can attest, the consequences of our pursuit of unlimited everything are very much consequential. That's the hangover, though. That came later. The party itself was fully catered by Nabisco, and it ruled.

My childhood wasn't happy only because of the snacks, just to be clear. While the odd bully would seize upon my obesity, most kids didn't care. Our desks at school had a fixed chair built into them, so I spent my entire day being uncomfortably bisected by plastic, but other than that I loved it. Also, math sucked. Besides math and the uncomfortable desk and the occasional bully, I loved school. What's not to like? Elementary school is essentially everything we spend our adult lives chasing: six hours of podcasts with a prepared lunch and a bougie gym class. But as I got a bit older, I could feel the cracks beginning to form. For example, you learn early that when someone farts and nobody claims it, everyone thinks it was the fat kid. The ancient rule "He who smelt it dealt it"—which I'm pretty sure is in the Bible—is chucked out when there's a fat person present. I'm not sure what logic this vile assumption follows. I guess you're fat because you eat more, and when you eat more your body needs to process gas, and if you're careless enough to let yourself get fat, then you're careless enough to just openly fart around other people? Maybe it's because, for a long time, fat people appeared in movies only as feasting, sweating, farting, and belching comedic devices, and we all just cruelly assumed it was true. Whatever the reasoning, I can tell you that it never stops sucking. You feel it. A tall, skinny kid could announce their intention to fart, hold a microphone up to their ass, fart, then declare that they were the one who farted, and still half the room would be, like, "Oh, gross, Ian." When it happens enough times, you can't help but internalize it, against all logic. I swear to God, you actually start to think, "Damn . . . maybe that *was* me who farted." You start to think of yourself as disgusting. You can rail against it with your words, embrace it for laughs, dress yourself up and apply the finest colognes, or even try to ignore it, but I'm not certain you can ever fully escape it.

It's all part of a complex system that leaves fat kids vulnerable to ridicule in nearly every situation. To be clear, "vulnerable" doesn't mean that someone is always making fun of us. I spent way more time playing Super Nintendo and admiring Clyde Drexler basketball cards than I did being humiliated by bullies, but the older I got, the more my innocence was chipped away. My awareness of my vulnerability became pronounced, and that vulnerability was very real. For example, let's say some kid accuses you of farting, and you're feeling good about yourself that day. You stand up for yourself and say, "No, Brendan [or whatever nineties-ass name you have], I didn't fart. You farted." You and Brendan (or Zach) start barking at each other. He doesn't back down, and neither do you. You squeeze yourself out of your desk. Brendan (or Cameron) glides out of his. You're walking toward each other. Tensions are high. He pushes you. You push him. You say something cool like "You wanna go?" and then Brendan (or Cody) looks at you and says, "What are you gonna do, sit on me?" and it breaks your heart. You can't even defend yourself without someone turning it against you. I'm now relitigating a thirty-year-old fight, but to even sit on this kid, you'd have to shove him to the ground in the first place. You'd have to be stronger, more agile, more balanced. The benefits of being fat don't even enter the equation until you've already got this dude on the floor, but forget all of that. You're fat if you do, and fat if you don't.

All the slights add up and they become a burden. If you count all the interactions you have when you're a little fat kid, the ones that revolve around your weight are a tiny percentage of the total. The stinging remarks stand out, though. They're heavy on your soul. You carry the weight in more ways than one. You spend your whole life anticipating the cruelty. The insults and humiliations, which could easily be written off as odd barbs tossed out by a handful of bullies, multiply in your mind. You imagine that people are whispering about you behind your back. You assume that they're making assumptions about you. You think that they're either pitying you or despising you, and honestly the pity feels worse. It's really only a few people, but it feels like everyone, and it starts happening right around puberty, too! I mean, my god, what a rub. It's a horror movie. The killer shows up just as the storm is knocking out the power. You've got to keep chugging along, too. You can't stay home from school because you're fat—not according to my mom, Sue Karmel, anyway.

Stretch marks started showing up just between my biceps and my forearms around middle school, and this is when I really started to hate my body. I wanted to rip my skin off. It felt like my body was already starting to do that on its own. The stretch marks quickly spread to my back, my belly, the backs of my knees. It was like my skin joined the choir of voices shouting, "You are bigger than you are supposed to be." The marks came in a variety of terrible, evident colors: purple, bright red, even a sort of "corpse dragged out of the Hudson" shade of pale blue. No matter the hue, they were horrible. I'd like nothing more than to tell you that I've come to love my stretch marks, that I see them as scars of a battle I fought and won against my own insecurity and society's cruelty. I do not feel like that. I don't feel anything about them. Like the mole on my face, they're just there. My adult feelings about my stretch marks are best summed up by the great stand-up comedian Katt Williams (and I paraphrase here): "Either you were skinny and you got fat, or you were fat and you got skinny. Either way, we fucking."

That apathy would be unimaginable to the younger version of me who first discovered the stretch marks on my arms. I was shocked when I first saw them. I didn't know that stretch marks existed until they showed up on my body, which is just about the worst way to find out about anything. I was consumed by my first stretch marks. They felt apocalyptic. They were irreversible. They were a sign that I had gone too far down a path to ever really turn around. My stretch marks preoccupied me to such a degree that I honestly don't even remember getting my first pubic hair. It's like when the government came out and basically admitted that UFOs were real, but they did it pretty early into Covid lockdown. Our collective response was something like "Yeah, yeah, okay, do the aliens have a vaccine? Because otherwise I don't really have room in my brain for that right now."

I have vivid memories of sitting in Mrs. Tannenbaum's science class at Meadow Park Middle School, yanking down on the sleeves of my T-shirt, hoping they'd cover the gouges in my arms. It worked about as well as the T-shirt I wore when I went swimming. As I pull at the thread of my childhood, it's easy to see why I was trying to cover myself up. I wanted to hide. You could fill a pool with the pain, and there were certainly times when I nearly drowned in the grief. My experiences were unique in their specificity, but I don't think they're all that different from what most fat kids go through. We chug along giggling, blissfully unaware that we're speeding toward classification. One day we find out that we're fat, and that it means something to be fat. We find out it's bad that we're fat. It explodes our anxiety, and it does so in a period of our lives when our emotions are already swinging wildly, and all we want to do is fit in. Maybe we eat more to deal with that anxiety. Maybe we curl up in a ball and try to get away from the world. Many of us do both and all sorts of other things to cope. We want to be like everyone else, but we can't be like everyone else because our particularities are sitting at the surface and bursting at the seams. So we hide. We hide in tragic ways, deflecting affection and attention. We hide in ridiculous ways, thinking a wet T-shirt is going to fool anyone into thinking we aren't chubby little children. We hide.

When I think back on childhood, though, it isn't only the hiding that I think about. It's certainly part of it, but it's so much bigger than that. When I think about that stupid T-shirt I was wearing in the pool, I can't help but look at the entire picture and see something more important. I see the shirt, sucked onto my torso, but I also see a kid having the time of his life despite that sopping wet cotton. I see myself splashing and laughing and body-slamming my little sister into the deep end. I feel myself speeding through the chlorine, the salt water, the lake water, the river behind my dad's house. I feel the warm sun beating down on my satisfied muscles and saturated shirt as I lay on the beach after a day spent fighting through the waves on the Oregon coast. I see joy. I see freedom. My life after that got more complicated. When you're fat, the world contorts itself into shapes that deprive you of that joy and freedom. It convinces you to deprive yourself of that joy and freedom. Sometimes it feels incidental, and you're just catching the shrapnel of a world that is unfair to nearly everyone. Sometimes, though, it feels personal. The joke really is on you, and everyone is laughing.

OVERWEIGHT.

Sometimes people use polite language because they think it means they get to freely express the contempt they have in their hearts for whatever makes you different. "Overweight" is just "fat" with an MFA.

CHAPTER 2

"Get in My Belly"

I still remember when I first saw Fat Bastard waddle onto the screen in *Austin Powers: The Spy Who Shagged Me.* It was in the Regal Cinemas off 185th on opening night, June 8, 1999. This date is important because it coincided with another incredibly important event—me being fourteen years old. A movie like *Austin Powers: The Spy Who Shagged Me* coming out when you're a fourteen-year-old boy is like Adele releasing an album the day after you get dumped. The synchronicity is divine.

Austin Powers: International Man of Mystery, the first movie in the series, was as funny as anything I had seen before in my dumb little life. At one point, the titular character pees for three minutes. There's a bald cat named Mr. Bigglesworth. The bad guy, Dr. Evil, puts his pinkie to his lip for no reason when he talks, and his voice sounds like Lorne Michaels's. In one scene, he made a comically paltry demand for "one million dollars," and when that shit dropped in 1997 it was everywhere. *Everywhere.* When you bought a Slurpee from 7-Eleven, you want to know how much it cost?

One million dollars. When your dad wanted to know how much money you needed to walk to Blockbuster and rent a movie? *One million dollars.* How much would I have paid to be in the theater for opening night of the *Austin Powers* sequel? I don't even need to say it.

I remember being nestled in my seat, a bucket of buttered popcorn cradled in my lap, a slightly smaller bucket of Sprite clenched in my hand, fully prepared for a religious experience. I was young, fat, and ready to laugh. And then I saw Fat Bastard for the first time. Well, I heard him before he appeared. His approaching footfalls shook the room like the T. rex from *Jurassic Park,* which at that point was a six-year-old reference, but nobody cared. The entire theater was already laughing. Once Fat Bastard stepped into the room, they were doubled over. He was a buckshot blast of fat jokes. His cankles were thicker than cold chili, his knees looked like topographic maps of Afghanistan, his body looked like somebody had stretched an American Girl doll outfit over a pumpkin, and any memory of a neck was as dead as the six cows who perished to make the belt screaming over his midsection.

He was a perfect weapon. I wish I could tell you I hated Fat Bastard. I'd love to say I stormed out in a cloud of self-respect. In truth, I was cackling as loud as anyone in the room. When he farted, I howled. When he said, "Get in my belly," I was levitating. He was hilarious. Mike Myers is a genius, and he played this character with the subtlety of an atom bomb. He was like a marching band made up entirely of tubas and slide whistles. Fat Bastard is a deep-fried Twinkie of a character, and his name, from a comedy standpoint, is as lean and athletic as the character isn't. I mean, it's all there. He's fat; he's a bastard; he has no other discernible character traits, and he doesn't need them. Fat Bastard is broad comedy's answer to Cruella de Vil and Batman. If Ernest Hemingway had written this script, the character's name would still be Fat Bastard.

These were the peak days of monoculture. When something hit, it hit up, down, and sideways. Your mother would say, "I'll be back," like Arnold Schwarzenegger, when she went to the grocery store, and you'd reply, "Alrighty then," like Jim Carrey, and each of you knew what the other was referencing. As true as this was for everyone, it was even more pronounced for kids, and that could be a disaster. When you're a kid, your personality is like a paper kite in a windstorm. You're trying to ride all these different waves and fit in as best you can, and even if you manage to pull it off at all, it's clumsy as hell. Any bridge you can build to your peers, even if it's just tossing movie quotes at one another, is invaluable. When the audience poured out of that screening of *Austin Powers: The Spy Who Shagged Me,* I knew all the kids were leaving with their cargo short pockets full of quotes that we'd be yelling at one another all year, but none of them caught on quite like "Get in my belly." Every single lunch: "Get in my belly." Every time a kid caught a touchdown in *Madden:* "Get in my belly." Every time a fat kid did so much as breathe: "Get in my belly." The first time I watched Fat Bastard waddle onto the screen, I couldn't stop laughing. A star was born. It turned into a black hole. Six months later, do you know how much I would have paid for that movie to disappear forever? . . . *One million dollars.*

Here's another thing that's as true as the fact that Fat Bastard is hilarious: Kids are mean. I don't know if it's motivated by cruelty, I think it's mostly motivated by terror. They're all just terrified. Truly terrified. The kind of terrified where all you can think about is self-preservation. So they find a target, the more obvious the better, and they throw them on the rack and sacrifice them to their own insecurities.

Kids are smart, too, and resourceful. A kid can take you apart in three moves, and you won't even know you're dead until your decapitated head is staring up at your collapsing body. Kids are John Wick—they can kill you with a ballpoint pen. When you give them some pop culture to play with, it's like tossing John Wick a flamethrower. There's never been a good time to be a fat kid, but when I was growing up, there were so many flamethrowers.

One of those flamethrowers was *South Park*. That show hit America like a mechanized Barbra Streisand. I mean, it was perfect, especially for kids like me. Poets spend their entire lives hoping to capture one moment that connects with the human soul the way that *South Park* connected with middle school boys every single week. I had two *South Park* posters in my room. One of them showed a kid sitting on a toilet with a note excusing him from class for having diarrhea. Look at my walls, ye Mighty, and despair.

But in addition to being one of my favorite shows, *South Park* was a disaster for my mental health. The Eric Cartman character, a brash fat kid, went back and forth between symbolizing everything wrong with America and just straight up being Hitler. In one episode, he was a police officer beating innocent people with a baton; in another, he was a modern embodiment of Titus Andronicus, feeding a kid a bowl of chili made out of his own murdered parents. Cartman has a voice like a coffee grinder. It's the kind of obnoxious voice that's begging to be imitated, and it came ready-made with a clip of catchphrases that tore through my fat little psyche like armor-piercing bullets.

One of Cartman's catchphrases was "I'm not fat, I'm bigboned." He'd usually say it after one of the other kids said, "Shut up, fat-ass." It was so devastating to have the fat kid respond to fat-based bullying by saying, "I'm not fat, I'm big-boned." Like all great comedy, it worked because it was the truth. It was ripped from the headlines. I tried that "big-boned" line more times than I could count. It was one of the only tools we fat kids had to deflect bullying based on our size. Of course, nobody ever actually had big bones. We were always just fat children with standard-issue skeletons. It didn't matter. The line never worked anyway. The whole thing was ridiculous from the jump. The bullies knew it. We knew it. Trey Parker and Matt Stone, the genius creators of *South Park*, knew it. They dropped it into their show, and it was a disaster for kids like me. It was a bomb that exploded if you tried to defuse it. It was like those antibiotic-resistant superbugs you hear about on the news, except it was hilarious.

South Park is an amazing show, and Cartman is hilarious. I think it's funny now, and I thought it was funny then, and I didn't just think that to help myself cope. Cartman is a cartoon, both literally and figuratively. I didn't watch that show and think, "Well, there I am: He's fat, I'm fat, that's a thing we have in common and therefore we are the same." I genuinely never thought that. I self-identified with Kyle, to be honest, because we're both Jewish, and in Beaverton, Oregon, that was a little more rare and exotic than being fat.

I knew then as I know now that I'm a complex and dynamic individual. I'm an amalgamation of everyone I've ever met and everyone they've ever met and every song I've ever heard and every movie I've ever seen and every book I've ever read and every experience, lived and imagined, that I've ever encountered, all mixed up with whatever divine sense of individualism we're all assigned at birth and are allowed to nourish as we grow. Other kids didn't think that, though; they thought I was Cartman.

When the other kids think you're Cartman, you have two options—listen to his catchphrases being screamed at you or scream those catchphrases yourself. Of course, you could do neither and punch the kids who make fun of you, and that's probably the right choice, but you know . . . society. Anyway, I chose the second option—if anyone was going to make fun of me, then it was going to be me. I don't know if I was owning it or simply doing the devil's work for him, but either way, I was involved and that felt better than being a target. I played the role and waited patiently for a more fair and nuanced reflection of fat people to appear in popular culture.

No, I'm kidding, I just eventually learned how to do a Peter Griffin voice. Thanks, *Family Guy.* You also get good at yelling "Hey, hey, hey!" like Fat Albert, which was a weird one because the show stopped airing in 1985 but somehow kids still knew about it, like it was a sacred story preserved in the oral tradition by generations of shithead middle school bullies. I bet people are still yelling "Hey, hey, hey!" at fat kids. I imagine it's the one thing we'll agree, as a culture, to save from Bill Cosby's legacy.

Not even the remote deserts of Tatooine were safe for fat people because in *Star Wars* there's a character called Jabba the Hutt. Jabba the Hutt is a murderer, a slave trader, a gangster, and yet the worst thing about him is that he's fat. And boy, is he fat. Jabba the Hutt is inescapably fat. He's fat in a human way even though he's a space slug with the face of a Persian kitty. He's sweaty, he has trouble breathing, he eats little living creatures as a snack, and he's fat. Also, they called him Jabba. The Hutt. They could have called him "Jabba the Space Gangster" or "Brandon the Hutt" and even children watching the movie would say, "Got it, he's a fat guy." Somewhere there's a piece of paper with the other names they thought about calling him and "Lardo the Tubb" is on that list. I love *Star Wars* and I love George Lucas for making it. I don't think his goal in creating Jabba the Hutt was to engineer a three-word thermal detonator that could be lobbed at fat kids to remind them that they're disgusting. Look at George Lucas. I'd never call him Jabba the Hutt, but I wouldn't exactly call him Han Solo either. So maybe it's self-loathing, maybe it's just repeating the cycles of abuse he experienced when he was a child, maybe he saw a big fat gangster in an old movie and stole the idea—probably it's a combination of all three—but the result is the same.

I'm not looking for nuance here. I know that *Star Wars* is a movie franchise full of outlandish characters who work because they play on broad archetypes that are as old as time itself. This is a universe full of pastiches in prosthetics, but Jabba the Hutt is the only big bad guy without any dignity. His only redeeming quality is that he knows Boba Fett, the bounty hunter who is coded as so cool that he got his own spin-off series nearly four decades after he first appeared in the movies. Meanwhile, Jabba the Hutt's superpowers are basically that he has money and a hot friend.

Darth Vader is evil personified, but Darth Vader is presented as extremely cool. He looks like an erect penis covered in BDSM latex and he talks like God. Darth Vader absolutely should have been fat, by the way. He's an asthmatic legacy kid who wears a cape, does magic, and owns a sword. That divine baritone voice was a gift from thick-boy legend James Earl Jones. Darth Vader is fat-dude cultural appropriation. We just can't have nice things even when they're evil nice things. Instead, we get Jabba the Hutt, who lolls around like his entire existence is mid–insulin spike, and an X-wing pilot named *Pork*ins, who immediately dies because this is a universe where anything is possible except a fat person being treated with even a shred of humanity.

Again, my goal in all this is not to ruin *Star Wars* or *South Park* or *Austin Powers* or any other form of entertainment. I don't currently have children, but if I do in the future, I'm going to show them *Star Wars,* and when I do, I'll be upset. Not because Jabba the Hutt is an insensitive caricature, but because I'll be showing them a sixty-year-old movie, they won't care, and that will remind me of death. I suppose my goal is just to tell you what it was like to be watching all of this as a little fat kid, in the hope that we can do better in the future.

I already think we are. If my kids are fat, I want them to look at pop culture and have more than just Santa Claus and Goldberg the Goalie from *The Mighty Ducks* as positive male role models. When I was a kid, one of my favorite shows had a character named Donkeylips who looked just like me; I'd love it if my kids could avoid situations like that, not to mention what I experienced one spring break in my early teens.

I was in middle school and I went on vacation to Florida with my dad, his wife, her kids, and my sister. While we were there, we went to an amusement park. I can't even remember which one, but I know it had roller coasters. I didn't even really like roller coasters, but you know, when in Orlando . . . The line was an hour and a half spent cooking in the sous vide of Floridian humidity. When I finally made it through to the front of the line, I squeezed into my seat and I was too fat for the safety bar to close. My gut was blocking it from clicking into place. The attendant tried to slam the bar down like he had crammed too many camping supplies into a car trunk, but all that did was call more attention to the fact that it wasn't going to happen. I physically could not ride. A crowd of people watched me skulk out of the seat, trying to hide my body without hiding my body, trying to hide my face without giving away the shame, trying to somehow make it look like it was all my decision. I don't remember what mix of family was with me, but I made them ride the roller coaster without me. Humiliation is one thing. Waiting in the sweltering heat for an hour and a half to experience that humiliation, in front of a crowd, is another. Making other people suffer because I was too fat for the ride was off the table entirely.

As I walked away, someone yelled, "I'm not fat, I'm big-boned," in a perfect Eric Cartman voice. Everyone laughed. The kids in line laughed, the adults in line laughed, the people working the ride laughed, the guy who tried to pull the bar down over my gut laughed loudly. So I shattered into a million pieces, and then I forced a laugh out, too. At least I had something in common with everyone else. We were all laughing. I was part of it.

I wish I hadn't laughed. I wish I had known then that I didn't deserve that, but what forces of the greater culture, what social norms, should have told me to think I deserved better? Fat Bastard? Fat Bastard, who said, "I eat because I'm unhappy; I'm unhappy because I eat"—a true and complicated and painful idea—and then farted? Eventually the Fat Bastard character lost a bunch of weight and, this is so stupid, I actually remember thinking, "Oh damn, good for him." Seconds later he collected all his loose skin and said his neck looked like a vagina. Hilarious joke. Sincerely hilarious joke. A sincerely hilarious joke that told fat people that they were a punch line no matter what. Damned if they do, damned if they diet.

BIG-BONED.

Calling someone "big-boned" is dumb as hell. You're just using language that supports the idea that being fat is an inherent character flaw rather than an occasional health concern. When you call someone "big-boned," you're saying, "Hey, look, man, I know you're gigantic . . . but you're not gigantic like those disgusting, lazy fat-asses. You're gigantic because of your big-ass skeleton." It's one of those terms that people use when they want to let you off the hook for being fat, but what if we just stopped putting fat people on hooks?

CHAPTER 3

I Was a Teenage Projectile

The Beaverton School District had the greatest chicken-fried steak on the planet. I first tasted it at Bethany Elementary School and then at Meadow Park Middle School and then at Westview High School, and it tasted the same no matter the cafeteria; it tasted perfect. There should be a *Chef's Table* about the succession of lunch ladies who crafted it: tense cello music and vanity shots of the meat defrosting in a sink; an old woman named Barbara ripping cigs while she talks about how she nearly destroyed herself in pursuit of the perfect congealed gravy. I've ordered chicken-fried steak all over the country and it's never tasted quite the same as it did back in school. It was so delicious that I genuinely didn't stop to think about what animal chicken-fried steak was until well into my twenties. It's steak, by the way. It's steak that they fry like chicken. They could have just called it "fried steak," but there's no poetry to that. Chicken-fried steak needs all three names, like a Gilded Age banker or a serial killer, because it sits perfectly at the intersection of the two. For all my years attending public school, the chicken-fried steak stayed the same, and it's nice to have that consistency when you're becoming a teenager, because everything else is confusing as shit.

I spent the bulk of my time in middle school hiding from that confusion by playing a computer game called *Ultima Online*. To give a description that would enrage my thirteen-year-old self in its oversimplification, the game was basically Dungeons & Dragons on the internet, played with thousands of other people all over the world. *Ultima* was entirely online, so there were plenty of idiots running around spouting KoЯn lyrics in all caps while they tried to murder you for no reason, but there were also dedicated communities of people trying to create an authentic role-playing experience. I was one of those people. I played a ranger with a Cockney accent that I'd type out like "well 'ello, wot 'ave we 'ere?" I had a small house and I belonged to a guild and I made real friends. I mean, not real-life friends—most of us didn't even know one another's actual names—but we spent thousands of hours together. We'd storm dungeons and fight demons and zombie wizards and lizardmen. We'd go on for hours talking, text appearing over the heads of our avatars. We'd laugh; we'd scheme; I'd flirt with women who I naïvely believed were being controlled by actual women. Every night I would log on to a new adventure and play deep into the night, peeling off hour after hour to fight digital dragons and then reminiscing over it in virtual taverns. Then I'd wake up the next day and go to middle school.

Middle school sucks. It's the main thing middle school does. In grade school you learn about multiplication and state capitals, in high school you study algebra and read an Ayn Rand book, and in middle school you cope. It's just the silliest time. It's deeply immoral that we use the word "awkward" to describe anything other than middle school. Puberty hits like a corgi race. There's no order or organization to it at all. You've got a kid with an R&B beard and an Adam's apple like he swallowed a Kleenex box sitting across the lunch table from Billy Elliot. I was the combination of both of those kids. By my thirteenth birthday I was the size of an Ivy League offensive lineman, but I had a sweet little baby face like I was carved out of marzipan. I didn't look like a man at all; I looked like America's largest boy, and man, was I ever a large boy. There's a picture of me hanging out with my friends at my Bar Mitzvah, and it looks like Shaquille O'Neal meeting BTS.

It is difficult being that big, that visible, when all you want to do is figure yourself out on the sly. There's no blending into the background; there's no hiding in plain sight. People were either delighted or challenged by my size. I mean, most people didn't care about my size at all—they were primarily worried about Marilyn Manson lyrics or English homework—but a significant number had weirdly strong reactions to it. The adults who were delighted were mostly innocuous. They'd call me "Big Man" and ask what they were feeding me back at home. Sometimes they would even hush their tone and ask how much I weighed. I always said I didn't know. I lied. I knew. I just wasn't going to tell them. I didn't want to watch them lean back, whistle, and admire the number as if I were some kind of sport fish. Those unsympathetic moments with adults are jarring when you're a kid. I had great parents and amazing teachers all the way through grade school, so when I got to middle school and encountered shithead grown-ups it was a shock. I was used to kids making fun of me; I had trained for that, honed my tools, sharpened my blade, learned how to yell, "I'm fat, but you're ugly. At least I can lose some weight." Cruel adults were another thing entirely, an enemy for whom I had failed to prepare. One spring afternoon, I was late for the bus leaving school. It was pulling out of the parking lot without me and I had to run after it to catch it. My backpack was wildly careening behind me as I sprinted over the blacktop. I waved my arms, exposing my stomach underneath my Big Dogs T-shirt. The backpack swinging one way, my belly swinging the other. The bus pulled away. I envisioned calling my mom and telling her I missed the bus. My mom, the saint, raising four children and several of their friends. My mom, already dealing with my self-destructive alcoholic stepdad. My mom, working graveyard shifts in the maternity ward of the hospital. My mom, dropping everything so she could come pick me up from school because I couldn't pull myself away from a conversation about Magic: The Gathering. Then, a miracle: The bus stopped. The brakes shrieked and the door hissed and whined and flopped open. I didn't break my stride and sprinted right up onto the bus. As I wandered back to an open seat, the bus driver grabbed the microphone to the loudspeaker. He looked in the rearview mirror and his eyes landed on me. I remember his face so clearly. He was old, white, craggy, thick glasses and eyebrows like far-off summer clouds. He wet his lips in anticipation, plunged the button, and cracked to his captive audience, "That's the hardest he's run in years!" I don't even remember if anyone on the bus laughed; I just remember how pleased with himself he looked. The old bastard was grinning like Chris Rock. I was humiliated, yes, but I was also shocked by the lack of decorum. The fat kid–decent adult treaty I'd enjoyed for most of my life had been ruptured. Also, yes! That *was* the hardest I'd run in years! Who's out here just running at top speed for no reason? I wasn't sitting at home thinking, "I'm in the mood for a Slurpee; I guess I'll just sprint to 7-Eleven as hard as I physically can like a cave bear is chasing me." I didn't say that, though. I just sat there and tried to hide, but I couldn't hide because I was gigantic. I felt terrible for the entire ride home. Then I got home and I told my mom what happened. Then I felt bad again, but for a different reason.

There's a look my mom gets that feels like a storm rolling in. The room gets colder. Birds take to the skies. Her eyebrows raise and God hides behind his throne. I don't know how she got the bus company on the phone so fast, and I might be misremembering this somewhat, but I swear she tore a hole in the fabric of reality, stepped through, and strangled the bus driver to death, while consigning ten generations of his ancestors and ten generations of his progeny to the hottest corner of the darkest hell. By the time she got off the phone, I'm telling you, I felt bad for the bus driver. I was, like, "Hey, look, Ma, comedy is hard, you know? You gotta walk up to the edge sometimes." The only other time I saw that bus driver again was when he apologized. Then again later when his Comedy Central half hour dropped. I'm kidding. He probably died shortly after that interaction. RIP, Bozo.

It wasn't just jokes in middle school. When you're big, sometimes people try to fight you just because you're big. You aren't even doing anything wrong—it's just Mount Everest rules. Why shove him? Because he's there, damn it! It's counterintuitive, I know, but it happens. People think they can prove something by bullying a big guy. To this day I don't understand it. I wore an Eeyore hat to school. I wasn't a big tough guy; I was just several little nerds rolled into one large body, but that logic was lost on them. Again, the kids I could handle. It was when an adult felt challenged by my size that things got interesting.

I had this gym teacher in seventh grade, let's call him Mr. Boyer because that was his name. Mr. Boyer didn't do anything crazy; he didn't try to fight me or anything. Mr. Boyer was a great guy. He wrestled in high school, and that identity suited him, so he just went ahead and stayed a high school wrestler well into his adulthood. By the time I met him, he had turned it into an art. He was horseshoe bald with a mustache groomed like the White House lawn. His body, even in middle age, was coiled and brimming with potential energy. He'd pace through class peppering us with enthusiastic aphorisms. There may have been a time when his voice wasn't hoarse, but it was long before I met him. He was pretty funny intentionally and extremely hilarious unintentionally. He was a great teacher, and if he'd had his way, we would have spent half of the gym class Greco-Roman wrestling and the other half freestyle wrestling, but this was a coed class at a public school in Oregon in the late 1990s, so wrestling was out of the question. The closest Mr. Boyer could get to wrestling was a gymnastics unit. He rolled out the tumbling mats, unfurled the rings from the ceiling, and issued us a challenge. As he wheeled out a pommel horse he told us that everyone in the class, yes everyone, would be vaulting over said pommel horse. There was a runway and a springboard and a pile of crash pads, and by the end of the semester we'd all be making the flight. I scoffed. He insisted. It was far enough away that I dropped the topic, but I knew one thing for a fact: I was not launching my body over that horse. The class proceeded, and over the weeks Mr. Boyer taught us cartwheels and walking handstands and all sorts of other workouts that strongmen would do on the Coney Island boardwalk in the 1920s. I mean, I didn't do any of those things; I sat on the floor and stretched, but the skinny kids did them. Every so often, Mr. Boyer would send a few kids over the pommel horse and every time it happened, I assured him I would not be doing it.

There were layers of reasons for my reluctance to vault over the pommel horse. A lasagna of reasons. First, simple self-preservation. I had no idea what would happen if I took a running jump off a springboard. I was twice as big as the next biggest kid in my class and three times bigger than anyone I'd seen go over that horse. There was no point of reference as far as physics was concerned. I could hit those springs, take to the skies, and never come down. I can see it now, smashing through the back wall of the gym, through the brick façade of the school, soaring over the Oregon evergreens, gaining altitude, Mr. Boyer pumping his fist triumphantly as I'm sucked into the engine of a passing 747. That actually wouldn't be so bad, because what if the springboard just didn't work at all? What if I jumped onto the board and the springs said, "That's it, I'm out," and quit like an overworked Starbucks barista who'd pumped one too many Torani syrups? I couldn't take that. I'd been there before. Too many shirts that didn't fit, too many rollercoaster bars that wouldn't close—I'd been humiliated too many times to have it happen in front of everyone in my gym class. Then there was the horrifying prospect of everything working out just fine. My feet hitting the springs, my body launching into the air like a rotund rocket, falling into the crash pads and popping up to my feet while the kids around me cheered. I hate overcoming things and I hate the encouragement to do so. I hate the way it makes me feel. Every clap makes me feel like a freak. Every whoop of encouragement makes me feel like more of a mascot than a peer. I know people think they're helping, but it's so embarrassing. It's a reminder that you can't hide, that even your most naked, vulnerable struggles are public property. Then there was Mr. Boyer. His encouragement was bordering on mania. He was certain I could do it. He was positive. At first it felt like he was being a good teacher, steely in his resolve to make sure that every child had the opportunity to succeed. Gradually, though, it started to feel like I was his white whale. He couldn't accept that I wouldn't do it. He wouldn't accept that I couldn't do it. I honestly had no desire to conquer the pommel horse, but even if I did, it wouldn't be my achievement. It would be something for the class to clap about; it would be Mr. Boyer conquering the unconquerable.

He wouldn't take no for an answer. He badgered me throughout the semester and then, at some point, I relented. I couldn't fight him off any longer. Maybe some part of me wanted to do it. Maybe some part of me wanted to prove to myself that I could do it, that I wanted to feel the thrill of flight. Mostly, though, I just wanted him to leave me alone. I wanted people to stop looking at me. The longer I fought him off, the bigger a deal it became for the class. So I agreed to do it.

It was the end of class. I'd been sitting on the floor stretching for forty-five minutes. It was time. I took my place at the top of the runway. Mr. Boyer positioned himself just behind the pommel horse. He told me he'd be there to catch me and help ferry me to the crash pads. In case anything went wrong, he'd be there to help protect my careening, out-of-control body. Hubris. I told him it was a bad idea, that he should just clear out and let me do it. He refused. I insisted. He refused. I didn't have any more fight in me. I took a deep breath and rumbled down the tumbling mat, my bare feet slapping loud against the surface. The approach was a blur; I hit the springboard and then everything slowed down. Liftoff. I was airborne. Slipping gravity and flying through the air, I felt a moment of euphoria. Then I saw Mr. Boyer's face. His drill-instructor enthusiasm was melting into a lizard-brained realization that he'd made a terrible mistake. I still felt euphoric, but now it was because justice was being served. This was an outcome I hadn't considered. Yes, it was a lose-lose, but hey, sometimes that's equality. I hit Mr. Boyer and it was like he was never standing there in the first place. I was already laughing before the gravity kicked in. By the time I hit the crash pads I was in hysterics. Mr. Boyer's face was as red as a matador's cape. His glasses were splayed out on his forehead like a teenager's bedsheets. He hadn't even taken his glasses off! The nerve of this adult man! The rest of the class was laughing, too. At me, with me, who could tell? It was humiliating, but so was everything in middle school—at least this was a novel way to feel it.

It's no wonder I spent every day of middle school waiting to go home so I could log on to *Ultima Online* and become someone else for the night. I felt more comfortable retreating into an identity I could control, even if it meant leaving my physical body and huge swaths of my personality behind. (Actually, probably *because* I was leaving my physical body and huge swaths of my personality behind.) Unfortunately, the things I left behind started to atrophy. I got fatter and sadder. I became a much worse student. My real life became an inconvenience. Nobody cares about their health in middle school, but I *especially* didn't care about my health in middle school because my body was just a thing that held the brain I used to play a video game. I started missing school because I was staying up until 4:00 A.M., running around in my preferred version of life. The bus would leave without me, and there was no way I was running after it anymore. School didn't have anything to offer me except an absolutely divine chicken-fried steak, and eventually even that lost its allure.

I stopped playing the computer game, but the damage was already done. I spent three years in middle school and I learned exactly one lesson: I could ignore my problems and grit my teeth through the parts of my life that I didn't like by focusing all my attention on playing a role. Of course, this is an incredibly literal example. *Ultima Online* was an actual game. Looking back, though, it doesn't feel all that different from the role I was on the verge of playing because I was about to enter high school, and brother . . . can I tell you something? Do you have a minute? Can I bend your ear? Are you someone who goes in for metaphors? Are you willing to let a man turn a phrase? Do you have room in your head for the traditions of human language? Do you have room in your heart? Because—brother? sister? cousin? friend?—high school is the biggest game of all.

FATSO.

A demeaning term with a patina of history! Finally, your dehumanization has that Jazz Age flair. If somebody calls you "fatso," they should have to live the rest of their life like it's the 1920s. You know, really commit to it! Wear a fedora, throw themselves from a window, that sort of thing.

CHAPTER 4

High School

I went to high school with a kid who wore Jedi robes in his senior pictures. I believe, without a doubt in my mind, that this is the guy who had the best time. Not the jocks, not the popular kids, not even the kids in the theater department. I think it was the Jedi. I'm not certain what high school is like now, but I know what it was like in the first few years of the 2000s, and the student body's main reaction to this kid wearing Jedi robes was a bunch of words that we don't use anymore. He did it anyway. To this day I find it amazing. Even then, I was blown away by how brave and honest it was. I wasn't shocked that he showed bravery in the face of a bunch of teenagers calling him names, though he did; I was shocked that he was brave enough to stick with it. He wasn't trying to be somebody he wasn't. . . . I mean, he was literally trying to be a Jedi, I guess, and I don't think he was *actually* a Jedi, but he wasn't trying to be someone who didn't want to be a Jedi.

Everybody is so worried about being cool in high school, but this was the coolest person on the planet—on several planets, if his robes are to be believed. He was actual cool, not the kind of cool you pay for with hair gel and Abercrombie T-shirts. He didn't care what other kids thought, or at least he cared about how he felt about himself more. How did he do that?! It honestly would have been less impressive to me if he was actually a Jedi. In high school, I contorted my personality to fit in. I loved *Star Wars,* too. I loved *Star Wars* more than I loved beer bongs, but I wasn't willing to let myself go through high school as the fat kid who loved *Star Wars.* This was the point in my life where I started caring more about what other people thought than about what I thought. I think a lot of kids do that in high school. It turns a lot of us into robots. But not the kid in the Jedi robes. He is not the droid you're looking for.

I don't want to give a false impression. I loved high school. I had a great time in high school. But I also worked really hard to make sure I "Had a Great Time in High School!" I was one of the popular kids. I was on the football team. I went to several school dances and I was invited to parties. I identified the game and then I found my role in the game and I played it to the best of my ability. The game sucks, though. The game isn't why I had a good time in high school. I don't have a ton of regrets in life, but I regret spending so much time trying to convince a bunch of people to accept me, the popular people, even though I resented them more than I ever liked them. I have no idea if they really liked me either. It's hard to say. I never gave them the opportunity to meet the real me, as corny as that sounds.

When I say I liked high school, I mean that I liked sitting around with friends playing *Madden* and skipping school to eat so much food at a sushi buffet that the buffet lost money on me. I liked reading Howard Zinn and then telling other people I had read Howard Zinn. I liked the way the grass smelled at football practice. I liked that sometimes homework meant you got to make a video with your friends, and as long as it connected, however tenuously, to *Atlas Shrugged,* you got full credit. I liked all the things that get lost in the mosaic of the monolithic idea of high school.

Sometimes, though, it felt like my enjoyment of high school was an act of defiance against everything that was conspiring against me, and in that way it was a personal triumph, but it was also an act of defiance against my own humanity. And because of that, I also hated high school. I know it isn't anything special to say you hated high school. Most American art is just people finding different ways to say "I hate high school."

I was one of the popular kids because I was funny and good at football and because I neglected any part of myself that would get in the way of being one of the popular kids. This got me into certain parties, and I felt like it won me the acceptance of the other cool kids, but it was always conditional on the expectation that I was sexless and self-deprecating. I got so good at being self-deprecating. I'd apologize to chairs before I sat on them, fill my mouth with impossible amounts of Laffy Taffy in the middle of class, throw back shots of ranch dressing in the cafeteria, and it made people laugh and I hated all of it. Okay, I didn't hate the ranch dressing, but I hated the rest of it. I hated it because that was neither the person I wanted to be nor the actual person I was inside. The person I wanted to be was tan and slim with a perfect center part and DiCaprio bangs. I wanted a laid-back California male vocal fry, a hemp necklace, and a Livestrong bracelet. That would have been a lie, too, but at least it would have been a sexy lie. The real me was into video games and *The Silmarillion* and telling jokes in class that only made the teacher laugh. I could never be the former option, and I wouldn't let myself be the latter option because I wanted to validate myself through the affection of the cool kids, no matter what I thought I had to do to get it. And that meant making these kids laugh, and letting these kids make themselves laugh, no matter what. I had to be okay with the jokes. I had to be okay with humiliation. I had to laugh when people slapped my belly, and I had to laugh even harder when they poked it and giggled like the Pillsbury Doughboy. I had to play football and I had to be good. And I could not get with any girls. That was not my role. There came a point during every party when people would start pairing off and retiring to bedrooms and laundry rooms and garages for whatever they were doing in there, and I'd be left sitting in the kitchen with a couple of other kids, a bottle of Captain Morgan, and a fifth repeat of that night's *SportsCenter.*

For nearly the entirety of high school, I sat on the outside and fantasized about girls liking me *like that.* Not even the sex, honestly, but the acceptance. The sex, too, but mostly the acceptance. Eventually I met Hailey, my first high school girlfriend. Senior year. Just in time for me to be a guy who had a girlfriend in high school, which was incredibly clutch for my campaign to feel like a normal kid who wasn't different just because I was fat.

We would drive around in my truck and listen to Blink-182, which doesn't sound romantic, but when I was in high school, Blink was basically Rūmī for people who think it's funny to chug a Mountain Dew and burp "I love you." Plus, Hailey was into skateboarding and punk rock, and that was not traditionally the kind of girl who liked a guy just because he played football and got invited to parties. I'd gone to great lengths to bury myself under several layers of Regular Popular Kid fail-safes, but I felt like maybe she saw the actual me under there, and that was such a huge relief.

Hailey was funny and sweet. She dressed cool—the specific kind of cool that is also cool again now, twenty years later. When friends post pictures of their teenagers, and they're dressed the way she dressed back then, it makes me feel older than the fact that I enjoy keeping a tomato garden in the summer. We were both kids, but I liked how grown-up she seemed. Those incremental slivers of maturity feel like chasms before age flattens everything out. I grew up at the bottom of a cul-de-sac and she lived in an apartment, and I know that was probably more a condition of economics, but for some reason it appeared so chic and mature at the time. It's not like she lived there alone either; she lived there with her mom, but her mom was gone more than my mom was gone, and sometimes it felt like Hailey lived there alone. It certainly felt like it on the nights she'd pull me into her front door and kiss me and take me to her bedroom.

I remember my first kiss with Hailey. We were sitting in the front seat of my truck, overlooking the football field. It's like we were cosplaying American high school romance. By the time our lips touched, I was ready for a girlfriend. I was so ready for a girlfriend. Aching for a girlfriend. I was longing at levels not seen since Regency England. If John Keats was Wilt Chamberlain, I was LeBron James. Then Hailey came along and she kissed me while Blink-182 filled the truck cabin and I liked her so much.

I liked the way she made me feel about myself even more. Hailey showed me, for the first time in my life, that I could be desired and what that would look like. She ran her hands over my naked shoulders and chest. Her fingers traced my stretch marks. They didn't have to look far. I was so embarrassed. I felt like my living ghost was being ripped from my body and slammed into the floor like a dirty rug. I thought that would be it for us. I thought that somehow it had eluded her that I was very fat. I thought she'd feel my stretch marks and then reach for my T-shirt, the light switch, and the door, in that order. Instead, she said they were beautiful. We sank into each other. I was in love. On the drive home that night I stopped at a Jack in the Box and gorged on tacos and cheeseburgers, because I reward myself with the exact same things I use as consolation.

The joy was not meant to last. A few weeks later Hailey told me that some other kids had asked her about us. They'd asked about our sex life. They said how disgusting it must be to have me lying on top of her sweating. Just because you're paranoid doesn't mean they aren't after you. We broke up not too long after that. She dumped me. In reality, the two things probably weren't related, but in my mind, they were directly related. I don't think I've ever again been so sad. I was pure, uncut teenager sad. The kind of sad feeling that, let's be honest, feels amazing in a way. I stopped listening to Blink-182. I started listening to Taking Back Sunday and Eels.

I cried so hard, so often, and so powerfully that I earnestly considered getting a job at Hot Topic. I was sure that Hailey had realized I was disgusting and broken. The whisper campaign to remind her that I was fat was successful. I felt like she had been lying to me about my stretch marks, and I hated her for doing that, and I hated myself for ever being stupid enough to believe her. Maybe there were traces of truth in those feelings, but probably not. I think she just lost interest in me because I was holding on to her so tight that she couldn't breathe. Just because you aren't suffocating someone with your body doesn't mean you aren't doing it emotionally. It would be ages before I realized that skinny people break up with each other all the time for reasons that don't include stretch marks or sweat or binge eating at Jack in the Box. Sometimes shit just doesn't work out, and it's not just because I don't work out.

She wasn't dating me as some kind of act of charity—she was doing it because she liked me—but when she left, I felt like I'd lost something greater than just the company of someone I had fallen in love with. I felt like my personhood had been revoked. I know now that this was never something she could have given me, and it was never fair of me to ask. I guess this is growing up.

At the time, I was devastated. I kept reliving the conversation she'd had with some unnamed classmates. Her realization that I was sweaty and disgusting. The spell breaking, reality setting in. There was a part of me that thought I deserved the breakup because I'd risen above my station. Part of the deal was that I was sexless, and what did I do? Try to have sex. I was so depressed. I hated the popular kids after that. I think they were all depressed, too. When I was hanging out with my regular friends, we ate ice cream and watched Mel Brooks movies; when I was hanging out with popular people, we drank whiskey out of a beer bong and boxed in living rooms. Does one of those evenings strike you as more desperate than the other? Not to diminish the grand tradition of bingeing a pint of Ben & Jerry's in a fog of depression, but the "cool kids" were microdosing suicide every weekend. Twenty years removed, more than a few of those "cool kids" went ahead and upped that dose. This is what happens when you get lost in a game. This is what happens when you sneak parts of yourself into the party and leave the rest at home. This is what happens when you compromise yourself and play a role.

I was like a mastodon in a tar pit with this acceptance stuff. The more I flailed, the deeper I sank. I was so determined to prove that I was an acceptable person that I couldn't ever just enjoy anything on its own. I was so warped that I'd take the things I genuinely loved and try to use them to prove to myself, and to other people, that I was okay. Like football, for instance. I loved playing football. Even with all the knock-on, knock-out effects, I loved it. I loved it for the camaraderie, the glory, and the work ethic it briefly instilled in me. I loved the way the drums sounded on a Friday night. I loved that the whole team walked like penguins after a leg day at the gym. It's an earnest and abiding love. I loved, mostly, that I felt like I belonged to something. I loved that it finally felt like my gigantic, fat body served a purpose. It had a defined role and a reason for existing. That the reason was the relatively unimportant cause of tackling smaller sixteen-year-olds from Beaverton didn't matter to me. I loved it.

I'm haunted by a feeling, though. I'm haunted by the fact that my body was only accepted on the condition that it absorbed and delivered pain for other people's amusement. I was more than accepted, actually; I was celebrated. Strange adults would come up to me and know that I was Ian Karmel, the football player, and they were rooting for me, and that cheeseburger I just ordered was on their tab, brother. My body actually became my ticket to humanity, *provided* I used it for pain. My body had been the only thing holding me back, and then I entered this bizarro reality where the only thing that mattered was that I had a gigantic, fat form that I was willing to fuck up for fun. I got to go to parties *because* I was huge. It became the reason I was popular. I passed Algebra 2 because the teacher was friends with one of the football coaches! Mathematics, the universal truth, bent to my girth.

It was awesome that I was fat.

As long as I hurled it at another fat teenager.

One time I tackled a kid and broke both of his legs. Some people on my sideline—adults!—celebrated. Overtly at first and then once they realized the kid was terribly hurt, covertly. They patted me on the helmet and the ass and carried on in hushed but happy spurts like someone watching the Super Bowl on their phone at a wedding. I'd love to tell you I was disgusted in the moment, but I was cheering right alongside them. I was so happy that my body was being celebrated that I didn't think about the awful reality facing this kid I'd hurt. He was staring down multiple surgeries, months of physical therapy, and a significant amount of bed rest, all before the advent of streaming television. I should have felt bad. I should have, at least, sent the kid some DVDs.

It gets even more messed up than that! For years I told that story like it was a good thing! On dates, with a combination of faux humility and even faux-er horror, I'd tell girls that I used to hurt people really bad during football games. I'd affect the pensive, far-off expression of a reluctant war hero and unspool the grisly tale, as though it continued to justify my body. Something like "You must be wondering why I currently weigh 375 pounds. Let me assure you, there's a very good reason that my body exists. A decade ago, I used it to hurt sixteen-year-olds." I felt like it was better to be dangerous than to be embarrassing because at least being dangerous gave me some control over how I was being perceived.

Every Saturday morning, the team had a little breakfast buffet, and that's where I discovered Go-Gurt. Go-Gurt was invented in 1999 and walked hand in hand with humanity into the new millennium. It's yogurt in a tube, so you can eat it without a spoon. Slurping down yogurt on the go. I don't have anything interesting to say about Go-Gurt, but I just talked about breaking kids' legs for so long that I feel like I needed a palate cleanser, and nothing cleanses the palate like a plastic sleeve of low-fat yogurt.

My time spent playing high school football was disgusting and beautiful. Very much like Go-Gurt. Even with all my complaining, though, I don't know that I'd go back and change it. Probably I'd try not to break both of that kid's legs, and there are a few other regrets, but it's a short list. Even while I was selling out my body for acceptance, I was having fun. Everything awful about high school football is true, but I spent the majority of every practice giggling like Winnie-the-Pooh. Having fun doesn't justify everything, but this was high school. You've got to have fun. The suck is going to come; there's no stopping it. You will squish like a grape underneath the cruelty of other children and your own hormone-heightened emotions, so in the margins, whenever you can, whatever it takes, you've got to have fun.

I had a friend on the team, a kid named Colin. He was a tall kid. The kind of kid who's so tall that he seemed to be skinny by accident. We played together for years, and after the last snap of our last game of our senior year, after the percussion of the drum had stopped echoing through the surrounding suburbs and the crowd had gone home and the stadium lights thudded to dark, we sat on the field and we held each other and we cried. At that moment it didn't matter that he had a concave chest and I had a gut that hung down over my belt; we were just two kids indulging our naked emotions and sitting in that concussive feeling of loss that only comes when something you truly love is truly gone.

When I look back on that memory, it plays in my head like a movie. It's saccharine and gilded, and so corny that it would have made Norman Rockwell drink his paint, but it's also pure and honest, and fat kids deserve to have those moments, too. Fat kids deserve to transcend all the bullshit that other people put on us and that we put on ourselves. We deserve to experience the euphoria of the massive pendulum of teenage emotion swooping into the ecstatic—and also the banality of sitting on the couch playing video games with friends. We deserve moments when we aren't overcoming ourselves, as though being fat is something that needs to be overcome in the first place.

I'm really happy that those authentic moments of joy slid in between all my attempts to manufacture it. I'm so lucky that I had friends and family who actually loved me, even while I was busy trying to impress people who maybe didn't. Looking back on high school, all the things I took for granted are the only things I really miss. It's fun to have fun, and it doesn't have to mean anything more than that. It's fun to be yourself, even if that accidentally happens while you're trying to be someone else. That's how you enjoy high school. That's how you win the game—by not playing it. That and you get yourself a Jedi robe.

BEEFY.

People will try to protect your feelings by calling you an adjective that should only be used for stew, and I think there's something almost beautiful about how dumb that is.

CHAPTER 5

No, But . . .

Freshman year of college was a full-blown identity crisis. I got into Southern Oregon University and entertained the idea of playing football there until, on a visit my senior year, the coach said the sentence "Practice starts in July" and I immediately staged a mental retirement ceremony right there in the student center. Small-school college football is bonkers. The coaches treat the program like it's the University of Alabama, even though most of the kids on the team have asthma and heavy ankles. Southern Oregon University's football team could play their games wearing jeans and it wouldn't change things that much. Practice should have started a week before the first game and it should have been at a Dave & Buster's.

Alas, this was not the case, and so my football career was gone, and with it went a huge chunk of my identity. Some things didn't change, of course. I still wore hoodies, basketball shorts, and slides to class every single day regardless of the weather. I still burped words. I still used my defensive tackle club-and-rip technique on doors, trees, stop signs, and anything else that could be clubbed and then ripped. But other things changed immediately. I didn't have a role I could play anymore. I was forced/set loose to pursue a new identity. I think that's one of the big appeals for a lot of people entering college, but for me, it was terrifying. I still thought I needed a justification I could give other people for why I was so fat, and I didn't have one that instantly created admiration and acceptance.

Of course, all the cool stuff that college changes happened, too. The intoxicating freedom, the intoxicating ideas, the intoxicating intoxicants. I explored them all, determined to enjoy myself despite the terror. My freshman year became one of extremes. Sometimes it felt like I was plagued with a paralysis of choice, trying to figure out who I was in the world, after "high school football player" cashed out early. I'd get stuck in periods of fear, confusion, and laziness—where I'd opt for the familiar comforts of stasis, food, beer, and Xbox. I didn't gain the Freshman 15, but only because I already weighed 350 pounds.

Other times, though, freshman year felt like my entire being was vibrating with the idea of endless possibility. I skipped class and wrote bad poems and read weird books and I started saying "film" instead of "movie" if I felt like the "film" deserved it. I developed a ridiculous sleep schedule, seemingly just because I could. There was one period where I just kept waking up one hour later every single day until I went all the way around the clock and back to normal. Southern Oregon is in a town called Ashland, and Ashland is home to some very whimsical public parks, and I'd go wander through them after midnight and sit by the creek and sketch out ideas for some unremembered flights of fancy. I also ate a lot of Hot Pockets, and one time this dude "Schmink" drank something like eighteen Red Bulls and had to go to the hospital. Life could also be pretty sweet.

As freshman year of college drew to a close, I'd learned two things definitively:

1. The German parliament is called the Bundestag.

2. I didn't know who I was going to be in life, but I was pretty sure I wasn't going to find out at Southern Oregon University.

So, I transferred up north, to Portland State University. Mostly, I just wanted to be in a city again. Ashland was nice, but I needed action, I needed life, I needed a Best Buy that wasn't a forty-five-minute car ride from campus. Portland offered all those things. The one thing Portland couldn't offer was an instant fix to my academically unmotivated self. Portland State is a wonderful college, but I can't say I was taking advantage of it. College was mainly something I was doing for the loan money and for the delayed arrival of adulthood. I saw friends and former high school classmates pick majors and discover passions, and my searching was starting to feel like flailing. I picked political science because it was easy and I heard it was a good major if you wanted to go to law school. I thought I wanted to go to law school because it sounded impressive and because it was three more years of school before entering the real world. It didn't move me, though. It didn't give me a sense of belonging or purpose the way football had. You aren't entitled to those feelings in your life, but I knew enough to feel their absence. I had no idea how I would find them, but I knew it was important to try.

I didn't realize it at the time, but looking back now, it's clear how not having any sense of purpose really did a number on me. I didn't have anything in my life to keep me from sliding into a total broke-boy bacchanalia. I didn't care about my classes, so why not go hungover? Why go at all? Drink until 4:00 A.M. on a Tuesday, play *Tiger Woods Golf* until 6:00 A.M. on a Wednesday, stay up until 7:00 A.M. on a Thursday writing a term paper that was due at 8:00 P.M. the day before. My self-esteem sucked anyway. It had been blown apart by being fat, by being mediocre in the face of expectation, by just generally being in my early twenties. You're a raw nerve in that era of your existence. Life hurts, and that isn't unique to fat people or to any one group, really. Pretty much everyone goes through some version of young-adult malaise. Those years are full of promise and pain, but my promise was spoiled, and I didn't have anywhere to put the pain. I couldn't spin it into anything positive. I wasn't riding a sense of accomplishment because I wasn't accomplishing shit. Every endorphin I experienced was the result of an unearned reward. I was hungover, so I ate a pizza; I drank a beer because that goes great with pizza; I drank nine more beers because that goes great with one beer; I went and got a burrito with my friends and then drank nine more beers and woke up and did it again.

One night, my three college roommates and I threw a house party, and I drank a fifth of Seagram's and a two-liter bottle of 7UP out of a Brita water filter pitcher and I got super drunk, which is what happens when you do that. There was a band playing in our unfinished basement, and while attempting to walk down the stairs to go see that, I missed a step and tumbled down, grinding my forehead against the concrete wall as I did. I didn't feel a thing (pitcher of 7&7). As a consequence, I took my shirt off and started rocking out while bleeding from the forehead. Right around this time, our landlord showed up with the police, and I decided that I was the perfect guy to make sure everything was chill. Shirtless and bleeding, I went and talked to the cops. According to less-drunk friends, I tried to put my arm around the most important-looking cop so I could tell him that my landlord was just being a prick and that it was totally okay that we were partying, and then my *also blackout drunk* roommates had to walk me away so I didn't get arrested. After the cops left, I started running in the vague direction of my landlord's house to . . . I guess beat him up . . . and my friend Nic had to lure me back to the house with a tub of imitation crab. I was a wild boy (total dumbass). It wasn't always that crazy—sometimes the only thing I was

bingeing was episodes of ~~Entourage~~—but everything in my life
was built to distract me from the fact that I didn't have anything
from which to be distracted.

Then I got lucky. Portland State is one of those liberal arts col-
leges that want you to get a well-rounded education. Even if you're
majoring in biochemistry, they want you to take a couple of classes
about *The Great Gatsby* or jazz or the art of the African mask, so
you'll be a well-rounded biochemist and you'll be able to drop
interesting facts about Charles Mingus at your biochemist dinners. I know a lot of people hate these curricula, but I'll defend
them forever, because I owe them my life.

I needed an arts credit to graduate, and though graduation
was a few years away, I thought I'd go ahead and knock the class
out early because it was probably going to be pretty easy. You always have to do the easy stuff first in life, because you could drop
dead at any moment, and it'd feel pretty silly if you did a bunch
of hard stuff and then died before it paid off. I was perusing the
arts classes, looking for the easiest one I could find, and I remem-
bered that my uncle taught improvisational theater at Portland
State. Improv. Literally just making stuff up. I couldn't paint, but
I could call a guy Harold even though his name was Keith. Improv sounded easy as hell, plus my uncle probably wouldn't fail
me, so I signed up.

I walked into that first class and within five minutes I knew
what I'd be doing for the rest of my life. We started doing improv
warm-ups and everything just clicked. I felt a profound sense of
belonging; I felt a calling; I felt like when you're putting together
a desk from IKEA and you can't get the drawer to slide onto its
tracks and you try to force it, and it won't relent, and you push
harder, and it almost breaks, and you pinch your finger and you're
going to scream and then all of a sudden the drawer just glides
effortlessly into place, except I felt that feeling in my soul. It felt
like kismet. I got to be quick; I got to be funny; I got to play a
bunch of different roles. Suddenly I had a use for all these skills I'd

developed to cope with being a fat kid in a world that hates fat people. I could use them to make people laugh, and that made them feel good, but more important, it made me feel powerful. For a long time, I'd just wanted to feel like a normal person, but making people laugh didn't make me feel like I was just a normal person; it made me feel bigger than that. I was addicted. I didn't care if it meant dying dead broke in a ditch. I was doing this.

Plus, it didn't hurt that there was a proud lineage of funny fat guys—John Candy, Chris Farley, John Goodman, Jack Black, John Belushi, Wayne Knight—yes, Wayne Knight. *Seinfeld, Dirty Dancing,* and *Jurassic Park* get you on the list. I saw that there was a place in the world for fat guys who could make people laugh, and with that came fame and money and power but also, most important, validation.

Comedy scratched every itch. There was another improv class, so I took it, then I repeated the first one, then I repeated the second one, then I TA'd them both, then I dropped out of school and moved to Los Angeles for a year to study with the Groundlings. I used my Bar Mitzvah money to finance the move to L.A., and I didn't know a single person in the city when I got there. I slept in hotels and used an internet café to scour Craigslist looking for a place to live. Writing the words "internet café" just made me feel a thousand years old. I eventually found a place to live, in South Central, with two USC students. I found a job, too, at a P.F. Chang's. I worked, slept, and took improv classes. In my free time, I sat alone in a Starbucks and wrote sketches. My drive consumed everything. My passion immolated my loneliness, my insecurities, and my desire to connect with women. Even in Los Angeles I was good, I was making people laugh, and that felt amazing. I breezed through the first two Groundlings classes and then slammed into a brick wall—there was a year's wait for the third level of classes, a sketch-writing class. My momentum was dead. I had no way to perform. I had no way to get validation. My loneliness and my insecurity caught up with me quick. I wasn't an up-and-coming comedian anymore; I was a college dropout who worked at P.F. Chang's.

I left Los Angeles in less than a year. I returned to Portland State with the intention of finishing my degree while I waited for a spot in the Groundlings to open back up. I started TA'ing improv classes again and even started my own improv group, but unlike in L.A., the speed of this scene couldn't help me outrun all of life's little needs. I developed crushes on girls and I couldn't do anything about them because I was so insecure. I was lonely and frustrated with myself and with my art. I wanted to rehearse four nights a week and everybody else wanted to . . . you know . . . be in college.

One day a local producer booked our improv group for a show, and she said, "You also do stand-up, right?" I lied and said I did. I don't know why. Three weeks later I did stand-up comedy for the first time. It was a blur, but I know I joked about NPR taking commercial breaks that were just thirty-five seconds of jazz, fighting a lion in hand-to-hand combat, and I definitely remember closing with a joke about how doctors should focus on the positive with fat people—I was more likely to get diabetes but was less likely to catch herpes. Despite how that might read, I was good at stand-up immediately and now I didn't have to rely on anyone else's work ethic. I got to decide how hard I wanted to work, and I wanted to work really hard. I got better at stand-up fast. I mined my pain for laughs. I don't know if this is a common experience for everyone who becomes funny for a living, but as I got more successful and skilled and confident onstage, my self-loathing and disgust and desire to self-destruct seemed to grow as well. Just in time for me to start dating.

CHUBBY.

When you absolutely, positively, 100 percent need to evoke the image of a cartoon bunny while describing your human body, you can't do better than "chubby." I describe myself as "chubby" a lot, but I'm married—it's okay for me to be adorable.

CHAPTER 6

This Isn't Gonna Work Out, and Neither Am I

Before we go any further, I just want to issue a blanket apology to everyone I ever dated, everyone I tried to date, everyone who tried to date me, everyone I matched with on a dating app, everyone I made eye contact with in the produce section of a grocery store, everyone reading this who thought I was a good guy, and my mom.

I'm a bundle of problems. I've spent years trying to untangle that mess, and I'll spend the rest of my life trying to untangle that mess, and that's how it should be. We're all fucked up, but there's beauty in the effort to be better. A lot of my problems, especially when it comes to relationships, are due to me being so fat. Some of those are directly tied to my weight; most of them are because of the massive lack of self-confidence, the constant need for validation, and the sheer volume of self-hate and self-harm that I built up around my body issues. I don't know if I'm messed up because I was fat, or I was fat because I'm messed up. That becomes a chicken-and-egg situation real fast. It doesn't matter anyway. I would never try to paint anyone else, fat or otherwise, with these problems. I'm only talking about it because I think there's a chance that people will recognize pieces of themselves in what I'm going to say. I think there's comfort in knowing that you aren't alone. My hope is that you can also find hope and some motivation to confront your demons and treat yourself with kindness. I've been down in some dark places, and things really can get better.

Oh, while I'm here, I also want to apologize for opening so many Tinder messages with "Hiiiiiiiii!" I don't know why I did that. It makes me sound like I'm trying to be chill about returning some shirts at Nordstrom.

Where to start? Up until I met my high school girlfriend, I was a straight-up virgin. Like, not "kind of a virgin," I was a full-blown virgin. You could appease a variety of different gods with my death, you know what I mean? I hadn't even really kissed anyone. I had a kindergarten girlfriend, which is like saying I was a chef because I had a plastic Fisher-Price kitchen set. Until I met my high school girlfriend, Hailey, that childhood role-play was the closest I'd been to a romantic relationship.

I really can't imagine when I would have scored that first kiss before that point. I had crushes, I guess, but I did very little about them. I spent every middle school dance in the computer lab playing a multiplayer game called *Bolo*, where you drove a little eight-bit tank around, and somehow nobody wanted to smooch me for being a pubescent Erwin Rommel.

I attended two Bar Mitzvahs, and those are hot spots for first kisses. I was too busy getting kissed by aunts at my own Bar Mitzvah, and my friend Marty's Bar Mitzvah was the first time I ever saw live sketch comedy, which should tell you all you need to know about anyone getting a smooch that night. I say that, but he could have had his party inside a Christina Aguilera music video and I still wouldn't have scored with anyone, because I had absolutely no game. When I say no game, I mean no game. A void

~~where the game is supposed to be.~~ I didn't suck at hitting on girls, I just didn't do it. I'm not sure if that's because I was chubby or thirteen. On the odd occasions when I tried to shoot my shot, it went over like bedtime at a slumber party. In second grade, I had a crush on a girl named Rachel, so I . . . hid . . . a rubber snake . . . in her . . . desk? On April Fools' Day? What were the steps between "Oh, look, a rubber snake in my desk" and "Let's go roller-blading and kiss" supposed to be? I truly have no idea why I thought that might work and I'm the same me who did it. There was a girl named Lorrie in middle school, and she was cool and beautiful and I had a few classes with her. I didn't even have a crush on her, but everybody else had a crush on her, so I just kind of went along with the prevailing opinion. One day in class, her backpack tumbled off the back of her chair, and her report card fell out and landed near my feet. I picked it up to hand it to her and yelled out, "You're getting a C– in English!" because I'd seen some of the attractive kids be mean to one another in a sexy way and I thought this was my opportunity to do the same. I can still remember how sad and ashamed she looked and how immediately I felt like the Archduke of Dickheads. No game. Negative game. I don't think it helped that the ideal boy was Jonathan Taylor Thomas and I looked more like John Rhys-Davies, but being fat wasn't my only problem then either.

I don't think I even wanted a girlfriend back then. I wanted the narcotic hit of acceptance that would come from a girl liking me. I wanted to use that feeling like a topical ointment. Normal people had girlfriends, I thought, so if I had one, I would feel a little bit more like everybody else. The external validation would nullify the internal doubt. I say "internal doubt" because that's really the demon here. I was the butt of the joke often enough. I took my fair share of bullying, but one of the most insidious things about bullying is how it makes you create paranoid fiction in your head. Every kid who calls you a fat-ass to your face means there's twenty more kids saying it behind your back. If you're seeing one termite, you're toast; they're all up in the foundation. Only it's not true. They're not talking about how you're fat; they're talking about Allen Iverson or what would happen if Batman fought Jesus. You couldn't tell me they weren't talking about my tits. I thought a girlfriend might shut down those conversations (that weren't happening anyway). A girlfriend might make me feel better about myself. In reality, a girlfriend in middle school would have just distracted me from online role-playing games and downloading pictures of *Tomb Raider*'s Lara Croft.

Anyway, I dated a girl in high school and I already told you about that. It was euphoric and then it was heartbreaking. I liked her and I liked how dating her made me feel normal, and then I lost her and I lost that sense of belonging I had unfairly pulled from her and that relationship.

After that, I made a sizable real estate investment in the friend zone. I mean, sizable: If you could Airbnb your romantic frustration, I'd be a billionaire. My early twenties were spent just waiting for girls to open their eyes, turn to me in slow motion, and see the perfect boyfriend standing right in front of them. I took girls to dinners, movies, Planned Parenthood appointments, always as a platonic escort.

People get mad at guys who complain about being "friend-zoned" and I understand that. They're right to be mad. Guys try to backdoor themselves into a relationship under false pretenses and then complain about something as lovely as the friendship they get instead. It certainly isn't fair for the women who thought they were just being good friends, only to find out that they are apparently actually withholding monsters who only value superficial qualities in a romantic partner. The ways that guys cope with being "friend-zoned" are stupid, too. One common complaint is that girls lie about wanting a nice guy, but then skip over their friend who is standing right there, being perfectly nice. Nice, you know, nice, like the kind of nice where you befriend someone hoping that you'll get to have sex with them. Trust me, I understand the animosity toward these guys, but I also spent a few years being one of them. I also feel bad for these dudes.

I never consciously started one of these relationships thinking, "I'm going to make her believe I'm a friend and then I'll somehow use that friendship to get her to have sex with me." Getting "friend-zoned" always happened the same way for me—I'd meet a girl, I'd like that girl, and a combination of terror and stupidity would get in the way of me ever making my romantic intentions known. Even if they were also interested in me romantically, I couldn't make the first move. I was paralyzed. I was just so afraid they'd reject me. I thought these girls would be insulted that I even harbored the dream that they might be interested in a big fat slob like me. I thought they'd laugh behind my back. The potential felt cataclysmic, so the mutual affection invariably settled into a friendship, whether that was always its destiny or not. It felt safer to just stay in their orbit and wait for some kind of miracle. Looking back now, it all seems so silly. These girls obviously liked me, and they certainly valued me as a person, if not as a potential boyfriend. They wouldn't have laughed; they were lovely people, not cruel caricatures plucked from internet message boards. Who knows what their reaction would have been? Maybe they would have been into it—that would have been cool. Maybe they wouldn't have been into it, and they would have rejected me, and I could have learned earlier that it wasn't the end of the world when a girl doesn't like you.

I see young guys going through this now and my heart breaks. They're lying to these girls, but they're also lying to themselves. They're hyper-fixating on their vulnerabilities and ignoring all of their own best qualities. They're suffocating themselves, their potential to grow and learn. They're severely stunting their ability to love and to accept love. Some of these guys call themselves incels, involuntary celibates, and some of them have more extreme views about women, but the playbook is always the same. These guys are afraid of getting hurt, so they only put a little bit of themselves out there. They expect women to guess their intentions. They expect women to infer that there must be whole galaxies happening inside these men, unlimited potential and untold kindness. The women never get there because the guys won't let them, because instead of actually talking to the women they purport to covet, they're playing out ten million worst-case scenarios in their heads. They want these women to see something in them that they aren't even willing to see in themselves. That's so fucking tragic because there *are* whole galaxies happening inside these men. These men are just too afraid to admit that they don't love themselves enough, so they blame it all on the women, and the hole gets deeper every time. I know this because I've gone through it.

Saying "you need to love yourself more" is some bullshit. I mean, it's true, but it's true the way "you need to lose some weight" is true. If you say it to me, even if I need to hear it, I hate you. So, I'm not going to say it. Instead, I'll say that I wish I had taken an honest self-inventory rather than fixating on my weight and the insecurities I built up around it. I think I would have liked what I saw. I was nice and funny and smart. I was a hard worker. I was tall. I had beautiful eyebrows. I had plenty to offer a girl, only I was too afraid to offer it. So I hated those girls, but nowhere near as much as I hated myself. All I had to do was look inward and I think I would have found my way out.

Of course, worrying about what other people were thinking was the dominant force in my romantic life for a long time. It's not a surprise that I didn't really care what I thought about myself. This is going to continue to make me look like a piece of garbage, so let's just jump right in. There were decades of my life, especially when I was at my fattest, when I never would have dated another fat person. I wouldn't even consider it. I couldn't. If I dated another fat person, people would think I was only able to attract another fat person. You know, because I'm fat, and therefore I'm disgusting, so my punishment for being fat and disgusting is dating another fat person because they're disgusting, too. Two fat dis-gusting people sitting in a tree, k-i-s-s-i—oh no, the branch broke. The fatphobia and self-hate that coiled within me was so unbe-lievably strong and resilient. I want to grab myself by the shoul-ders and scream back through the decades that I was participating in the very system that vilified my body. I want to shake it out of me. It's still in me. The scar is too deep. It's haunted my life and every relationship I've had since. When I started performing stand-up comedy, I'd go onstage and joke that I couldn't fuck an-other fat person because neither one of us could see our genitalia. We'd have to have sex like how a fighter jet refuels mid-flight, all guesswork and near misses. That joke was an act of self-immolation to try and shield my good nature from the awful, embarrassing truth. I hated how other people's fat reminded me of my own.

It's the kind of problem that you hope time wrings out of you. You hope that as you leave behind the awkward-baby-giraffe phases of your life, and you become a more self-assured and suc-cessful person, the rest of your life will follow suit. You'd like to think you get better as you get older. I got worse.

Stand-up had gone well for me in Portland. I won the very first Portland's Funniest Person contest. I had a weekly column for the *Portland Mercury* called "Portland as Fuck," where I wrote about whatever was floating in the local zeitgeist from week to week. They gave me the column because I wrote an article for the paper in which I tried to look at Voodoo Doughnut and our legendary strip clubs with fresh eyes. When I was growing up in Portland, they were just part of the furniture, but they were also the first things people asked me about whenever I did comedy out of town. It was a beautiful time to be a creative person in Portland. The city was in love with itself. The comedians loved the cooks loved the bands loved the writers loved the burlesque dancers loved the bartenders loved the poets loved the people welding to-gether insane rideable bicycle sculptures. Portland felt alive and people were starting to notice.

Because of stand-up, I had the opportunity to do television for our NBA team, the 1977 World Champion Portland Trail Blazers. Somebody from the local cable news network saw me at Helium Comedy Club and asked the owners, "Hey, can some of your comedians come on some of our shows?" and all of a sudden I was on a panel cracking jokes with players I'd grown up idolizing.

I'd fly to New York and L.A. and I'd get big laughs on their best shows. On one trip to Los Angeles, I was booked on a show called "Holy Fuck." Right before my set, the host told me that Aziz Ansari was going to do a quick set before I went up. This was an alt-comedy show in the mid-2010s. Going up after Aziz Ansari was like going up after God, but a more hip, American Apparel version of God. Aziz was friends with Kanye West. I was wearing cargo shorts. He went up and he had a pretty good set. I went up after and I crushed it. (He was doing brand-new stuff and I was doing jokes I'd practiced a million times, but I would never tell anyone that.)

The set went so well that I got a manager. A big Hollywood manager! While I still lived in Portland, if you can even believe that! And then I was selected as a "New Face" at the Just for Laughs comedy festival, which is like being an NBA draft pick for stand-up comedians. You know who else was in my class? Pete Davidson! I imagine he's in Saint-Tropez with Dua Lipa or Zendaya or Dame Judi Dench also bragging about how he once did a comedy festival with workmanlike television writer Ian Karmel.

After the festival, I moved to Los Angeles with a bunch of momentum and then, literally within days, secured an appearance on Chelsea Handler's late-night show *Chelsea Lately*, and that went so well that she immediately hired me to be a writer and a panelist. Shortly after that, I did my first late-night set on *Conan*. It was like what somebody's aunt thinks will happen to their nephew when they move to Hollywood, except it actually happened to me. I went from my first stand-up set to working on *Chelsea Lately* in less than five years.

I present this tepidly impressive résumé to give a sense of what I was doing at the time and how it made me think of myself. I thought I was an absolute lord. I felt like I was living the prologue to season one of *Entourage*. When I stepped onstage, I had power over the entire room, and people in the entertainment industry treated me accordingly. I got high on the feeling. The good kind of high, like how it feels when you listen to a song by The Weeknd. I also got the bad kind of high, like what happens if you read the actual lyrics to a song by The Weeknd. Anyway, I felt like a big fat tiny little god.

All this bravado was fueled by a yawning chasm of insecurity, of course. It always is. It didn't matter to me. I was feeling good about myself. I was rolling. I was . . . well, I was sitting in an office for twelve hours a day trying to come up with funny things for Chelsea Handler to say about Charlie Sheen yelling "Tiger Blood!" It was an office job. It was a very fun office job, but it was an office job. It didn't matter to me. I bought into my own hype, and I assumed that everyone else was buying into it, too.

It was with this energy that I got myself into a series of relationships that all had two things in common: The women were beautiful and the situations were impossible.

I saw these women as a reward. I never consciously said that to myself, but looking back now, it's pretty clear. I took all the bullshit in my life—all the fat jokes, all the girls who just wanted to be friends, all the gouging pain of being on the outside looking in, and I turned it into a career, and that career was thriving, and on some level I thought I deserved the attention of these women. Everyone deserves to be loved, but when you start to think of that "deserves" in transactional terms, you're fucked. I was fucked.

I can't generalize because I don't live in anyone else's head, but I can tell you what happened to me and what I think happens to a lot of guys when their romantic fortunes are suddenly reversed. You go your whole life wishing you were more attractive to the people you find attractive. You wish that you'd been born with a faster metabolism or higher cheekbones, that you were taller or stronger. You're sad about it, but also you're angry about it. Why do you have to deal with this shit when that guy over there just happened to be born perfect? You see all the pretty people being pretty together. Maybe they'll let you into their world, but never the way you want to be let in. You'll never be one of them. You might get invited to their parties, but not the way that they're going to those parties. You feel like a prop. You feel like a journalist from the planet of the virgins. Maybe they don't even invite you to the parties.

You feel stripped of your humanity, so you strip them of their humanity, only you feel justified in doing it because you think they did it first. They're shallow, stupid; this is their peak and they don't even know it. You, meanwhile, you're pursuing your own shit. You don't have a date on Friday night, so you stay in and work on your script or your book or your YouTube channel or whatever it is that you love, that they'll never get because they're too busy being pretty.

People start to like what you do. A few of them at first, but then more and more and more. They don't just like it, they love it. They love you. They validate you. They talk about you. They tell their friends about you. Their friends notice you. It's intoxicating. Then maybe a little money comes. People you looked up to start to respect you. Somebody writes about you. People want to be near you. Some of those people might even want to have sex with you. A pretty person might even want to have sex with you. Look at them. Look at how pretty they are. Look at how highly that speaks of you. Look. You earned it! Enjoy! You're still in that system that made you feel like an ugly, fat piece of shit, but look at you now! You played the long game and now you're winning the whole thing. You're sleeping with a pretty person. She has a name, yes, but that isn't what matters here. She's a pretty person. The same kind of pretty person who wouldn't have given you the time of day before. So even though you're certain she only likes you because of what you represent, be with her. Because you deserve it. You're entitled to it. Think about what you went through to get here, to this place, where this pretty person wants to have sex with you.

It never occurs to you, at the time, that you might be more attractive because you're more confident because you've worked hard and it's paying off. You have a passion and you've pursued it and that's attractive, too. But you can't distinguish between that and someone just wanting to use your success to validate their own feelings. Probably because that's exactly what you're doing with their beauty. It's a math you do in your head to cope with your own perceived shortcomings. You think you lack their beauty, so they must lack your . . . something.

You need to tell yourself that you've got something that they don't; you didn't get their good looks, but you got some stuff they didn't, and now the arrow is pointing up on your qualities while their beauty slowly fades. You tell yourself this so you don't just feel like a genetic loser or a broken person. It's an awful trap. You're dehumanizing yourself and everyone else you meet. You're balancing the numbers on some ledger of social values that you've created in your insecurity rather than, you know, actually getting to know people and see if you hit it off.

The relationships I sought out were impossible. Most of them were long-distance. Some people get into long-distance relationships because they want to make the relationship work; I got into them because I wanted to make sure it didn't. I dated a woman who lived in Portland with both of her kids. Then I dated a woman who lived in Portland, but *her* kid lived with the dad in Washington State. Then I dated the first woman again. Then I dated another woman who lived in Portland, but this one had no kids. We had an incredibly volatile relationship and eventually she moved to Los Angeles, and as soon as she did, we started sleeping in separate bedrooms and we never had sex or really any kind of physical contact. She moved back to Oregon and then she dumped me over the phone. Somewhere in there I dated a couple of women who lived in Los Angeles. One of those relationships ended because we spent so much of our time together getting blackout drunk and she realized we weren't good for each other. The other relationship ended because things were going too well, and I started to become disgusted with her for liking me. I broke up with her one night, weeping, telling her that I had to get my health under control. It was an honest reason, in a kind of roundabout way. I did need to become a healthier person, but in that moment, what I really needed was to be far away from her. I couldn't be in a relationship where things were going well, because then I would have to think about the future. I would have to think about getting married and having children. I'd have to think about being a 400-pound binge-drinking food addict who hadn't been to the doctor in, like, a decade. I'd have to think about putting a partner through that reality. I'd have to think about putting kids through that. I'd have to think about their graduation and how unlikely it was that I'd be alive for it, unless I made some big changes in my life, and that was too much to think about. So, instead, I broke up with her and dated another mother. She lived in Boise with her three children.

These women were lovely people, by the way. All of them full of incredibly attractive qualities and wonderful personalities. I'm the schmuck here. I mean, a few of them were also shitty, but they were micro-shitty within a larger lovely ecosystem. I had grand, intoxicating love affairs with some of them. That's the nature of long-distance dating. It's a boom-bust dynamic. The fatalism of everything is romantic in a self-destructive sort of way, and I had a subconscious attraction to expiration dates.

Other than the breakup I described, every single one of these women dumped me and I hated them for it, even though I deserved it and even though it was exactly what I wanted on a subconscious level. I was so used to being romantically frustrated and overlooked in my life that I couldn't recognize my own destructive behavior. When you're an underdog for so long, you can't ever think of yourself as anything but an underdog, even when you're being a total piece of shit. I can see it clearly now. I was toxic. I was a terrible, drunken mess. I had so many things I needed to work out before I could be in a healthy relationship, but I kept trying to skip over those issues by jumping right to the relationship part. It doesn't work like that. Your bullshit is not *Super Mario Bros. 3* and women are not a warp whistle.

I wish I could say that my old habits died with those impossible relationships, but instead that string of heartbreak kicked off a run of despicable behavior. I have no other choice here; I have to invoke a truly exhausted term because there is no better description. I behaved like a fuckboy. The only immediate lesson I took from those relationships was that it felt good when pretty women liked me. I kept chasing that feeling. I didn't need the last three months of those relationships, just the first three weeks, just the thrill of it. I didn't even need three weeks. I could get that feeling in a week, or a weekend, or a night. I let women think I wanted more than just sex, that maybe I'd want a relationship. I didn't actively lie to anyone; I just let them believe whatever they wanted to believe. I bet a few of the women also just wanted to have sex, but even if that was the case, I'd never let myself see it. Again, I poisoned myself and, in turn, poisoned my relationships with other people. I didn't think anyone could be sexually attracted to me because I was so fat. I thought they were just sucking it up and gritting their teeth through the sex so that they'd get the thrill of dating me. Like dating a binge-drinking, sleep-apnea-snoring stand-up comedian was some kind of grand prize.

It got to such a weird, warped point with me that I didn't even want to have sex anymore. I just needed to prove to myself that I could have sex with someone if I wanted to. That's how I got the validation I needed. The sex didn't matter half as much. Sometimes I'd match with someone on Tinder or Bumble or Raya, and I'd text myself into a place where I thought sex was a sure thing, and then I'd fall off the face of the earth.

The partners came and went, some for a night, some for longer.

I went on serial dating, bumming out people's daughters all over America's golden West. I started to realize that I was the problem. I mean, it's obvious now, but back then I was in a fog of weed, alcohol, high blood pressure, and self-pity. Sometimes I had trouble realizing what day it was, so realizing that I was engaging in a pattern of antisocial, self-destructive behavior that was hurting innocent people was monumental. I didn't do anything about it at first, but I did realize it. I tried to be better. Trying counts, but it only really counts for the person who's doing the trying. It doesn't count so much for the poor woman wondering why I ubered home from the party and passed out in bed without telling her goodbye, even though I was the person who invited her to the party. I was trying to be better, but I hadn't done a single thing about my root problems. I hadn't examined my anxiety or my insecurity or my history of self-destructive behavior. I hadn't done anything about my old problems, so despite my trying, I slipped into those same awful habits. By the time I had the language to communicate that, and to try to apologize, most of those women had stopped responding to my text messages.

For a long time, I had been punishing any woman who actually liked me and idolizing any woman who rejected me. Gradually, I walled myself off while I tried to work on myself, but it took years to get there. I started treating myself better. As hokey as it sounds, the more I loved myself, the more I felt like I was able to actually love another person. I know I already said it's stupid to talk about loving yourself more, and it's a massive cliché, but sometimes a cliché is a cliché because it's true. It's easy to paint it on a sign and hang it in your mom's kitchen; it's much harder to actually love yourself. It takes work and commitment, and you have to be willing to forgive yourself and earn that forgiveness by not being such a jerk. It takes being able to look in the mirror, see yourself honestly, and with hope in your voice say, "Jesus, what a mess."

When I met my wife, I was trying to grow as a person. I was especially trying to respect myself more and, as a consequence of that, respect my romantic partners more. I'd just recently been reckless with someone's affection and I could feel myself sliding. I drew a line in the sand. I wasn't going to let myself pursue someone romantically simply because I thought it would be a challenge to win them over. I wasn't going to get caught up in validating myself through someone else's affection. I'd hurt myself too much doing that. I'd hurt too many other people doing that. I didn't want to fuck up again. It was the first time in a long time that I was focusing on how I felt about another person rather than how that person made me feel about myself. It worked.

But you don't stop fucking up just because you tell yourself you're done fucking up. The part of you that wants to self-destruct doesn't just go away. When I met my wife, I was already on my way to a healthier lifestyle. I was losing weight. I'd faced down some serious health scares. I'd overcome my fear of the doctor. I was committed to being a healthier person. This was such a massive shift for me. The gravity of these positive changes pulled my self-esteem with them. I was feeling good about myself in a real, sustainable way because I was being good to myself in a real, sustainable way. This wasn't the temporary euphoria of a career milestone. This wasn't the dopamine hit of a good stand-up set. This was steamed broccoli and long walks. This was blood pressure medicine. This was telehealth therapy and meditation.

I'm so grateful that we met during this period of my life. Three months earlier, maybe things don't go so well for us. Three months earlier, maybe I mess it up.

Even in this better place, I found myself trying to sabotage the relationship. Inside, I was still terrified by how good things were going. Inside, I was tantalized by the familiar comfort of not having anything to lose. Inside, I was still figuring out how to be a healthy person in a healthy relationship. Wanting to be better isn't enough. You have to have someone in your life who is patient enough to let you try and fail and then try again. My decades of mangled self-esteem and horrible relationships did a number on me. I didn't know how to communicate what I was feeling unless it was good. That would be bad enough, but I also didn't know how to accept feedback in our relationship without catastrophizing it. Anytime a relationship wasn't perfect, I thought it was going to end. I'm a child of divorce. It's part of the territory. It's the price we have to pay for two sets of Christmas presents. I could see this bullshit happening even as I was doing it, and the frustration of being trapped in that same cycle would drive me further down into it. I was trying to be better, and it was still slipping away from me. After the emotion wore off, I'd feel like a werewolf the morning after a full moon—just sitting there, agonized by regret. Only this time, my wife was sitting there next to me. She met my mania with love. I was thrashing and she was patient. I've never felt that kind of love from a partner, and I was only able to receive it because she's an amazing person and because I finally started to feel like I deserved it.

You aren't entitled to someone who will put up with your bullshit. You aren't entitled to anything from another person. In my experience, though, a good partner can see that you're trying. That trying is self-love in action. I want to make a masturbation joke here. I won't. Instead, let's switch from the metaphorical heart to the literal one. Let's talk about the doctor.

OBESITY.

"Obesity" is a beautiful word when you consider it free of any context, isn't it?

"Where are you going on vacation this summer?"

"Oh, my wife and I are getting a little place in Obesity. Just going to drink wine and swim and really connect with each other."

Obesity would be a great name for the following things: son, daughter, Mazda hybrid SUV, racehorse, perfume, schooner.

CHAPTER 7

Regarding the Heart Attack I Thought I Was Having

I'm pretty sure I'll die from being fat. It sits forever in the back of my mind like a love seat that doesn't quite go with the rest of the room. It blends in when I'm busy, but when I'm still, sometimes it's all that I can think about. I never used to think about it before I lost weight. Maybe it was too big to hold in my head while I was living in a state of denial about the damage I was doing to my body. Maybe I was eating garbage and chugging booze to distract myself from those thoughts and it worked. Maybe those thoughts have quickened as I've steadily reached middle age. I hope it's middle age, anyway. Life isn't promised in the best of situations. Healthy people's lives are cut short all the time. You're more drastically aware of your finite time when you've sat in an urgent care and had the nurse practitioner read your blood pressure, and the first words out of her mouth are "Oh wow" followed by "So it's 211 over . . ." (forgotten).

I found myself in that urgent care because twelve hours earlier, at 5:45 in the morning, I was standing on the sidewalk in north-east Portland with my iPhone clutched in my hand. I'd typed 911 into the screen, and my thumb was hovering over the little green phone circle that would have landed me in the back of an ambulance. My other hand was moving rapidly between my neck and my chest, one moment pressed against the carotid artery, the next placed firmly over my sternum. My heart was slamming against my ribs like the double bass drum in a Metallica song. My pulse was spasming against my finger like a freshly caught fish.

Twelve hours before that I was in my car, driving toward a chicken wing restaurant, fresh off an afternoon of patio ciders with one of my best friends. I was on a liberation trip. It was the summer of 2020, and I'd road-tripped up Interstate 5, back to my hometown, to visit the friends and family I'd only seen over FaceTime for the last six months. It was more than just liberation from the Sheetrock dungeon of quarantine, though. For months I'd been meticulous about my diet. Stricter than strict. After spending the first couple of weeks of Covid eating like Postmates was delivering directly to my electric chair, I'd tightened up. I'd decided to lose weight once and for all, now or never.

I'd dieted before, more times than I can count. I'd tried every gimmick, including willpower, and they'd all failed at varying stages for varying reasons, but this one was sticking. It was working. The pounds were slicking off, and I was converting discipline into pride in a way I'd never experienced before. I was feeling a level of satisfaction from commanding my addiction that was almost as good as biting into a grilled cheese sandwich. But then I set out for a week or two of friends, family, fun, a reminder of everything that life could be before we locked ourselves inside our houses. Surely I could take a little break from grilled chicken rolled up in lettuce. Besides, I'd earned it. So I found myself going back to one of my favorite restaurants in the world and picking up a to-go order of chicken wings and fried pickles. Another tier on the celebration cake I'd decided to make of the evening.

I was sucking chicken wings clean as I was parking the car in front of the apartment my friends were letting me borrow for the trip. I pride myself on my chicken-wing-eating ability. I like to think that there's a nobility in my complete deconstruction of the wings and drums that honors the chicken to whom they once belonged. There isn't even a whisper of meat on there once I'm done. Not even a hint, an allegation, a rumor of meat once having been there in the first place. I use every tooth in my mouth like they're clubs in Tiger's bag at Augusta. The incisors cutting, stripping, peeling. The molars popping the cartilaginous caps and grinding out the marrow. It might be the thing I'm best at in the whole world. If there was a chicken-wing-eating contest and it was based on quality instead of quantity, I'd be in a very different line of work right now. I kept eating the wings as I traipsed up the stairs and flopped onto the couch, and I washed them down with some fried pickles dipped into a chipotle mayonnaise concoction that may well be illegal by the time this book is published. This was a new me, of course, so I saved a few of the dozen wings I'd ordered for later. I was quickly joined at the apartment by another one of my best friends, and we proceeded to drink hard seltzer and listen to music and laugh late into the night. It was wonderful in the way that any relapse is wonderful for a while. She left. I finished the wings. I stumbled to bed. I fell asleep. My heart woke me up.

It's funny what goes through your mind at a time like that. I was terribly afraid, of course. Afraid in an animalistic sort of way. Mortally afraid, I suppose. Amid all the terror, there was a measure of utilitarian calm floating above the churn, trying to assess the nature of the threat and tow me out of the danger. Grab your phone. Put on your pants. Go outside because you still weigh more than 300 pounds and you want to make this as easy on the paramedics as you possibly can. They're going to be mad at you anyway; give them a reason to like you and maybe they'll try harder to save your life. There was more than just terror coursing through my constricted veins; there was also skepticism and denial. Even in this moment that should have been completely clear and sober, a part of my brain was trying to bargain. A part of me was trying to stop myself from calling for help, because if I did that, then it'd be a whole big thing and nobody would be chill about it. I was standing there thinking, "There's a chance this isn't a heart attack, and if I take an ambulance to the hospital, I'll have to tell my parents, I probably won't be able to get anything good for lunch, but more than that, I'll have to deal with a doctor. This might not be a heart attack, and still I'd have to deal with a doctor. I'd have to pull my head out of the sand and I'd have to confront everything I'd been ignoring for years. And, again, I'd have to deal with an overeducated, undersocialized, trash-handwriting, God-complex-having, Hawaii-condo-with-the-new-wife-owning nemesis, the doctor."

Plenty of ink has been spilled about the acrimonious relationship between fat people and doctors, and for good reason. There is so much fear, resentment, and loathing baked into so many of the interactions we have with medical professionals, and it's a two-way street. Some doctors deliver bad news to fat people with an attitude of "Well, what did you expect?" and we repay the favor by removing ourselves from the system entirely, going years between visits and never just for a checkup. It hurts to be spoken to like that. It's dehumanizing in a place that is already terrifying. When you're fat and you're at a doctor's appointment, you're already harboring the notion that you're not exactly a marathon runner with an adagio resting heart rate and immaculate blood work. The news is bad enough; you don't have to spit it at me. The pain of those interactions hurts for another reason, though. I'm going to speak only for myself here, because I don't want to generalize the way fat people behave, and because plenty of people are "overweight" while also being healthy, but still I suspect I'm not alone in what I'm about to say. Going to the doctor hurt for me because it disturbed the artificial "reality" I built around myself that told me it was okay to be living the way I was living. It ripped open the blinds, tore off the comforter, and screamed at me to wake up, and that was the last thing I wanted, even if it was closer to what I needed than the life I was living in ignorant bliss.

I knew I was unhealthy, but I was able to smudge that fact into the background because the alternative seemed impossible. I don't think I can adequately describe how daunting it feels to know you need to lose a lot of weight. It's very difficult and it takes a long time. I did it, and I'm not going to dip it in chocolate for you: It's the hardest thing I've ever done in my entire life. Before I did it, it seemed unfathomable. You can think of it as a "one day at a time" proposition, but then you start thinking about how many one days you have to take at a time and it's agonizing. The enormity of the task snuffs out your best intentions the same way an avalanche, which is really just a whole lot of harmless little snowflakes, buries you for good. So, for the longest time, I didn't think about it. I lived my life, and nothing catastrophic happened. I was fine. I felt strong. On occasion, I would entertain the thought that maybe I was immune to the deleterious effects of my obesity. Maybe I was some new kind of human who could be as fat as I was and die peacefully in my sleep on the eve of my ninety-fifth birthday, surrounded by great-grandchildren playing the Xbox Omega that I'd had installed in their retinas for Chanukah.

Even when I wasn't floating in those delusions, I'd do a sort of morbid math to give myself time to delay my reckoning. I'd look at famous fat people, figure out when and how they died, and work backward from there. John Candy died at forty-three, heart attack, and we were around the same size, but I didn't smoke, so maybe add a year or two for me. James Gandolfini died at fifty-one, heart attack, and he was less fat than me, but he yelled a lot on *The Sopranos,* so maybe that evened it out. John Belushi, less fat, more cocaine. Chris Farley, same deal. (That probably should have stopped me from ever doing cocaine, but by that point, well . . . it's not like I was trying to kill myself, but I don't think I was actively trying *not* to die either.) In my twenties and early thirties, I'd look at these people and think, "What's the rush? I've got a few years before I need to get my act together." Even now, after I lost weight, this kind of thinking is seared into my brain. I look at all the famous fat people who lost weight and nervously cross-reference their age, when they lost the weight, how fat they were for how long, and try to plot out my odds of survival. Al Roker, Al Sharpton, John Goodman, every offensive lineman who transitioned to a studio show on ESPN, all lost a bunch of weight, all chugging along, diluting my anxiety, but not enough to keep me from searching out the cause of death anytime I see a tweet about somebody dying, celebrity or otherwise.

I have a vague vestigial fantasy about my own death that I developed when I was bigger and haven't been able to shake. If I'm ever stabbed to death or I fall out of a hot-air balloon or I meet my end by failing to notice a mountain lion, I want you to know that I'll be lying in a pool of my own blood with the hint of a smile on my face, because in the most morbid way, I will have beat the odds. The people clicking on the GoFundMe for my funeral will be expecting to find the word "stroke" or "heart attack" or something else they can easily assign to my own easily observable destructive behavior and they will be left wanting.

Needless to say, I'm fixated on death now. I didn't start this book thinking I was ever going to quote Lin-Manuel Miranda, but there's a line in *Hamilton:* "I imagine death so much it feels more like a memory." That line fucked me up. I felt it like a cold wind. I used to hardly think about death at all. I long for that peace of mind, even though it was a complete fabrication that I maintained, at all costs, to the detriment of my health. Little problems occasionally popped up. Little problems that were easy to ignore. As the problems continued to grow, it became harder to ignore them, but humans are remarkable creatures and I somehow mustered up the focus and energy to ignore them all the same.

Ten years ago, I got two things right around the same time: gout and health insurance. You'd think the presence of the latter would have helped me address the presence of the former, but nah. Such was my steadfast dedication to avoiding the doctor. If you've ever had a gout flare-up, you know how serious I was about not being serious about my health. If you haven't had gout, wait until January, fly to Los Angeles, take a car to Pasadena, secure front row seats to the Rose Parade, and proceed to let every single float drive over your big toe. Let the marching bands stomp on it, too. Any horses, Buffalo Soldiers, police motorcycles, Hondas full of *The Bachelor* contestants—make them get in on it, too. If Rita Moreno is there being honored, ask her to stomp on your big toe. If LeVar Burton is celebrating his storied career by marshaling the parade, don't just take my word for it, have him drop a heel on your digit. Have Mario Lopez stand directly on the front of your shoe and not get off until he introduces the Harlem Globetrotters, who delight the crowd with their basketball antics, all while also standing on your big toe. Take this experience and then spread it out over a week, and that's how gout feels the first time you have it. The condition is caused by a buildup of uric acid in the blood, which then bottlenecks at your joints and causes incredibly painful swelling. What triggers gout? I'm glad you asked.

- Preserved meat
- Game meat
- Organ meat
- Probably easier to just say all red meat
- Oh, also turkey
- And seafood
- Sugar
- Corn syrup
- Yeast
- Alcohol
- Especially beer
- But all alcohol, so don't get any big ideas
- Gravy

It's everything wonderful that there is to eat and drink. You're basically allowed to eat milk and cherries, but that's how President Zachary Taylor died, so watch your fucking back on that, too. Gout is poetic in its cruelty. If Shakespeare, Aesop, and Zeus sat down together and came up with a disease for fat people, it would be gout. Oh, you like rich food and sitting around? Well then, let's make sure an excess of the first thing leads to a totality of the second. You can have as much salami as you want, but it's going to turn you into a wailing statue in agonized repose.

I thought I had sprained my toe the first time I had a flare-up. I couldn't recall any actual traumatic event where a sprain could have happened, but at that point I only knew gout as something that afflicted members of the various royal families of Europe. I assumed you caught gout through inbreeding and witnessing a joust and I had no idea what the symptoms even were. The pain was intense. Ibuprofen helped, but only a bit. The second night it hurt so bad that I chased the ibuprofen with whiskey, which is like treating a leg cramp with a marathon, but I had no idea. Finally the pain went away on its own. Then the flare-ups kept happening. I didn't go to the doctor. I didn't have a doctor. I went to urgent care and they concurred with my armchair sprain diagnosis. They gave me a bottle of Vicodin and instructions to stay off my feet, and I indulged in both of those instructions happily. And then the flare-ups started spreading, first to the other big toe and then to the knees. Gout in your toe is painful but ultimately manageable; gout in your knee is fucking hell. I'm not going to dignify it with an elaborate analogy; it's just fucking hell. You can't walk without a massive limp, and it was only magnified in severity by my considerable size. I was hobbling around at 350 pounds on a knee that wouldn't bend and hurt like it was full of glass even when I wasn't walking on it. I explained it all away as further sprains caused by overcompensating for the earlier sprains, all of which was also always, of course, just gout.

Eventually, I realized that all these flare-ups couldn't just be sprains, so I did what any reasonable American would do—I went to WebMD. After eliminating "toe cancer" from the list of possible suspects, I surmised that I must have gout. There are dozens of times in this story when I should have just sucked it up, confronted my mortality, and gone to the doctor, but this is the most glaring. I had a condition and, yes, it was a self-diagnosis, but at this point it was like googling "Have I been bit by a shark?" and then looking down at your leg where a shark is currently biting you. I was 99.9 percent sure I knew what was going on, and there was medicine I could take for gout! It would help ease the worst pain I'd ever felt in my entire life. It would, in fact, stop me from ever really experiencing it again. Instead, I treated the gout by popping tart cherry pills by the fistful and drinking an "Oh my god, I have a drug test tomorrow" amount of water. I could get the cherry pills at Whole Foods. You don't need to have a prescription to shop at Whole Foods. You only need to have a Prius.

Untreated by medicine and unmitigated by any significant changes in my lifestyle, the gout got worse. It started spreading even more, touring all the joints in my body and rendering them temporarily useless and shockingly painful. It showed up in my fingers and my thumbs. It struck my elbows. A couple of times, I had gout outbreaks in my shoulders, and the least painful way to hold your body when that happens is to walk around with your arms out like you're a buff dude at the gym, so look, it's not all bad. It is mostly bad, though. The gout permanently changed the physiology of my body. It threw things out of place. There are weird bumps and nodules in my elbow and my shoulder. My knees don't bend the way they're supposed to bend. My consumption of tart cherry pills is responsible for 11 percent of Jeff Bezos's personal wealth, and still gout ravaged my body. I should have gone to the doctor. The idea that my body was somehow impervious to the way I was treating it had been dashed over and over and over again, in one of the most painful ways possible. Why, even then, didn't I go to the doctor?

There's a joke fat people tell about doctors, hard-won through unhelpful humiliations. The details change, but the essence is the same: A fat person is rushed to the hospital with a broken leg. They're speeding through the emergency room on a stretcher. They're in agony, screaming, moaning, pleading for help. As they writhe in pain, waiting for the morphine to kick in, a doctor walks in, places his hand on the fat patient's shoulder, and says, "First things first—you should really lose some weight." Motherfucker, we know. We know, we know, we know, we know, we know. Every single time I went to the doctor as a fat person, from when I was a child getting a mumps vaccine, to when I got a bad concussion playing high school football, to when I got my wisdom teeth removed, to the extremely rare occasions I went as an adult, they told me I needed to lose some weight. When I was just a little dude, I went to a specialist who checked my blood sugar with a finger prick. He told me, a twelve-year-old, that type 2 diabetes was running up on me like an Olympic sprinter. He gave me a device so I could prick my finger and read my blood sugar in the comfort and splendor of my own home. It was, by far, my least favorite video game. It was so frustrating and humiliating. It made me think about my health as a fait accompli. It was doom, delayed, and it was easier just to dash it from my mind completely than to obsess over my blood sugar until the inevitable happened. It still hasn't happened. I'm old enough now to know that it doesn't mean that the doctor was wrong; he just wasn't doing anything to get me the information that I needed. He was administering his opinion in a way that would never get to where it needed to go. It's like giving someone 10 cc of medicine by pouring it into a wineglass and tossing it into their face like the whole thing is happening on Bravo.

These visits to the doctor wouldn't strike such a nerve if the doctors were wrong. They often miss the point of the visit entirely, with terrible timing, while being inconsiderate, off-putting, ugly, rude, blunt, boorish, unfeeling, and unhelpful, but they are not wrong. That's what makes the whole ordeal so perilous. For both the sake of being correct and the sake of being humane, I have to say that you can be fat and be healthy. You can be trim and be unhealthy. "Fat" is an amorphous word in general, and its definition can change from person to person, from metric to metric, in a way that diminishes its practical use in a general discussion about overall health. At the same time, I don't think doctors and scientists are in on some grand age-old conspiracy against fat people because one of us snagged the last spanakopita from Hippocrates at a Grecian cocktail party. I don't want to recite the long list of ways that being too fat can be harmful to your health. I'm not a doctor; I *barely* have a bachelor's degree. All of which is to say, we know fat can kill you. We can, and should, talk about how BMI is bad and biased, but biased studies don't make you more susceptible to heart attacks and strokes. Sometimes it feels like doctors are giving you CPR with a sledgehammer, but they're trying to help you. Sometimes they're bad at it, but doctors are trying to help you. A suggestion that you lose some weight is not an attempt to dissolve your personhood, no matter how much it feels like that at the time.

Doctors are fucking awkward. Not all of them, okay? But they're fucking awkward. They've had to read so many books and not one of them has a wizard in it. They have to memorize the bones in the hand, even if they're planning on specializing in the foot. These are the same people who have to send a robotic snake up your ass and then later on talk to you like they didn't just send a robotic snake up your ass. There is one doctor who is good at talking to people—Dr. Oz, and look at how that turned out. Doctors are also busy, frazzled, and—it's important to remember this—at work. Are you ever at work? It's terrible. I spent eight years writing for a late-night show, where my job was literally coming up with silly little ideas and making jokes, and there were mornings when I felt like I was being deployed to Vietnam. Sometimes you're just catching a doctor on a shit day, and you don't deserve to be treated like the ninety-fifth email of the morning, but sometimes you are.

I'm not so much apologizing for doctors here as I'm telling you it's not your fault. You have to remember that it's not your fault. It's important to drill that information into your head because, in my experience, the other thing that can keep you from visiting the doctor—more than how rude they can be, more than a desire to keep your head buried in the sand—is shame. To be fat in America is to be subject to a ceaseless and powerful campaign to make you feel ashamed of yourself. It happens directly, it happens indirectly, on purpose and by happenstance, but no matter how it happens, it's cruel and constant and consistent. I didn't go to the doctor for years. I let the wrenching pain of gout tour my joints for the better part of a decade.

I let it all happen for a number of reasons, but the one I keep returning to in my head is that I thought I deserved it. On some level, the agony in my toes and knees and fucking collarbones felt like a physical manifestation of the pain I was feeling in my mind. Don't get me wrong—I was not sitting in a dark room painting my fingernails black and muttering Dashboard Confessional lyrics to myself. I was living my life. The happy memories outweigh all the sick, sad, somber shit. I was not a prisoner of constant grief, but I could order without looking at the menu, if you feel what I'm saying. Whenever the first hints of stiffness in my knee would turn into days of radiating, excruciating pain, I thought, "This is what I deserve." I want to tell you it was just a part of me that thought that, but it was all of me. I kept drinking too much, I kept eating the "wrong" foods, and I cast aside conventional wisdom and my own better judgment to do it. I deserved to be in agony the way you deserve to have a hangover the morning after a high school reunion. I deserved everything that was coming to me.

I stood on the sidewalk in beautiful Portland, Oregon, with 911 typed into my phone, sure I was about to have a heart attack, and all I could really think was "So this is where it happens." I was losing weight, but it was too little, too late. Everything I'd put out of my head, everything I'd worked so hard to avoid, was here; it was happening. Then it didn't happen. I didn't have a heart attack. I don't really know what it was—probably my first panic attack mixed with an elevated heart rate from drinking for the first time in months mixed with a sense of doom from the pandemic, but it wasn't a heart attack. I didn't hit the green button to send the 911 call to the dispatcher. I went back upstairs to the apartment. I sat on the couch. I felt the gravity of convenience and shame and rude doctors pulling me back toward my old habits. Write it off; wait it out; it'll all be fine and everything will work itself out. This time, I couldn't. *A Christmas Carol* happened to my central nervous system. I reached out for help. Well, I reached out for a compromised, chill, "none of this is a big deal, I bet I'm okay" version of help. I did a telehealth session with a bougie, hipster walk-in clinic. They told me to come in. I did. Then they told me that my blood pressure was higher than any NBA team has ever scored in a single game. Salt, alcohol, size, years of being too fat, years of sitting still, years of shrugging off "I'm a little worried about your blood pressure" at the urgent care, years of avoiding the doctor because I knew that they were just going to tell me to lose weight anyway, all staring me systolically in the face. I remember the kind voice of the nurse, telling me I would be okay, that they'd get that number down. I remember the worry in my mother's voice when she asked me to repeat how high it was. I remember the fluorescent lights inside the twenty-four-hour pharmacy cooking me as I filled a basket with baby aspirin and a blood pressure cuff.

Nobody likes a wake-up call, but it's better than sleeping through all the fun stuff. I went to a doctor, finally. He was a fucking prick, I don't mind telling you, so I went to a different doctor. She was wonderful. She told me some serious stuff, but it's all in the telling with that kind of information, isn't it? *Poltergeist* and *Casper* are both ghost stories. I was ready to listen. I was ready to face my reality. I lost 120 more pounds. I got that blood pressure down. I went to the doctor. I liked going to the doctor so much, in fact, that I got another doctor *just* for the heart. I went to that doctor *a lot.* The amount of times my cardiologist has said to me, "I'm not worried, but I can tell you are, so let's take a look" is staggering. My cardiologist rules, and I can't believe I'm saying this, but I always leave his office feeling better than when I walked in. Even before I lost all the rest of the weight, I felt better after seeing the doctor. Let me say that again. Even while I was tipping the scale well in excess of 300 pounds, I felt better after seeing the doctor. Read that one more time because it's important—*I felt better after leaving the doctor even when I was, by medicine or media or God's definition, a great big fat guy.* Wonder of wonders, miracle of miracles! It's possible.

Some things had to change for me to have this experience. I had to find the right doctor. I had to go to the doctor in the first place. I had to confront the reality that I needed help. I had to convince myself I deserved it. None of these things are easy, but they're worth doing, even when they're hard. Even when they're the hardest things you've ever done in your life. Life isn't all peaches and nonfat Greek yogurt since I lost the weight and started going to the doctor either. I went from ignoring my mortality to being borderline obsessed with it. I check my pulse a hundred times a day. I dart off to the emergency room like I used to dart off to the Go-Go Taquitos roller at 7-Eleven. The pendulum has swung wide in the other direction. I'm fighting to pull it as close to the middle as I can. I suppose I've thought about death a normal amount for someone my age; it's just that I've crammed it all into the last three years. The more time that I spend with my head out of the sand, the less intense it gets, and I suppose that will continue to be true the longer I go on. My health isn't a monster under the bed anymore; it's something that I'll have a steady relationship with for the rest of my life, until that mountain lion finally tracks me down and takes me out for good.

BIG GUY.

If you are going to call someone "Big Guy," the entire group better have fun nicknames. If there's a "Big Guy," we also need somebody named "Wheels," somebody named "Rattlesnake," a set of identical twins who go by "Truth and Consequences," and a person you've only ever spoken to over the phone who answers to the handle "Dr. Theodore Everything."

And you need to be coming together for one last job.

CHAPTER 8

Down and Out in the Big and Tall

I've got a pair of polyester pants hanging in my closet that serves as a reminder that losing weight comes with its own set of risks. They're light blue, they're covered in palm fronds, they're beautiful—I've worn them once. I can't pull them off; they're too cool. They look like Henri Rousseau designed a fashion line for cocaine dealers. If they made 500 pairs of these pants, the other 499 are on Steve Harvey's yacht right now.

I made some wild choices when I first let loose in a clothing store after I dropped some pounds. The world is incredibly restrictive for fat people, and if that restriction is all you're used to, the sudden presence of choice is dizzying. I hit the racks like Templeton the rat hit the snacks. I was buying stuff just because it fit. Not even a second of consideration, just the unfamiliar high of walking out of a dressing room with options. My wardrobe is now an incoherent collection of Pendleton print hoodies, Gwen Stefani–ass ska pants, and floral print jackets that I bought just because I could. Most people go through this phase of their life in high school, when the combination of bullies and budget forces them into something resembling a reasonable theme. I was a thirty-five-year-old television writer—all I had was disposable income and friends who'd recently started meditating. I realize now that I wasn't just buying clothes for thirty-five-year-old me, I was buying clothes for every single version of me that had existed and that might have existed had it been allowed to exist. So much of the restriction I'd experienced in my life as a fat man had been existential, but the restriction I felt at the mall was real. No stores carried anything close to my size.

For slender people, the mall is a world of endless possibilities. They can walk out as someone completely different from the person who walked in. The only thing standing between them and an entirely new identity conceived and constructed at Wilsons Leather is the courage to see it through. Outside of size, there aren't a ton of other restrictions. An Orthodox Jew could walk into the mall wearing a tallit and a fur hat and walk out with Rollerblades and a Kyrie Irving jersey. An emo kid could walk in wearing a Jack Skellington hoodie with thumb holes in the sleeve and walk out wearing a different Jack Skellington hoodie with thumb holes in the sleeve. It's a portal to whatever identity you desire. Big date/job interview/undercover police assignment on the horizon? Your fashion montage, ripped straight from a rom-com, is waiting for you inside the mall. Unless you're the fat best friend in the rom-com, in which case the mall is just a bunch of empty rooms surrounding a collection of pretzel stands.

Here's how it feels being fat at the mall. In most stores, you know you're out of luck right off the bat. An employee will give you a look that lands somewhere between "I'm sorry, sweetheart" and "We don't carry your size in store, but you could always try buying a burlap sack at Home Depot, you fat fucking tub of walrus shit." That is, if they acknowledge your presence at all. Oftentimes they don't. Sometimes they just stand in the corner and fold shirts that you should know, intuitively, would never be in your size. Do you know what it's like to walk into a J.Crew as a fat person? They've got three different shades of pink chinos, but not a single waist size over thirty-four. That's the line. Salmon pants with dogs on them? Normal. Forty-inch waist? Sir, we can't be expected to carry everything.

Some stores have a Big and Tall section, though, and let me just stop a minute to say God bless them for throwing "tall" in there. Never once in my long and storied career of ill-fitting polo shirts have I seen a tall person in the Big and Tall section. It's never been me, Kareem Abdul-Jabbar, and the guy who played Chewbacca digging through a pile of Carhartt workwear. They could have easily and honestly called that dark corner of the Sears "Big and Bigger" and they didn't. It would be the last kindness they cared to extend. Shopping the Big and Tall is like going vegan at a Jack in the Box. They have options, but honestly, that shit is so condescending that it'd be less offensive if they straight up had nothing. The Big and Tall clothing section tends to break into a few different categories. This is not an exhaustive list, but it is an exhausting one.

WE THINK IT'S FUNNY THAT YOU'RE FAT

It's not enough to joke about your weight when you're ordering dinner, when you're stepping off a treadmill, settling into an airplane seat, when it's hot out ("Sweating through your shirt? Hey! Welcome to my world!"), or when it's cold out ("Don't worry about me, I'm already wearing nature's jacket!"). Every piece of your dwindling existence must be dedicated to making everyone else comfortable with how fat you are, and that includes the clothing on your torso. I saw a T-shirt for sale, available to the public, for purchase, yours for a fair price, that said "Here Comes Big Daddy." The size of that shirt was 5XL. They know Big Daddy is coming. Everything else about your existence tells them that Big Daddy Is Coming. The shirt is redundant. It's like Steve Buscemi wearing a T-shirt that says "Steve Buscemi" on it. Nobody didn't think that was Steve Buscemi. I'm not trying to write this shirt off completely; I don't speak for everybody. Maybe you're a Ruben-esque lover whose romantic partner calls you Big Daddy. Maybe you're Adam Sandler. He isn't a fat guy, but based on every pa-parazzi photo of him that I've seen, he'd absolutely wear a 5XL T-shirt that says "Here Comes Big Daddy." It wasn't the existence of that shirt that bummed me out, so much as it was the existence of that shirt in lieu of others. When you're stripping the shelves in search of something you can wear on a date, "Here Comes Big Daddy" doesn't feel like an option; it feels like a wrecking ball.

That was just one shirt, and I wish I could tell you it was an aberration, but it was quite the opposite. Entire companies thrived on the idea that fat people should wear clothing that comments on how fat they are. Big Dog Sportswear was founded in Santa Barbara, California, in 1983—which is weird because Santa Bar-bara looks like it was written and directed by Nancy Meyers, and Big Dogs is a clothing brand that Turtle would have started in an episode of *Entourage*. Big Dogs did two things better than anyone else in the 1990s—expanded sizes and sassy little slogans, and this was a competitive era for sassy little slogans. No Fear, Big John-son, Coed Naked, AND1, everybody wanted you to lead, follow, or get out of the way, and they were sassy as hell about it. They put up numbers. Patrick Ewing put up numbers, too. Unfortunately, he did it during Michael Jordan's prime, and that's what we're talking about with Big Dogs. They stuck a big, furry Saint Ber-nard finger in your chest and screamed their slogan "If you can't run with the Big Dogs, stay on the porch!"

It always seemed like a very silly slogan to me, because the last thing I was doing in any of my 3XL Big Dog Sportswear clothing was running. I was never running. If the shirt had said "If You Can't House an Entire Meat Lover's Pizza While Dominating *GoldenEye* 64, Stay on the Porch!" it would have been a little bit closer to *my* truth, but it didn't. And it's kind of surprising that it didn't, actually, because other than sass, Big Dogs' chief interest was pop culture parody. If it was happening in the nineties, Big Dogs was going to cram a dog into it and throw it on a T-shirt. "Jurassic Bark," "Seinfetch," " 'Bone Cold' StevePawstin"—they had their finger on America's dangerously elevated pulse.

Big Dogs even parodied shows that nobody liked. My mom once bought me a T-shirt that said "Dogs Behaving Badly," which was a parody of the short-lived sitcom *Men Behaving Badly.* She bought the shirt because it was on sale at the Lincoln City Big Dogs outlet store. You can't beat "on sale at an outlet" when it comes to fat-guy clothing because fat-guy clothing is expensive. Small, medium, extra large, it's all the same price, but once you start getting any girthier than that all of a sudden they're charging by the square inch. It's the same principle behind the prices at remote gas stations. What are you gonna do, go somewhere else? This is your only option. If you don't like it, stay on the porch.

WHAT IS A BALTIMORE ORIOLES T-SHIRT DOING HERE?

If you're a fat guy, you can always get officially licensed sports clothing. It's a twist of irony that would make Alanis Morissette blush. You can't find a button-up in your size, but you can find a replica of a professional athlete's work shirt. When I lost weight, I started piling up my old big-guy clothes so I could donate them and it looked like a tornado hit Nelly's house. I had pieces of clothing affiliated with the following sports teams: the Pittsburgh Pirates, the Seattle Mariners, the Houston Astros, the Texas Rangers, the Baltimore Orioles, the New York Mets, the New York Yankees, the Brooklyn Dodgers, the Los Angeles Dodgers, the Los Angeles Rams, the Los Angeles Kings, the Phoenix Suns, the Oregon Ducks, the Georgetown Hoyas, the USC Trojans, the Arizona State Sun Devils, the U.S. men's Olympic basketball team, the Vancouver Grizzlies, the Portland Beavers, the Kansas City

Katz, and the Toledo Mud Hens. I was a fan of none of those teams, not even the last three, which are all minor league baseball teams. I also had about forty pieces of clothing from the Portland Trail Blazers, including a very slick black satin jacket. I am a fan of the Portland Trail Blazers. It crushed me to give away that jacket.

MAGICIANS LOOK VERY DAPPER, DON'T THEY?

I don't know who told the clothing industry that fat guys like vests, but they must have screamed it like a dying god, because let me tell you something, vests are available. Vests are available in such abundance that sleeves must be the hard part. There must be some tortured designer, slumped over a desk in a forest of fabric bolts. The veins on his forehead bulge like corridors, his eyes turned pink by frustration. A temple of stale coffee cups sits in quiet reflection of a mountain of stubbed-out cigarettes. The only sound in the room: a metronomic repetition of rip, crumple, toss, rip, crumple, toss, rip, crumple, toss. His understanding of the body is like nothing seen since Michelangelo summoned a man from marble. The idiosyncrasies of the fat male torso bloom in his mind like wildflowers: the love handles, the rolling neck, the swoon of the breast as it curves to meet the back, all of them as familiar as a Wednesday. Mastery. More than mastery. All of it. Except the sleeves. He can't nail the fucking sleeves.

CHEST PAINS ON THE GOLF COURSE

There's a lot of pressure when you're a fat guy. Aside from health concerns, societal perception, and dating, there's also an expectation that you hold an upper-tier management position at Enterprise Rent-A-Car. Nobody will ever come up to you and say, "Hey, you're a fat guy, it's weird that you don't have an upper-tier management position at Enterprise Rent-A-Car," but one twirl through the Big and Tall section and it becomes clear. Otherwise, why on earth would there be so much golf clothing for fat guys?

I'm just not ready to wear that much moisture-wicking stretch fabric. I'll wear some of it, I'm not a monster, but a man has limits. I'm in my thirties. I'm not meant to wear a polo shirt made out of the same material that Usain Bolt wore when he broke the world record in the 100-meter dash. Athletic fabric has no business being in league with polo shirts. I know that polo is technically a sport, but it's a sport where the horse does all the work. If the horse wants to wear a moisture-wicking stretch-fabric polo shirt, that's fine, but I'm not going to wear one until I'm at least fifty.

In reality, it's just a piece of clothing. It's not that serious. That's not what it feels like, though. Every golf shirt that you slide out of the way feels like a reminder of who you're allowed to be as a fat man. It feels like a declaration of which archetypes society has decided to accept: fat, middle-aged, corporate, hitting the links, crushing three Michelobs and a club sandwich at the nineteenth hole. Look, that sounds like a great afternoon to me, but what about the twentieth hole? *What about the rest of my life?*

ALOHA!

The people making Hawaiian shirts have always had our back. Our relationship goes all the way back to the loom. Shout-out to Tommy Bahama. Shout-out to Hilo Hattie. Wearing a Hawaiian shirt is luxurious, festive, and pleasurable. It's the sartorial equivalent of fried chicken and caviar. It's casual, it's fun, it says "I'm down to have a good time," but it's got buttons on the front, so it also says "Not so much fun that I'm going to end up barfing in your sink."

Is there a correlation between the Hawaiian shirt's prevalence in areas with strong Polynesian culture and those cultures' acceptance and even celebration of fat bodies? I can't tell you for certain.

I went to Portland State University, which isn't even the best college in Southwest Portland. It doesn't seem far-fetched to think that a culture will take more care with the things they accept than they will with the things they want to hide away, but again, Portland State University. Our most famous alumna is Courtney Love.

WE SAW GUY FIERI WEARING THIS

They saw Guy Fieri Wearing This.

I guess what I'm getting at here is that the scant variety of clothes offered to fat people have nothing in common except for the fact that they fit fat people. It doesn't make any sense. There's no vision. The commonalities are superficial and not the kind of superficial you're looking for at a clothing store. The offerings in a Big and Tall section are like a group of people who only hang out because they're all named Daryl. Maybe they can find some stuff in common, but it's going to be a coincidence. I've gone on journeys to put together a cohesive outfit that J.R.R. Tolkien could write a book about. A shirt here, some pants there, a belt crafted in the hellfire of Mordor.

The experience echoes a defeating refrain that the world lobs at fat people again and again—the thing that makes you unique is that you're fat. Your identity is that you are fat. I wanted so badly to be the one who dictated what makes me unique.

Sometimes when the clothes I wanted didn't fit I bought them anyway. Aspirational clothing. I know this isn't a phenomenon unique to fat people. Everybody buys clothes that almost fit right. I'm sure somewhere in Chris Pine's teakwood-and-tobacco-scented closet, next to a reclaimed wood bench and an antique saddle, there's a shirt that would look perfect if his delts were just a bit more sculpted. Ultimately, though, aspirational clothing is like gout. You can get it if you're skinny, but it's mostly for fat people. I'm no stranger to aspirational clothing (or gout, for that matter). There have been times in my life when my closet housed more clothing that I hoped to wear someday than clothing that actually fit my body. Some people have "fat clothes" for when they pack on some extra weight during the holidays. I had "maybe one day I'll change my whole entire life" clothes.

You buy aspirational clothes for a lot of reasons. Sometimes you'll bring three pairs of pants into the dressing room, and the guy working at Nordstrom gives you a look like he knows they don't fit, you know they don't fit, and he knows you know they don't fit, so why are you wasting everyone's time? Sometimes he gives you a look like you're going to ruin the pants just by being fat in them during your futile attempt to unite the button and the hole. So you take the pants into the dressing room, unsuccessfully strain to button the pants, and walk out, like, "I'll take the most expensive pair, please." You showed that prick, by buying an expensive pair of pants that he gets a commission on. It's your "big mistake, huge" Julia Roberts moment from *Pretty Woman*. You're the person making the big, huge mistake—because the pants will sit in three different closets through three different moving days, before you finally pop the tags so the people at Goodwill don't know you're donating aspirational pants.

Sometimes you buy the clothes because they alllmooooosssssst fit. They're so close. Yes, right now, one of the buttons doesn't button. And yes, when you button the rest of the buttons you kind of look like a houndstooth cannoli. And yes, the particular button right above your belly button viscerally reminds you of Tobey Maguire in *Spider-Man 2* when he's trying to stop that subway train from going off the rails, but still, you're so close. You can see it fitting. You can imagine the person you'll be when it does fit.

Sometimes you buy the clothes because it's easier than actually getting less fat. Sometimes you buy a 2XL because you just want to tell yourself you're the kind of person who wears a 2XL, and really, you're not all that fat. Actually, you don't have a problem at all, because as you can see, you just bought a regular shirt in a regular store. It's always a little bit this last rationalization. I remember in the early 2000s, baggy clothing was in style. Rappers, especially, were wearing massive T-shirts and throwback jerseys and basketball shorts, and young Ian Karmel was thrilled. I could walk into a Champs Sports and buy a 3XL tall T-shirt and some shorts and walk back into the mall like I wasn't prediabetic. I was fucking devastated when Kanye started wearing clothes that fit. I know it wasn't personal, but have you heard what he's got to say about the Jews? Maybe it was.

It's hard not to take the *entire* fashion industry personally when you're fat. It certainly feels personal when you're sweating through ill-fitting button-ups in a dressing room at Sears. I suppose it's helpful to remember that it can be hard to design for fat people. Tailors go from small to extra large by steadily increasing uniform measurements across the garment. The length of the shirt grows by one amount in conjunction with the width of the sleeve growing by another amount, and that's how fat people sometimes end up with a shirt that fits their torso perfectly and sleeves that would accommodate the Rock's thighs.

I feel for the designers. Not as much as I feel for fat people, but still, I feel for the designers a little bit. Every fat person is fat in a different way, and that can be impossible to plan for. Some people carry it on their legs, their butt, their back; I carry mine on my gut. People even carry their fat on their gut in different ways. Some people go wide; some people get that big, hard belly that makes them look like they coached Mississippi State to three straight Cotton Bowls in the early 1980s. My gut fat is long. It's like a sheet cake that starts under my boobs. At my fattest I was so fat that the gut fat kind of built an addendum to the house, so the bottom of my gut actually extends down like Jay Leno's chin, with a cleft and everything. It hangs there. I really don't mean to dwell on this; I know this level of anatomical detail might put some people off, but I'm trying to paint you a picture here, and I'm more Hieronymus Bosch than John Singer Sargent, so you'll have to forgive me.

Anyway, some people have big hard fat guts, but my gut is more like a natural boob that you'd see at a hot spring. When a shirt isn't long enough, I'm showing the fat-gut equivalent of underboob. I hate the way it looks on me. Even at my most body-positive, bucking against social norms, loving myself and even my imperfections, it's a bad look. There are entire family vacations that I choose not to remember because my gut chin is peekabooing in all the photos.

When I was a cast member on the comedy sports game show *Game On!* on CBS, I danced at halftime of a Lakers game with Rob Gronkowski, Venus Williams, James Corden, and the Laker Girls. I hate the Lakers more than I hate my metabolism, and even still, it was a singularly amazing moment in my life. It went viral before the show even aired and then it went viral again when it did air. If I have kids, it's the kind of thing I'd want to share with them. Look, there's your dad dancing with one of the greatest football players of all time, one of the greatest tennis players of all time, and that guy from *Ocean's 8*. But I don't know if I'll ever be able to show my kids that footage because my Jay Leno gut chin pulls a "Here's Johnny" nine different times during the clip, and it still causes me visceral discomfort to see it. I feel like the story is out of my hands and hanging out of the bottom of my shirt.

I think a lot of fat guys want to figure out a way to express themselves and dictate the terms of their identity through their clothing. They want to use the same palette that is available to everyone else. I think that's why you see so many fat guys who are into sneakers. It's the one clothing store in the mall whose doors are always open to fat people. If they don't have your size, it doesn't feel like a value judgment. If they're out of size 13s, they're out of size 13s. It doesn't mean you're a disgusting monster who doesn't belong on this planet. If anything, it just means you have good taste.

For the uninitiated, I know that sneakers seem like a confined resource from which to pluck an identity. They go on your feet;

how different can they be? What can they really say? But sneakers are one of those subcultures that allow a person to become as obsessed as their time, budget, and storage space will allow. The deeper you go, the more there is to discover, and the feeling of inclusivity amid all that variety is intoxicating. It's especially intoxicating for fat people, who've been denied inclusivity by nearly every other kind of clothing subculture. To some, the variations might seem superficial, but there's a world of difference between a pair of Joe Freshgoods x New Balance 993s and a pair of royal-blue Nike Air Foamposite Ones. You're telling the world one thing with a pair of Adidas x Gucci Gazelles and a completely different thing with a pair of beat-up Reebok Club C 85s. It's a pair of shoes, but it's also a declaration of what you value and prioritize in life. You're telling people what kind of music you like, what kind of bars you drink at, what kind of movies you watch. You're broadcasting the idea that you're on trend, or ahead of the trend, or you don't care about the trends, or you care deeply about the trends but you want people to think you don't actually care about the trends at all because caring is thirsty. You can wear those shoes with individual toes and tell people you're into polyamory and improv. Whatever you choose, you're granted the ability to say "I've thought about what I look like and I've put some care into it," which is something too many people assume that fat people don't think about at all.

I can tell you this from personal experience, because my garage looks like a city skyline of sneaker box towers. Every box contains a pair of shoes and a shred of idealized identity. I've got a pair of Nikes in there that I spent $750 on. It's the most money I've ever spent on a pair of sneakers. Depending on how into sneaker culture you are, you're thinking either "How could you spend that much money on a single pair of sneakers?" or "How is that the most amount of money you've spent on a single pair of sneakers!" I bought them because I was performing stand-up on television and I wanted to have something nice. I wanted something declarative. I wanted something that said "Yeah, I'm a big fat fuck, but I'm a big fat fuck on your television screen." I went to a store called Flight Club on Fairfax in Los Angeles, and I bought a pair of Nike Off-White Blazer Mids—the "Grim Reaper" colorway. They cost more than my share of the rent, but I didn't care because they were tough as hell. Black-and-white, high-top, they elongated the leg and made me look almost graceful. The shoes were adorned with Virgil Abloh's signature print and a Swoosh that looked like Death's scythe in leather. They were rare. They were exclusive and I had them, on my feet, on television. The camera only caught the shoes for a fraction of a moment, but it was enough to net me a flurry of tweets. Strangers were complimenting my shoes, telling me they saw me, and most important, asking me how I got them. Sneakers let me have something that money couldn't buy me at any other store in the mall—jealousy. I could cultivate desire and taste with sneakers. I could say "Here Comes Big Daddy" without writing it on my shirt.

HEAVY.

Has someone described your body the same way an old hippie describes Vietnam? If so, you may be entitled to compensation.

CHAPTER 9

Want to Lose Weight? Ask a Fat Person

I eventually found a way to lose weight that worked for me. The whir of the motor in a blood pressure cuff is a good motivator, but even still, it feels like a miracle that I was able to get it done. I don't know how trying to lose weight feels for everyone, but for me it felt like trying every single key on a janitor's key ring. You try a key, it doesn't work, you try a key, it doesn't work, you try another key, it seems like it's working, you think you're in the clear, the bolt won't turn, you throw the key ring into the trash, and you get a deli sandwich and some Fritos. Then you fish the keys out of the garbage and you start over.

It's because of this that I truly believe there isn't a group of people on this planet who knows how to lose weight better than fat people. Perhaps it seems counterintuitive, but fat people know how to lose weight. Fat people know how to lose weight intimately and in perfect detail. Fat people know how to lose weight the way a contractor knows load-bearing walls; the way a chef in a movie knows how to make an amazing sandwich to reconnect with why they got into cooking in the first place; the way an off-duty cop knows Oakley wraparound sunglasses. If you want to know how to lose weight, ask a fat person.

Don't get me wrong—there are plenty of skinny people who will tell you how to lose weight: nutritionists, doctors, personal trainers, and women who wear seven hundred dollars' worth of athleisure to their job at the juice bar. Sure, they've got degrees, diagrams, bronze medals from the 2014 CrossFit championships, and bulk bags of goji berries, but having them tell you how to lose weight always feels a little bit like having LeBron James tell you how to dunk. Oh, do I just jump, LeBron? I just do a little run and then I jump? Great.

When it comes to losing weight, it's not the knowing, it's the doing. Every fat person knows how to lose weight because we've tried so many different methods that fail for one reason or another (the one reason is that the methods are insane; the other reason is also that they're insane). We're like pirate skeletons clutching treasure maps. So close to the treasure! If only they'd kept going; if only they'd followed the map! What marvelous treasure would they now hold, were it not for that giant swinging boulder or that pit full of snakes or that ghost who somehow had a real sword standing in front of the thirty-foot chasm? Even if you time the boulder perfectly and use it to swing over the pit of snakes and answer the sword ghost's riddle, what are you supposed to do about the thirty-foot chasm?

What I'm saying is, every diet works, if you do it. The problem is in doing it. They're unsustainable, and many come prepackaged with disastrous side effects that reveal themselves during the diet, right after the diet has failed, and long after the diet has failed. Many diets leave you worse off than you were when you started them. It's like moving out of your apartment and into a sandcastle on the beach. You're glad to be out of your apartment, but eventually the tide will come in. I'm not telling you that with the high-cheekboned confidence of someone handing you a sixteen-dollar smoothie either. I'm telling you as someone who has watched an uncountable number of sandcastles swept out to sea.

I think what makes this whole losing-weight thing so fraught and, at its worst, malignant is that the diet industry is a monster who eats good intentions. You have people who want to get varying degrees of less fat for reasons that range from "I want to look good at my daughter's wedding" to "I don't want to die." The desperation in those desires vacillates wildly and isn't always tied to what outside observers would identify as reasonable urgency. Sometimes the person who wants to lose weight for their daughter's wedding is treating it as more life-and-death than the person who is facing an actual life-and-death situation.

The diet industry is also full of evil. There's money to be made off people's fear and insecurity, and evil loves that shit. That is like a wine-and-cheese mixer for evil. It's an engraved invitation for evil. The diet industry is a summer camp, at midnight, thirty years to the *day* all those horny teenagers were murdered. You can't avoid the evil. Having said that, I think it's important to remember, both as a precaution and for the well-being of all of our souls, that not everyone who makes money off trying to help you lose weight is evil.

I had a personal trainer named Jason. Jason is straight out of central casting. He's so buff that it makes him seem dumb—like there can't possibly be enough blood in his body for all those muscles and his brain. He's so buff he walks wrong, you know? He walks like he's covered in a bunch of sleeping bees that he's trying not to wake up. Jason was hired by my mom and my sister to help me lose weight when I was at my unhealthiest. He was a Hail Mary for extending my life expectancy. I worked out with Jason three days a week, and it became clear he wasn't dumb at all. He'd talk my ear off while we went through our circuits in the gym, and yes, we'd mostly communicate in dumb dude-movie quotes, but the hour sessions would fly by with me barely noticing I'd been working my ass off. He knew what he was doing. After a couple of weeks, he noticed I wasn't really losing any weight and then we talked about my diet. He took time out of his life, off the clock, to take me to two different grocery stores and help me learn how to buy healthy foods that I'd actually enjoy eating. He showed me what to look for on labels. He built a food plan for me that I could actually follow. He taught me about spaghetti squash and how to cook it so you almost believe you're eating spaghetti (as long as it's been a while since you had actual spaghetti). Jason is a guy who makes a living because people want to lose weight. Jason is a really good guy. They're out there. They're rare, but they're out there. It's important for you to remember that, because there are also a lot of bastards out there trying to sell you a quick fix.

Looking back on the many diets I've attempted, I've learned one thing for sure: There are no shortcuts to being healthier. They're like the sleeves on Vin Diesel's shirt—they do not exist. Even if you want something to not be a scheme, and the person telling you about the scheme doesn't want it to be a scheme, it might still be a scheme, and that's what makes the diet industry so damn evil. Diets are terrible, *but* if you know that, they're kind of fun to talk about. The way a bad date is kind of fun to talk about after you're safely at home watching *Gilmore Girls* and eating a moderate amount of pistachios. Here are some of the worst ones I've ever tried.

THE *FAT, SICK & NEARLY DEAD* ALL-JUICE REBOOT

When I think about this diet, I think, "I have no poop and yet I must shit."

In 2010, there was a documentary called *Fat, Sick & Nearly Dead*. It followed Joe Cross, a guy who had an autoimmune disease and weighed 310 pounds. Joe lost 80 pounds in sixty days by drinking only a specially blended combination of vegetable and fruit juices. As a result, he was able to stop taking all medications, his cholesterol plummeted, and he started a business to market the diet called Reboot with Joe. To be fair to Joe and this diet, he did the entire thing under close medical supervision, and he never intended his "only drink vegetable juice" diet to be something people did for the rest of their lives, only for sixty days to help "reboot" their health and perhaps—oh, perhaps—change their relationship with food. Noble goals all.

I don't think Joe Cross had a cross bone in his body. When you find something that works for you, you want to tell everyone. After I got to a healthier weight, I wanted to grab fat people on the street, pull them aside, and tell them how I did it. Have you heard the good news? Are you ready to walk the path of light? Are you ready to walk that path of light for *at least* ten thousand steps a day? You want to help other people. In a way beyond reason, I think you're somehow hoping you can reach through time to an earlier version of yourself and say, "It's actually possible. I know it seems impossible, but look, you did it. Also, don't buy a Tesla. Just wait that whole thing out."

I get that Joe Cross, in his way, only wants to help people. I believe that is his primary motivation. And he helped me, alright. He helped me have something that I can only describe as "ghost diarrhea." While I was on this juice diet, I would regularly be hit with the sensation that I had to take a shit that was both extremely urgent and structurally unsound. I would find a bathroom as fast as possible. I would sit there on the toilet, prepared to have the kind of diarrhea that makes you believe in the Old Testament's version of God, and yet no diarrhea would come. All the doom of the affair, none of the relief. Ghost diarrhea.

I lost weight. Not a ton, but it was noticeable. I also didn't make it the entire sixty days. I made it three weeks. In those three weeks I experienced insane cramps, including onstage at a comedy club, where I had to style out a thigh cramp while telling a joke about cheeseburgers to a bunch of drunk people in Tacoma. On the other hand, I had an incredible amount of energy. Like, Bradley Cooper in *Limitless* levels of energy. I don't know the science behind it. Maybe my body was finally freed from the burden of digesting processed foods. Maybe my brain thought my body was dying, so it was flooding me with primeval injections of adrenaline originally designed to help humans kill mastodons. Who knows? But I've done this diet and I've done cocaine and they aren't dissimilar experiences. The diet didn't make me want to open a high-concept restaurant/Criterion Collection Blu-ray rental library, though, and that's one of the main things about doing cocaine, so I guess they aren't *that* similar.

All told, I lost a bit of weight, all of which I gained back, and then a little more weight on top of that, because full-blown deprivation does change your relationship with food. I believe it *can* change it for the better because I believe it worked for Joe Cross, and I've seen it work with other people, but for me it changed it for the worse. It reinforced a binary for me, one that I still struggle with. Either you're being healthy or you're not being healthy, and if you're being healthy, you have a monastic devotion to kale, and if you're not being healthy, you eat like you're on death row. The deprivation sucks and the bingeing sucks even worse. You aren't eating the sandwich; you're eating the fact that you're allowed to have the sandwich. You're eating the idea that, soon, you won't be allowed to have that sandwich, so you don't even taste the sandwich. You never feel satiated; you only feel frustrated that you can't fit more contraband in your system before prohibition hits. Every meal feels like you're packing bags as your city is falling, the enemy at the gates, pounding banh mi on the last helicopter out of Saigon.

Oh, you also have to buy a three-hundred-dollar juicer. You have to make your own juice. That's part of it. Incidentally, I have a lightly used Breville juicer for sale. A hundred dollars out the door, and I'll throw in some kale.

SOME KIND OF WEIRD ATKINS-ISH HIGH-PROTEIN, LOW-CARB DIET

I'm not sure how fair it is to call this the Atkins diet, because I did it in high school and I can't remember how devoted I was to a faithful reading of Dr. Atkins's scripture—but this was still a high-protein, low-carb diet. This diet felt amazing, which I probably should have taken as a sign I wasn't doing it correctly, but hey, you're always looking for miracles, right? The year was 2001, *Super Troopers* was in theaters, Lee Ann Womack was hoping we'd dance, and I was sitting in the cafeteria at Westview High School in Portland, Oregon, eating a bagful of cheese. "Bagful" is a top-five way to eat cheese, by the way. It's decadent but grounded. Here are the top five ways to eat cheese:

1. Grilled, on a sandwich

2. Melted, on a pizza, so it gets all stretchy when you bite into it. The ideal version of this is illustrated in the *Teenage Mutant Ninja Turtles* cartoon or the 1995 motion picture *A Goofy Movie.*

3. Out of a bag

4. Passed apps at a wedding after you've starved yourself for three days so you look good in pictures

5. Nine Kraft Singles in a row, standing in front of an open fridge

Here are the five worst ways to eat cheese:

1. N/A

2. N/A

3. N/A

4. N/A

5. N/A

The high-protein diet seems like it shouldn't work at all. It's like something a popular kid would use to run for class president:

"Mountain Dew in all of the water fountains, and you can eat cheese and meat all day, and guess what? It's good for you. Also, Principal BARF-ield has to move his office to the bathroom." I'm not certain a high-protein diet is good for you. It's supposed to put you into ketosis or something. Tricking your body into a metabolic state that happens to people with diabetes seems as short-sighted as making Principal Garfield sit in the bathroom while he's going through a divorce.

I think my high school appetite broke whatever math makes ketosis work. I was eating enough meat and cheese to collapse the system. I was like John Henry lunch-meating against the steam-powered diet, and luckily I stopped early enough, or else the result would have likely been the same—my heart giving out in a tunnel of Swiss cheese.

SLIMFAST

SlimFast needs no introduction; it's one of the OGs of the diet industry. It's the grande dame of worried moms. We had these little cans of SlimFast in the cupboard. The liquid was thick and chalky, and the idea was that you'd drink them instead of a meal. But meal-replacement shakes turn into meal-accompaniment shakes real quick unless you have Olympic-figure-skater levels of discipline. Maybe SlimFast worked for somebody; that person wasn't me. The problem was, whenever we had cans in the house, we also had other food, and the cycle would be the same every single time: I'd drink a SlimFast. I'd sit back down on the couch. I'd get up, open the fridge, and look for actual food.

MEDIFAST

Medifast was a multilevel-marketed diet that I can best describe as 1960s NASA meals for obese astronauts. During the day, you'd eat a bar, or some crackers that tasted like a plaster wall, or something

you'd have to add water to, and then at night you got to have a
protein and some vegetables, and holy shit, it worked. It worked!
I didn't weigh myself at the beginning of the diet, but from when
my mother brought it home in the spring of 2008 until the end of
the summer, I went from kind of fitting into 3XL clothing to kind
of fitting into 2XL clothing, and I felt fantastic. I remember somebody commenting that it changed the way I walked! That stuck
with me because I hadn't considered that I "walked fat" before.
Once I put the weight back on, and then some, I practiced walking "not fat" in the mirror, which just made me look like a bear at
a circus wearing person clothes. I get ahead of myself, though.
Medifast was working. Every couple of weeks, my mother would
buy a fresh supply from her work friend and we would continue
losing weight—I say "we," because my mother was also using
Medifast and so was another familiar face, Dr. Alisa Karmel, all of
nineteen years old at the time. We were hooked as a family.

I know the lesson of Medifast, of every diet, *should* be that you
can get less fat by eating less and eating better-quality food, but
I'm not sure that's the lesson that Medifast wanted to teach us,
because the lesson we all seemed to learn was "You need Medifast
to get less fat and you definitely need it to stay less fat." At this
point, I'm singing a familiar tune, but the destination of any plan
that starts with "all or nothing" is nothing. It's always going to be
nothing. I had a summer of powered Medifast milkshakes and
zero ice cream and then in August I had some ice cream and my
brain exploded and reignited my addiction to food. Like a re-
lapsed heroin addict, I went back to the dose I was doing before I
kicked the habit, and chased twelve chicken wings with a brownie
and chased that with twenty-four years' worth of shame so thick
you could stand up a spoon in it, if only you weren't using that
spoon to inhale a pint of Bunny Tracks ice cream as soon as you
could fit it in your stomach without wet burping.

I didn't trail off the Medifast diet, I jumped off it like it was a
train barreling toward a brick wall (incidentally, you could also get

Medifast crackers in brick-wall flavor). I steadily gained the weight back and then I quickly gained more than I lost. I was living at home when I started the Medifast diet and when the diet failed. Or when I failed. Whichever, they're both true. What is also true is, my mom kept buying the Medifast food and giving it to me and she did so at my request. In my mind, I wasn't giving in; I was just taking a breather and stocking up for the long road to health that lay ahead. When I left home, I took boxes of DVDs, graphic novels, 2XL clothes that would never fit again, and several months' worth of Medifast. My quick-fix miracle cure, my meat-sweats methadone. Anytime I wanted to get less fat, I had the key in my cupboard. I started to hate it. Every time I went to get a pan, the Medifast was staring me in my gradually swelling face. It was a painful reminder. I had been so close. Everything was going so right. Then I slipped up, let the diet lapse, and careened off a cliff, back into unhealthy habits. Every time I looked at those boxes, I felt a wave of self-loathing. It was as if the boxes were saying, "Hey, bro, we're ready when you are. Ope! Going for Top Ramen drowned in sriracha again. Got it. Well . . . you know . . . we're here!" One night, I had a moment of clarity, and I tossed all that Medifast into a trash bag and carried it out to the dumpster in the parking lot of the apartment. So long, purgatory; hello, hell!

Then, a couple of years later, I moved to Los Angeles and ordered *more* Medifast and tried to do it again. If you want a book about someone who's good at learning lessons, buy yourself a plane ticket, walk yourself to the Hudson News, and check out whatever Malcolm Gladwell is talking about these days. Or, even better, skip down to my sister's section, where you'll actually find something helpful.

The only miracle present in miracle diets is that it's a miracle that we keep falling for them. It just speaks to the power of fear and insecurity. It speaks to how intimidating it is to lose weight. There are a lot of jerks out there who like to say that fat people are fat because they're lazy. Oh yeah? Explain Grover Cleveland. Dude was fat as hell and he was president two different times. The truth is, everybody is lazy sometimes. One time I tried to turn my television off by throwing a shoe at the power button. We've all done stuff like that. People don't stay fat because getting to a healthier weight seems hard; people stay fat because getting to a healthier weight seems impossible. People don't reach for miracle diets because they're lazy; they do it because it's terrifying, confusing, and more difficult than you can imagine to lose weight. They want help. Well, I lost a bunch of weight, and I don't have any miracles to report, but maybe I can help.

RUBENESQUE, ZAFTIG, PORTLY.

If you use these words, it legit sounds like you want to cook a fat person in a giant kettle and eat them. If something is Rubenesque, it had better be a sandwich.

CHAPTER 10

Eat Less, Eat Better, Work Out

This book isn't really about how to lose weight, but I lost around 200 pounds and so far I've kept it off, so let's talk about getting less fat.

You can do it in three simple steps:

1. Overcome everything in society.

2. Rise above billions of years of genetic evolution based on the concept of scarcity.

3. Don't eat after 8:00 P.M.

Okay, sorry, sorry. I actively do not want to dwell on exactly how I lost weight. I don't want it to feel prescriptive, and I definitely don't want it to become a thing that people try to emulate, fail at, and write off. Most important, I don't want to sell the hope of a quick fix that preys on insecurity because I know how that feels (like shit). The motivation and drive to actually see it through and lose weight has to come from within. The "enough" moment, if you even want or need to have one, can't come from a book or anywhere else.

I didn't take any weight-loss drugs and I didn't get any surgeries, but I also don't look down on any of that stuff at all, because again—you have to find what works for you, and that's only if you've decided that you want to lose any weight at all. Also, just because I didn't get medical help doesn't mean I didn't get any help. When losing weight finally stuck for me, I had plenty of help. At the beginning, the world was shut down because of Covid-19. No bars, no big family dinners, fewer temptations. More important, I was the head writer and onscreen sidekick of *The Late Late Show with James Corden*. I had a great job and plenty of money. I could afford to sign up for a service that would deliver healthy food right to my doorstep. The flip side of that job is that I had to go on television every night with my changing body, regularly looking like a toddler wearing his father's clothes while James Corden looked amazing in bespoke Gucci suits, but these are the sacrifices I made. Your sacrifices will be different, but there will always be sacrifices.

There are going to be people who will tell you that it's easy to lose weight. These people fall into two groups. Either they've always been skinny and they'll speak to you with the confidence of an heir to a fortune so old their ancestor originally won it by inventing the color orange or something. Or they're somebody who lost a bunch of weight, and for whatever reason, they drastically oversimplify the process like Leif Eriksson saying, "I dunno, I just pointed the boat to the west, and next thing you know, bada bing bada boom, Canada."

Losing weight is not easy. Losing weight is like skiing up a hill. Losing weight is throwing a punch in a dream. Losing weight is kicking heroin, except also, you need a little bit of heroin every day or else you'll die. Losing weight is the twenty hardest things I've ever done, and I mean it's one through twenty, because I've tried to get less fat at least that many times and every single time it was like taking the SATs blackout drunk and in French. Even now, looking back, having gotten to a weight that feels healthy and right for me, I can't believe I did it, but I did do it, and I hate to belabor the point—it was not easy.

But it was simple. There's a difference between easy and simple. Dunking a basketball is simple; it is not easy. Playing the Settlers of Catan is easy, but it isn't simple. Or fun. But that's a fight for another day. For me, when it stuck, losing weight was simple. It really broke down to three steps: eat less, eat better, work out. That's it. Eat less, eat better, work out. If I were a cynical asshole, I could call this entire book *Eat Less, Eat Better, Work Out,* and I'd pose on the cover wearing gigantic jeans, holding the yawning waist at arm's length and making a face like I'd just been bit by a radioactive Peloton instructor and instantly lost 200 pounds—unfortunately for my bank account and my prospect of owning two Jet Skis that I ride behind in a third Jet Ski like an ancient Roman chariot, I'm not that cynical.

Also, I say "simple," and I mean it, but it's also "simple" the way Earth is "a blue marble floating in the cosmos." It's true, it is, but then you zoom in and there's weather systems and giraffes and people ambushing you with the Settlers of Catan at dinner parties, and all of a sudden simple looks a lot more complicated.

"Eat less." I straight up hate those words, and it's an ancient hate. "Eat less" is one of the first weapons formed against the chubby child. Yelped on the playground by kids who didn't have to shop in the husky section and then discovered anew every year of your life by a different crop of assholes, like it's the Velvet Underground—and always suggested with the same spirit, a whisper-thin veneer of concern spread across a brick of disdain. "Eat less" is the kind of insult people eventually arrive at, after thirty tweets, when you initially disagree with them about the best season of *The Wire*. Telling a fat person to eat less is like blasting them in the temples with a defibrillator, all the more painful because in the right hands those words could save a life. Because to lose weight, I really needed to eat less. It's the horrible, unassailable truth of mathematics. If you want to lose weight, you need to use more calories than you consume, and calories add up quick. *Quick*. Calories add up like the cost of a wedding, nickel-and-dimed until you're 300 pounds and you haven't even factored in the cake yet. Conversely, burning calories adds up like snowflakes falling on a school-day morning. It's agonizing.

Let's take a spoonful of almond butter, for example. It's a sweet treat, but it's a healthy fat, as far as fats go. It's the kind of thing you eat instead of a candy bar and then you think to yourself, "Look at me, this *and* I had a glass of water earlier. I'm basically an Olympic athlete." But a hefty spoonful of almond butter is 250 calories. That's an eighth of the calories they recommend you consume on an average day. Maybe that makes sense to someone who has a healthy relationship with food, but to me, it seems absolutely abhorrent. Insulting, even. It feels like a personal affront that something as insignificant as a spoonful of almond butter should contain an eighth of the calories you're supposed to have in a day. You're telling me that eight spoonfuls of almond butter is all it takes to maintain the status quo? "Eight spoons of almond butter a day" seems like it'd be Christian Bale's secret to losing a ton of weight for an Oscar-bait movie role. I've eaten eight honking spoonfuls of almond butter standing over a sink because my Postmates delivery was taking longer than I expected. I've eaten eight spoonfuls of almond butter on good days—not even depressed, not anxious, not even stoned—just at home, vibing.

Do you know what it takes to burn 250 calories? There are many ways, and they're all equally godawful. One way is to run for thirty minutes. Did you even know you could run for thirty minutes? Well, apparently it's possible. Thirty minutes—that's one-half of one hour. That's an entire episode of *The Office*, and that's with commercials. If you watched that episode on a streaming platform, you only ran for twenty-two minutes, and now you have to keep running for eight minutes, which is also an insane amount of time for which to run.

Now, don't worry, running isn't the only way you can burn 250 calories. Another way to use the calories present in one (1) spoonful of almond butter is to swim for twenty-five consecutive minutes. If I was starving to death on a desert island and a note washed ashore that said a Las Vegas buffet was a twenty-five-minute swim away, I would eat the note and make peace with God.

There's a chance that swimming and running aren't for you. Maybe you need something a little more whimsical, a little more lighthearted, a little more something you can do like no one is watching, and if that's the case you're in luck, because another way to burn 250 calories, *which is the amount of calories in a single spoonful of the butter of an almond,* is to dance for forty-five minutes. That's right. Dancing for only(?) forty-five minutes can burn more than 250 calories. I don't know who did the math on this one. If you're dancing for forty-five or more minutes, you're either

- on Molly, or
- trying to win a car in a twenty-four-hour dance marathon, last person legging leaves with a Lincoln, or
- both, on a *very* special episode of *I Love Lucy.*

What I'm saying is, 250 calories—easy come, impossible go, and that's so daunting that it becomes discouraging. It makes getting to a healthier weight seem impossible, and when you get to that point mentally, it just seems easier to say, "Fuck it, why even try?" Thinking about how restrictive you have to be to be healthy doesn't just make me want to eat a spoonful of almond butter, it makes me want to eat a tray of lasagna. Fuck it, if almond butter is bad for me, Panda Express is bad for me, too, but at least it's actually a treat, I'm going to eat the Panda Express. Fuck it, if I have to run for half an hour to burn off a bite of that orange chicken, I'm not even gonna get off the couch and go for a walk. Fuck it—I'm ordering two appetizers with my dinner, because I want egg rolls and crab rangoon, and it's delivery anyway, so I never have to look anyone in the eye, just leave it on the porch, I forgot to mention it wasn't just two appetizers, it was two entrées, too, and chow mein, because that's basically a vegetable, and sure they put four sets of utensils in this bag, that's probably just how many they put into every bag, plus, you know, I weigh as much as three healthy people anyway, but fuck it, don't think about that, think about how good this egg roll is, except you didn't remember to even register the taste of it until the last bite of the fourth egg roll, but fuck it, there's more in the kitchen, grab a second plate, *enjoy* that second plate, taste it this time, treat yourself to something nice because the world fucking sucks for fat people, don't think about how you can't find clothes, don't think about breaking chairs, don't think about how you look in pictures, don't think about how everyone either stares daggers or doesn't see you at all, don't think about how you don't fit in the seats on airplanes and definitely don't think about how the flight attendants walk over with a seatbelt extender—displayed a bit too prominently—their faces barely concealing their pity and disdain, don't think about your blood pressure, don't think about death, don't think about death, DON'T THINK ABOUT DEATH, DO NOT THINK ABOUT WHO MIGHT FIND YOU OR HOW LONG IT WILL TAKE OR HOW NOBODY WILL BE SURPRISED THAT YOU'RE DEAD BEFORE YOU'RE FORTY BECAUSE, I MEAN, LOOK AT HIM, THINK ABOUT THAT ZESTY ORANGE CHICKEN, THAT SHIT IS ZESTY, IT'S ZESTY AND YOU DESERVE SOMETHING NICE, and never mind the fact that now the food is gone, you're so full that for the rest of the night you'll be puking in your mouth every time you try to burp to ease the discomfort of your gorging, and the best-case scenario is that now you feel numb, because if the fear starts to creep back in, you're too full to chase it away with more food. So you go to bed. You go to bed with a full-day's-work-for-a-lumberjack's worth of calories in your stomach. You get up the next day, and you do it again, because now you're that much farther from the impossible dream of being healthier. The idea that you could ever possibly be less fat seems so far away, but the estimated delivery time for that Panda Express is still just about twenty-five minutes, so you let yourself drown because can you even imagine swimming for that long?

I know that feeling with the intimacy and clarity that I know what Honey Walnut Shrimp tastes like the third time you've thrown it up into your own clenched mouth, so when I say you might need to eat less, I don't say it lightly or flippantly or with the faintest implication that it might be easy. I do say it, however, with the knowledge that it works. However fraught with complication and complexity, it works. And your average body burns somewhere between 1,500 and 2,000 calories a day simply by existing. That's just what your guts and bones and brain need to keep you bopping around all day. Isn't that great? I think that's great.

Moving on to the next old chestnut (77 calories in a quarter cup of chestnuts) of wisdom—eat better. It's a confusing suggestion because what does "better" mean? Better than what? Even when you're doing better, there is always better than better, and when there's always better than better and you're trying to better your better, sometimes you decide you're better off just eating butter. I live in Los Angeles, and let me tell you, the "better" here is full-blown bonkers. There are empires here built on the idea that top-shelf cheekbones are the result of cucumber-romaine-spinach-parsley phytonutrient-dense green juice, and not centuries of the hottest Scandinavian people boning each other until they produce children who are basically a collection of forty-five-degree angles. Not that there's anything wrong with being acute—I'm just saying, they don't sell that at Whole Foods. They do sell apples, though. And they sell them at the less-bougie grocery stores, too, the grocery stores that are named after dudes with strong handshakes like Ralph and Fred and Howard Edward Butt. Apples are a *better* path to full than, say, a handful of Doritos that I cram into my mouth all at once like a toddler yawning. That's what eating better really boils down to for me, finding a better path to full. Yes, there is always going to be a better better, but that kind of thinking is a treadmill—it keeps moving and it doesn't get you anywhere, and nothing feels better than getting off a treadmill. You don't have to figure out what it means to "activate" a walnut to realize that some broccoli with hot sauce is a better path to full than some fettuccine with Alfredo sauce.

I need to admit that I was only able to accomplish "eating better" by being two people, and one of those people had to be vigilant and conniving in an effort to set the other person up for success. In pursuit of simplification, let's call the two people "Really Wants Some Ben & Jerry's Ian" and "Really Wants to Not Have a Heart Attack Ian." I love both of these people, by the way, and both of these people have my best interest in mind. For instance, Ice Cream Ian wants me to have a whole pint of ice cream while I sit on the couch and look at my phone for the entire duration of a movie, and Don't Have a Heart Attack Ian wants me to delay having a heart attack, or even prevent one entirely. It's tough, though, because I really like both of these things, and depending on the time of the day and how stressful everything was up until that point, it's hard for me to decide which one I like better. That's an insane thought in the abstract, but if I just worked all day and work sucked and nobody left me flowers by the stairs and I get home and I'm tired and anxious, No Heart Attack Ian is going to be shouted down and expeditiously exiled until well after Ben & Jerry's Ian has had his way. I mean, you have to realize that Ben & Jerry's is really doing some wild things in the ice cream space. They'll put a whirl of marshmallow in chocolate ice cream and then little pieces of candy swimming around it, and while you may not actually be able to visit Willy Wonka's chocolate factory, these two dudes make it feel like you can bring a little bit of it home with you. Plus, they just seem chill, you know? Ben and Jerry don't mind if you use their cabin for the weekend, just make sure you strip the bedsheets. Ben and Jerry show up to your wedding in a linen suit and sandals, and you know what? It works.

On the other hand, having a heart attack seems like it would suck. I know we live in an all-or-nothing world now, and social media has stripped the very idea of nuance out of our daily lives, but heart attacks straight up have terrible vibes. Heart attacks have no homies. Heart attacks loud-talk into their cellphones at dinner while their wives sit there mentally examining the pertinent details of the prenup. Every day I don't have a heart attack, it rocks, and it never gets old.

So, how do you find the balance between a life lived long and a life well lived? Like I said earlier, I have to trick myself—Ice Cream Ian can't be a part of the shopping, because Ice Cream Ian is a charismatic bon vivant with a sweet tooth, a silver tongue, and no concept of tomorrow. No Heart Attack Ian has to fill the house with cauliflower rice and pears and radishes and other bummers to protect Ice Cream Ian from himself, but look, sometimes Ice Cream Ian is right. Diets, to the extent that they work at all, work for a million different reasons, but they all fail for the same reason. They're unsustainable. Your willpower will burn hot, but it will burn fast and then you'll falter and "fail," and you'll start to associate the concept of "eating better" with deprivation instead of nutrition. You can't lock Ice Cream Ian in the dungeon, because he'll kick open the door and then toss No Heart Attack Ian down there and lock the door, and that's no way to live with yourself. This isn't *Spy vs. Spy;* this is your life and you need to let yourself live it. If I want ice cream, I may not keep it in the freezer, but I'll go get it and I'll try to walk if I can. I'll have cake on your birthday. I'll have that fettuccine Alfredo sometimes because part of eating better is knowing better, and I've dieted enough times to know that an abstinence-only education always leads to a food baby.

Finally, there's working out. Getting swole. Cut. Stacked. Diesel, bro. Getting vascular. Brolic. Buff. Built. Trim. Lean. Jacked. Stalwart. Strapping. Hitting the fucking gym. The iron church. The beef palace. The thunderdome. Navigating the Cuban Muscle Crisis with John F. Shreddedy and Fidel Blastro. I'm talking about slowly building up to the point where you get ten thousand steps a day and then integrating other physical activities that pique your interest. That's what worked for me, anyway, and I did all that other shit. I was a star athlete in high school, and by "star" I mean asterisk.* (*I was a six-foot-three, 350-pound seventeen-year-old and nobody else was that big, so I was pretty good at football.) Being a jock meant a lot of things: I listened to that song "Last Resort" by Papa Roach a lot, even though those dudes probably hated the football team, and, most germane to this discussion, I worked out. I worked out a lot. We were constantly squatting, benching, deadlifting (all workouts whose names properly convey their unpleasantness), and I never really burned through any fat. I got a lot stronger, and I'm sure there were plenty of positive side effects to that, but I remained massive. We didn't just lift either. We ran so much. One of my coaches came up with something called "The 280-Yard Dash," and it's exactly what it sounds like, and we did twenty of them, and that wasn't the only running we did that year, week, day, or even afternoon. I'm sure I would have lost weight, but before football practice, I would fuel up with two Big Cheeseburgers from Jack in the Box. They cost only a dollar each at the time, and if you think ketchup is the tastiest condiment you can put on a burger, you're wrong, because that honorific belongs to *value*. This is the place, though, to tell you that health and wellness are a parking-lot carnival of aphorisms, but one I've found to be useful is that you can't out-train a bad diet. Maybe Michael Phelps could have done it, but there are so many things that he can do that we can't (win twenty-three gold medals, clear a bong in one breath, simultaneously have no neck and have the longest neck you've ever seen in your whole life). You can try to burn 3,000 calories in a day, and if you eat 4,000 you're up a creek, and again, Michael Phelps doesn't need a paddle, but we do.

I've spent the last fifteen years trying to "Be Like Mike," by the way. Not just weight lifting or running but also, well, everything else. You name it, I probably tried it. Did you just say, "Oh yeah, Ian? Even rhythmic gymnastics?" and yeah, pal, even that! I was elegant and beautiful, but I wasn't trim. None of it made me trim, but even when it didn't, it made me feel better. It made me feel like there was something I could control about my health, even when I found myself uncontrollable in front of the fridge later that night. That sense of control, even amid this hurricane of my own self-destruction, gave me hope and self-esteem, and when I finally learned to group the working out together with the eating less and the eating better, that's when I started to get where I wanted to be. And I wasn't in the gym doing dead lifts when everything clicked either. I wasn't getting diesel or lean; I was taking five thousand steps a day. Then I started taking six thousand and then seven thousand and then ten thousand steps a day and I was getting healthier; I was enjoying exercise instead of dreading it. I started biking; I started lifting again. I got a medicine ball, which I thought was like a penny-farthing bicycle and people only used them in the 1880s, but apparently they're still a good way to angry up the blood, and so I toss a medicine ball around. I'm not saying ten thousand steps a day is some kind of magic bullet, but all I can tell you is what I feel, and I feel like you need to have something. You need to have some kind of activity that reminds you that you are not a brain riding around inside a fleshy-looking robot. Working out releases endorphins, and that's really nice, but it can also remind you that you are you. The mind that is comprehending this sentence is the same you as the hands that are holding whatever you're using to read this; the eyes you're rolling at this seemingly obvious sentiment are the same you as the heart and pancreas and kidneys that are chugging along inside your body. Your body doesn't have to be a temple, but it shouldn't be a

U-Haul trailer either, and I say this as someone who dragged my-self around for decades. You can't out-train a bad diet, but in my experience, training definitely helps you stick to a good or even just okay diet. Plus, if you do enough push-ups, you can do that thing where you make your pectoral muscles dance. That's house money, baby.

So there it is. Through eating less, eating better, and working out I managed to get less fat. I'm sorry—I wish I actually had a secret method. I wish I'd found a magic flute or something, but no, it's the horrible truth. All that stuff they told us was good for us turned out to work for me. I'm so sorry.

They say that being a professional writer is like winning a pie-eating contest where the prize is more pie. Well, the same is true for losing weight, except instead of pie, the prize is ancient grains. You've formed new healthy habits, but you have to figure out how to stretch them out over the rest of your life. If you want to get less fat, and you manage to do it, that's great—but that's just the be-ginning of the journey. Up next, a new challenge awaits. A Hell in a Cell, winner-take-all match with "Stone Cold" Steve Austin. Wait, sorry, no. Keeping the weight off, that's the next challenge. Keeping the weight off.

HUSKY.

Please don't call someone "husky" unless you can also offer them a full-ride scholarship to play on the offensive line for the University of Wisconsin football team. It's a very specific term that should only be used in that exact circumstance. It's like champagne. Outside of Madison, it's just sparkling fat.

CHAPTER 11

Maintenance Phase

For years my stand-up comedy routine opened with the following introduction:

> My name is Ian Karmel, which is ridiculous, because I am a six-foot-three-inch 350-pound Jewish man, and my name sounds like a whimsical British candy store. My name should be Shlomo Puddingtits. Or just something like "Hamhock" and I just come up onstage and say, "Better put some butter on it!"

There was a little dance that accompanied "Better put some butter on it." It was essentially a fully clothed truffle shuffle. I did that joke in front of three people at open mics, I did that joke in front of six thousand people opening for Chelsea Handler, I did that joke in Portland, Los Angeles, New York, and Kansas City, Kansas, and it killed every time. When I did my first ever late-night set on television, on *Conan,* I opened with that joke. I proceeded to talk about, among other things, self-diagnosing depression by telling the Jack in the Box employee to give me tacos until my dad was proud of me. When you're a big fat stand-up comedian, you quickly figure out that audiences want to hear you talk about how you're a big fat stand-up comedian. They'll laugh about other stuff, but they want the fat jokes. They're at the circus; they want to see the elephants. I like dignity, but not half as much as I like attention, so I happily obliged. I built a career on fat jokes. I like to think they were clever fat jokes. I wanted my shtick to be like my triglyceride count: elevated. They were fat jokes all the same, though. I rode that shit with the same regularity that I didn't ride a bike. I talked about the best way to prepare kale (throw it in the garbage; order a pizza). I had a six-minute joke where I described a Juicy Lucy cheeseburger I'd had in the style of the long-dead horror author H. P. Lovecraft (pickles and sautéed onions lurking underneath a burger patty filled with molten cheese, rolling in tumult). These weren't my only jokes, but they were the backbone of my act. They were the parachute I pulled when my jokes about *Pimp My Ride* or NPR's weird world music "commercial breaks" weren't hitting with the crowd.

I lost weight. I dropped from 420 pounds down to around 230. Wonderful for my health, an absolute disaster for my comedy. The act was obsolete, sure, but that wasn't my biggest problem. I could write jokes, but I didn't know who I was anymore. I didn't know who the audience saw when I walked onstage. I know it wasn't Shlomo Puddingtits, but I'm also not quite funny enough to come up with a silly name for a guy who could stand to lose 15 to 20 pounds. (Randolph Frogurt-Tits? No, see, that's awful.) I was lost. Up my sleeve, there was no ace. For a while I got by on joking about how I had nothing to joke about because I'd lost so much weight. Sometimes I'd try to shift my old fat jokes to the past tense. The audiences full of kindhearted people didn't laugh at all, and the audiences full of pricks laughed a little too loud.

After one set an audience member, a fat woman, found me and she told me I probably shouldn't tell those jokes anymore. I agreed. I'd already felt that instinct deep in my heart, but I was flustered and confused and, for the very first time in my career, frightened onstage. It used to be the place where I felt the most comfortable.

I'm still figuring out who I am onstage. That's because I'm still figuring out who I am offstage. So much of my identity was tied up in being a very fat person. I was so wrapped up in beating people to the punch in their perception of me that I lost quite a bit of who I actually was in that pursuit. I knew they mostly saw me as a fat person, so I self-identified in the same way. That's how I could own it, shape it, define it as much as possible on my own terms. As I got bigger, I got smaller. I cleaved away parts of myself that I thought would trample on other people's conception of me.

This is my maintenance phase. Finding out who I am, free of the gravity that being fat imposed and the force generated by losing a whole lot of weight. Make no mistake, I'm also going to talk about exercise endorphins and eating routines and what to do in the wild when you're confronted with an absolutely gorgeous bakery display, but this is first, because I think it's the most important. When I look in the mirror, I see the same person I've always seen. I don't see skinny me. When I was fatter, I didn't see fat me. I just saw me. Part of that is my unparalleled ability to find a flattering angle in literally any mirror. Seriously, any mirror. I'll find my light in a piece of dental equipment. Part of that is the gradual nature of weight loss, even relatively rapid weight loss. There isn't a grand reveal. There isn't a spinning-chair barbershop-mirror moment. You're an archaeologist unearthing whatever version of yourself is sitting under the sands of thyme. Brushes, picks, tiny little mouse chisels. Part of seeing the same man in the mirror, 200 pounds apart, is the simple reality that, for the most part, I'm the same person. Same gorgeous brown eyes, lush eyelashes, perfect eyebrows, proud nose, bountiful lips, regal nostrils, learned earlobes, auspicious asymmetrical sideburns because I'm still pretty bad at shaving, erudite rapidly receding hairline. Senatorial little stubby teeth that are perfectly aligned but mostly due to erosion because I've ground them for decades. It's more than just the physical traits, though. It's, well, whatever the ineffable quality of "me" is. Soul or identity or consciousness or weird little alien sitting in a cockpit inside my skull. I'm not sure where the science is on this right now. That's me and it's been there for the whole ride and it'll be there until the line goes flat and I'm a ghost or an angel or a tiny little alien scurrying around, looking for another meat ship.

I take a lot of comfort in seeing the same me in the mirror. Losing weight feels great in a lot of ways, but the schism in my identity is unmooring. I feel that most when I look at an old picture of me, one where I'm much heavier. I don't get a sense of "Goddamn, look at me now."

It's more a sense of "Goddamn, look at me then." It's a much different goddamn. It feels like looking at a different person. The dissonance between the consistency of the image in the mirror and the concussive blow of seeing an old picture can be explained by all the things I just described, the gradual versus the sudden, but I don't think it can all be tied to that. I think a lot of that feeling can be explained by what parts of myself I allowed myself to acknowledge and what parts of myself I ignored so I could adequately get through the daily rigors of life. I see a person who is physically much bigger than I am right now. That's the most striking, but I think the difference that resonates with me the most when I see those old pictures is that I see a person who still had so much to work through mentally, emotionally, and, for lack of a less trite term, spiritually. It doesn't make sense on its face, but for me, there were so many things about being very fat that I couldn't deal with until I wasn't very fat anymore.

I couldn't see the warping effects that being very fat had on my identity until I no longer had that governing force in my life. I couldn't see the toll it took on my relationships until I fully engaged with the legacy of distortion it had on my self-worth and ability to take myself seriously. I could not let myself process the catastrophic burden on my health that was created and sustained by being very fat. I spent years trying to pretend there wasn't a wolf scratching at the door, and now that the scratching has stopped, I can't stop screaming. This is part of the maintenance phase, too. Trying not to scream so fucking much. Trying not to dwell on the things I ignored about being so fat, and the legacy they leave, while remaining aware of them and acknowledging the way they echo through me still. There's a part of me that is trying to retcon the appropriate amount of considered trauma for the past few decades by overloading on it now. Did you ever fall so far behind in math class that you had to write an essay about Archimedes and watch a documentary about Rubik's Cubes just to get a passing grade? I'm doing that, but with freaking out about my shit instead of algebra. It doesn't work, by the way. You can't throw off the average, and you can't game your own trauma. In the words of that same algebra teacher, you can try to make up the work, but you're only cheating yourself.

Easy to say, extremely challenging to execute. I continue to spread yesterday's share of anxiety onto today's behavior. Sometimes I meditate three times a day, and even when I do, I get myself stuck in psychic loops worrying about a vein bulging in my forehead. I've let my imagination drag me through so many potential strokes and heart attacks that if they ever do happen, it's gonna feel like an old friend swinging by. I'll eat a dry chicken breast with my bare hands in my car, huddled in the dark like a raccoon, and then hop out and walk to a restaurant where I watch my wife and her friends eat a delicious Italian dinner while I pretend to be satisfied with a cup of tea. Do you understand how big of a gulf there is between chicken parmigiana and a cup of herbal tea? Even if it's the worst chicken parm, even if it's the greatest cup of peppermint tea? If there existed a cup of tea that was even one hundredth as delicious as tomato sauce and melted cheese, you'd know about it, because it would lead every single news broadcast, even if that same day the pope assassinated the president with a sword crafted by aliens and given to him, this year, by Tupac Shakur, Bigfoot, and Elvis. I love tea. I drink five glasses of tea a day. Tea rules, but next to anything that's actually, like . . . good, it just can't stand up.

This is the maintenance phase, too. Figuring out if you're sacrificing the present in order to give yourself to the future or if you're doing it because you're giving yourself to the past. Sometimes it's absolutely appropriate to skip the big Italian dinner. Maybe you just got back from a long, indulgent vacation. Maybe you're going to a friend's birthday the next night and you want to eat pizza and cake. Maybe you've been indulging for a few too many days in a row, you're in a stressful place in your life, and you can feel yourself slipping back into old habits. Or maybe you're being a dinner fascist, and you're trying to fix your blood pressure in 2018 by skipping dinner tonight, and you should just loosen up and get that fucking chicken parmigiana, you dingbat. You haven't heard a single word your wife's friends have said because you're staring daggers at their dinner plates, and your hand has been in the decorative table candle for the last three minutes because you're afraid it might end up in the bread basket.

Now we're talking about the actual boots-on-the-ground, day-to-die grind of maintaining your weight loss, but you can't think about keeping the weight off until you think about who you've become. You aren't as fat anymore, but in a lot of ways, you are. You're the person in the mirror and you're the person in the picture. I'm the person who went from 8 pounds to 420 pounds, and I'm the person who went from 420 pounds down to 219 pounds, and back up to 240 pounds, and back down to 223 pounds, and back up to 250 pounds, and back down to 230. I contain the poison and the antidote. I contain a lot of different poisons and a lot of different antidotes. I . . . am trying not to think of these things as poisons and antidotes. It's a work in progress, and I think the most important part of that work is not sticking my head back in the sand. I don't know how people who have been fit their entire lives think about dinner, but I imagine it's a lot more casual than how I think about dinner.

I hesitate to give specific advice on keeping weight off. Every person is so different. Brains and bodies are unique, and what keeps me on course might send you spinning into oblivion (Taco Bell). I will say what works for me, and I'll try to explain why it works for me.

I WEIGH MYSELF

I know that body weight is a pretty lousy indication of your health; I know that. It has a harmful legacy both generally in the world and specifically in the life of anyone who's been any degree of fat. I weigh myself anyway. I weigh myself the way I use rosemary. It would be insane to sit at a table and eat sprig after sprig of rosemary like a goat or a performance art installation or something, but if you toss a little bit of that stuff on some chicken, it can really sing. The scale isn't the main ingredient, but it helps the other ones make more sense. If I start treating myself with a cup of popcorn every night, and that cup slowly becomes a bowl, and that bowl becomes two bowls, and I notice that the number on the scale starts to creep up, I can check in with myself. Am I enjoying that popcorn enough to justify what it's doing to my body? Am I really enjoying that bowl more than I'm enjoying that cup, or is this show I'm bingeing just kind of boring? Do I need this popcorn every night, or am I creating a ritual to act as a crutch instead of addressing what's really bothering me? Oftentimes when I notice my weight start to creep up, it correlates directly to how stressed I am in life. Part of that is what being stressed does to your body, part of that is that I get stressed when I notice myself putting on weight, but a big part of that is my habit of stress eating. Bowls of popcorn, handfuls of almonds, multiplying, expanding, spinning out of control, and sending me into a spiral.

Seeing that expressed as a number on a scale is like splashing cold water on your face—it sucks, but it can wake you up.

There are plenty of times when I won't weigh myself. If I pop off on that big Italian dinner and chase chicken parm with tiramisu, I'll take a couple of days to let the dust settle and the dairy digest. I'm trying to keep myself on track, not trying to flagellate myself for the grievous sin of enjoying food. I got married in the month of September. After my wedding came my honeymoon, and after that a deluge of holidays, birthdays, visits home, and all the indulgences that accompany a celebration. I let myself celebrate. I didn't weigh myself for a couple of months. Once I finally stepped on a scale, I'd gained 20 pounds. It fucking sucked. But I'd gotten to enjoy cake at my wedding. And cake during my honeymoon. And cake during my birthday. And then cake on a different day celebrating my birthday. And cake on Halloween. And cake when we visited my wife's family. And cake when we visited my family. And cake on Thanksgiving. And cake during Chanukah. And cake during Christmas. And cake at New Year's. And cake for my wife's birthday. And then cake for a different day celebrating my wife's birthday. And then even more cake for my wife's birthday. It was a big birthday. Then I had some cake for my mom's birthday. It feels like it should have been more than 20 pounds, but it was 20 pounds. You know what I did when I saw that bigger number on the scale? I felt like shit and then, after I processed that feeling, I went without cake for a while. That number on the scale started to fall. That felt good.

I STARTED LISTENING TO MY BODY

Sometimes an idea can be obvious in the abstract and a bit more complicated in the execution. Listening to your body is one of those things. There's a lot of static in the signal, so it can be a challenge, but paying attention to how I feel has really helped to give me a sense of positive participation in my health. Really being honest about it, though, sometimes I feel sluggish, and I reflect on how I've been treating my body, and I can usually find some correlation. If I've been eating too much processed sugar or I've been having big meals late at night, I feel it. I feel bloated; I sleep weird; I get cranky; my brain feels foggy; I get into insanely personal arguments about NBA free agency on Twitter. I feel like trash, and when I start feeling like trash, it often becomes a self-perpetuating cycle, so awareness is key. When you're out of sorts, you're tempted to throw quick fixes at it: a candy bar, a beer. If you feel like doing that, who am I to stop you? But if you want to actually feel better, I've found that it helps to treat yourself better. Emphasis on the better, not on the treat.

Here's what I do when I feel myself spiraling out of control with my eating. I give myself a few days of eating very clean. I try to get a good night's sleep. I make sure to exercise, or at least walk. I shake the Etch A Sketch. If you've been housing cookies like Santa Claus, your body is going to crave more of that sugar. It's going to lie to you. I try to give myself a little space from it, even if it's hard, and then I listen to what my body is telling me. I've found that my body knows exactly what it needs to feel good; I've just got to listen. Portion size, protein, carbs, fat, exercise—your body will give you clues. Education is important; the more context you can give yourself for the choices you're making, the better. Mindfulness is key; be aware of what you're doing and how it's making you feel. There's nothing wrong with eating a big-ass scoop of ice cream every now and then, but the next morning, when you're a little bit bloated and your brain feels like it's wearing a mitten, remind yourself that that's part of the ice cream, too.

I DEVELOPED BORING HABITS

Maintaining a healthy weight is a total yawnfest, and that mundanity is a gift and a curse. There are probably ways to keep it interesting: A week of getting your lean protein exclusively from exotic bird meats. Your personal trainer waking you up at 4:00 A.M. with a treadmill and a chain saw. Personally ending the Soviet Union by running up that mountain in *Rocky IV.* Eventually, though, it's Wednesday. Unless you've economically graduated from Wednesdays, they come for us all, and to get through a Wednesday, you need to be boring. It's hard enough to keep healthy habits in a perfectly placid environment, but sometimes life sucks. You slept on your neck weird, your cat barfed in your shoe, your boss is being a prick, your job's a joke, you're broke, your love life's DOA (RIP Chandler Bing). The world has turned on you, and you crave the comfort that only cream cheese is capable of providing. I'm not telling you not to have that bagel, but if you're trying to tell yourself not to have that bagel, you're going to need your boring habits.

Preparing your meals in advance is about as dull as it gets. I mean, Tupperware is involved. Nothing exciting has ever involved Tupperware. If you put cocaine in Tupperware, the cocaine stops working. You aren't putting cocaine in this Tupperware either. You're stashing baked chicken breasts and steamed broccoli. The only white powder in your pot is cauliflower rice. Cauliflower rice! Not even cauliflower rice you're planning on eating at that very moment; this is planned cauliflower rice. Infrastructure cauliflower rice. Is there a more boring proposition than "Cauliflower rice . . . for later"? Cauliflower rice is socks for Chanukah. It's so boring in the moment that you barely even notice it, but once Wednesday rolls around, you're going to be glad you've got it in your arsenal. Again, I'm not telling you not to have that bagel if you really want to have that bagel, but if you're anything like me, you've had your share of stress bagels. You've realized that the bagel didn't fix a goddamn thing, you're still stressed, and now you've got a bunch of sesame seeds stuck in that treacherous little canyon between your laptop's keyboard and its screen. I can only tell you what's been true for me, but I find that I'm happier when I bagel with purpose, not panic. Meal prepping helps me do that.

Meal prepping may feel like it's overly strict, limiting your choices to what you cooked up on Sunday night while you blasted through HBO's offerings. The truth is, you're actually giving yourself more options. The drive-through is always going to be there. Postmates isn't declining your order because you've got some salmon in the fridge. But if you find yourself stressed out of your gourd on a Wednesday, let's be honest, you probably aren't going to swing through the grocery store to buy yourself a bunch of ingredients you're then going to have to take home and cook, using pans you're then going to have to wash. Give yourself the healthy option and you'll be surprised by how often you find yourself going for it. Pop open that Tupperware, baby, it's time to get boring.

Meal prepping isn't my only agonizingly mundane habit. I also walk. I walk all the time. In the mornings, evenings, during breaks at work, after meals, before meals, I walk. I'll walk to a destination; I'll walk when the walking *is* the destination. I try to get ten thousand steps a day, which is easy to record, because your phone is a snitch. I say "I try" because I want to seem chill. That's not true. I make sure I get ten thousand steps a day unless I'm physically unable to do it. I am, honestly, a little too weird about it. Sometimes I'll come home from work late, I haven't seen my wife all day, and yet I still can't sit down and enjoy her company unless I've seen that number on my phone tick up above ten thousand. Part of my devotion is the fiction that I can control my mortality by hitting a somewhat arbitrary number of steps, and it is an arbitrary amount (and it isn't). The magical number ten thousand is based on a Japanese pedometer from the 1960s that has managed to survive to this current age of fitness trackers and quick fixes. While the number has endured mostly because it's pleasantly round, actual science has shown that walking more is still very good for you. A study reported in the *Journal of the American Medical Association* (*JAMA*) in March 2020 found that people who walked for around eight thousand steps a day were half as likely to die early as those who walked only around four thousand steps a day. There weren't really any extra benefits between eight thousand and ten thousand. For me, though, there's one big benefit—I like it. I like seeing that number on my phone. It reminds me that I've achieved something wonderful for myself. It reminds me that in a world that is wildly out of my control, there are still things I can control, specifically my effort. Ten thousand is dumb, but it's my dumb. I can give myself the benefits, physical and psychic, provided by hitting that number, even when I'm feeling self-destructive. That's what's nice about having a hard number rather than a feeling as a goal. There will be days when you don't feel like giving a shit about yourself. We've all been at the gym, done three curls, and decided "Nah, I'm out." Having a goal lets you push through that feeling and reap the benefits, often when you most need them.

The benefits from walking extend beyond things that can be quantified with scientific studies. It helps me clear my head. It helps me control my cravings. It helps keep my thigh meat chiseled like a beef castle. I find the very act of caring for myself to be nourishing in a spiritual way.

I STOPPED PRETENDING LIKE NOTHING WAS WRONG

I'm screwed up in the head. By now, that should be clear. We're all screwed up, though. We're all bonkers and we're just trying to get through the day, and sometimes we develop unhealthy habits to help us cope. Our broken bones don't heal wrong out of spite, but they can still trip us up all the same. Those habits we develop to help us cope can hurt us in the long run. Admitting that is the first step to helping yourself out; the next steps can be a little bit trickier, but they're something worth considering all the same.

I feel like a lot of people toss around "Mental health is important" or "Go to therapy" with the same spirit that Marie Antoinette once encouraged starving peasants to eat cake. In the United States, therapy is expensive and often inaccessible. There's a stigma to it, too, that slides in severity from person to person, community to community, but it's everywhere. Even in circles that binge-watch *Frasier* and take mental health days, you've got this stigma. I was someone who was very open to other people going to therapy, but I thought that I didn't personally need it, or deserve it, or that it wouldn't work on me. I still don't regularly see a therapist. I have in the past, though, and I know I will in the future. It helps. Having someone to just listen, as trite as that might sound, can be wonderful. A good therapist will help guide you through yourself. As I've spelunked through the most warped parts of my own psyche to write this book, I've noticed the lack of help in the past, and I feel the absence of it in my present.

Unfortunately, I'm too busy to go to therapy right now. My last therapist didn't want to do Zoom meetings anymore, and I couldn't make the trip across town before work. He couldn't see me on Saturday mornings, and I can't find anyone new who will do that either. These are excuses, but excuses are going to happen when you first try to go to therapy and when you try to continue going to therapy. Not going doesn't make you a failure or an uncaring mess, but persevering through periods where you aren't receiving help doesn't mean the help isn't worth it. It's a headache getting help. I'm also dreading the idea of a new therapist because I'm going to have to rehash all my bullshit and get them up to speed: Fucked-Up Ian 101, 102, 103; Advanced Fucked-Up Ian; Applied Fucked-Up Ian. It's like a bizarro first date, where you're actively highlighting your problems instead of hiding them behind conversations about prestige television and wild anecdotes from high school football. It's hard. Going to therapy is hard. But, in my experience, it helps.

There is more than one way to take care of your head, though. The only wrong way is not doing anything at all. I meditate. My cardiologist prescribed meditation. That sentence is so Los Angeles that my computer started playing the *Entourage* theme halfway through typing it. It's true, though. He sat me down, and in his relaxed, reassuring, and perfectly tanned voice told me that I should start meditating for my health: simple, ten-minute guided meditations. It could lower my blood pressure, it might help my anxiety, and there was even a chance it'd put a stop to my panic attacks. It did all three of those things. The lower blood pressure and the fewer panic attacks speak for themselves, but meditation's ability to help me to chop through the suffocating vines of anxiety is the feature I most often appreciate. As I mentioned earlier, my anxiety has a profound impact on my life. My anxiety fuels my most self-destructive habits: my overeating, binge drinking, drug use, and thoughtless sex. All of them pop a road flare and wave at the monster; none of them do anything more useful than distract.

It took a while to realize I was anxious because I never thought of myself as an anxious person. I thought anxious people were mostly nerds who fidgeted around, dropping armfuls of schematics, while chill party dudes like me blasted half-racks of light beer. Anxious people hung out with other anxious people and talked about their therapists over black coffee. Anxious people needed help. I didn't need help. I needed two joints and 3,600 calories of orange chicken. I guess I thought that anxiety was like Beetlejuice. You could only summon it by acknowledging it. I was self-medicating my anxiety with things that society had deemed fun. I was drinking, eating, snorting, smoking, fucking through my fears—rather than confronting them head-on—and thus I was not an anxious person. I'm not even sure if you could call what I was doing self-deception. There's too much agency in the word "deception." I'd been pulling this ruse on myself for so long that I don't think any part of me was even remotely aware of it. Once I started peeling away my methods of self-medication, it became extremely clear extremely fast that I am an extremely anxious person. Meditation helps with my anxiety. It helps in a preventive way, and it helps when I feel my chest tightening and the panic bubbling up through my bones.

Your mileage may vary, of course, such is life, but I recommend meditation to nearly everyone I meet. I use an app, one of the big brands. It guides me through a daily ten-minute meditation. The teacher ends every episode with a quote about mindfulness and one time it was a Lenny Kravitz quote. I can't remember the exact line, but it was Lenny Kravitz, so it was probably something about how once when he was performing his leather pants split open and his penis flopped out like the emergency slide on a jetliner. It can be difficult to meditate. Life comes up and the momentum of your day will barrel through any attempt to slow it down. That's part of why it's so important to pursue it. It's radically kind to take ten minutes to yourself. Make it the ten minutes you would have spent scrolling through Instagram or cycling through shit on Netflix before you land back on the same sitcom you've already watched through to completion ten different times. It's okay if you don't meditate every day. I don't. I go months without it sometimes. I always feel better when I do make that time, though. It feels like gently dipping my brain in a pool. Sometimes meditation can lead you to important realizations. Sometimes it's just sitting there quietly for ten minutes while you think about how it's weird that both Ronald *and* Donald are names. Either way, it's time well spent.

At the heart of maintenance is the notion of self-respect and love, but I mean, like, real self-respect and love. Figure out what's messing you up and do the best you can to put a stop to it. What's that old joke? A man walks into a doctor's office, his arm bent at the elbow, and he says, "Doctor, it hurts when I do this, what should I do?" The doctor replies, "Stop doing that." Look, it's not the perfect joke for this situation, but I told you, I had to throw out my entire act; I'm a work in progress.

FLABBY.

You know how they say the Inuit have over one hundred different words for snow? America is so obsessed with being fat that we've somehow let "flabby" be a word. And yet there's only one word for Xanax. Interesting.

CHAPTER 12

Cheat Days

Some folks lose a bunch of weight and seemingly turn into completely different people. I follow this guy on Instagram who used to be fat and now he posts videos like "Five Reasons to Get Stoked About Brazil Nuts." I love this guy, by the way. He's great. I've learned a lot about healthy eating by watching his videos. I have not learned how to be genuinely stoked about Brazil nuts—at least not compared to how stoked I get about calzones. I need to have a calzone every now and then. I need a cupcake. I need five glasses of wine. I need to have an entire day where I'm not asking the waiter, "Can I get that salmon without the miso glaze?" I need cheat days.

I feel like the world opens up on a cheat day. I live in between two amazing bakeries, and when I'm eating healthy, they might as well be H&R Blocks. I need them to be. I can't think of them as places that sell food, so I create a fictional world and damn myself to live inside it. Entire sections of the grocery store cease to exist entirely. There aren't twelve different flavors of Doritos; there is one flavor of Doritos: Forbidden. Postmates and Grubhub get about as much action as that Shazam for Plants app I downloaded and have used exactly once. (Coulter's Matilija poppy: It looks like a fried egg.)

When I'm eating healthy, I do my best to think of food as a fuel, and I know that's probably the best way to think of food, but sometimes that feels so limiting. It's like you're cordoning off an entire wing of human expression. Like you're screaming, "The *Mona Lisa* is frivolous! Paint should only be used on freeways, tanks, and jumbo jets!" My body feels so much better when I'm eating better, but I get this nagging feeling that I'm going to live a longer, healthier life with no life in it. Then I arrive at a cheat day and it's like I'm slapped awake by a cartoon hand of steam from a pie cooling on a windowsill. Those bakeries are open for business. The sheer variety of confections and delights available is overwhelming. I'm like an East German staggering into a West Berlin grocery store just hours after the wall fell. All my friends exist again, all the canelés, the croissants, the madeleines, the kouign-amanns, and yes, I also just found out it's not spelled "Queen Iman." When I'm on a cheat day, every restaurant vibrates with tantalizing possibility, like the unread books on a shelf *right after* you finish reading a book. Even restaurants I would never normally eat at become deeply intriguing. A ceviche restaurant with a C health rating is just a misunderstood masterpiece waiting to be rediscovered. The diarrhea is part of the overall dining experience! It gives you time alone to reflect on how extremely room temperature that shrimp was.

Of course, I'm not going to eat at a midrange ceviche restaurant; I've got a tasting menu all lined up and planned out. I remember being in the middle of a long run of eating exclusively healthy foods when an image of a pastrami sandwich on white bread entered my brain so clearly and fully that if it had been Jesus I'd have bought an Under Armour polo shirt and moved to Phoenix to start a megachurch. I could hold the experience of that divine sandwich with all five of my senses. I remember fixating on the first bite, my nose getting there before my taste buds, the smell of the pastrami sending saliva flooding into my mouth like it's a wedding dance floor when the DJ finally plays "I Wanna Dance with Somebody." The pillowy bread relenting under my teeth, the flavor of the pastrami, salty and deep and rich, fat melted and soaked into the tender meat, the sensation unrolling down my palate before the yellow mustard cuts through, a condiment Errol Flynn slicing open a sail of cured beef brisket. The flavors mix as I chew, overpowering each other, empowering each other, doing so much more together than they could ever do alone. I swallow and I look down at my hands and I nearly start crying because I'm still holding, like, 80 percent of a perfect pastrami sandwich. When I finally did eat that sandwich, it wasn't as good as the image I had constructed in my brain. It was better. Pastrami is so fucking delicious. We talk about it a lot and we still don't talk about it nearly enough. It's the best thing we Jews have given America, and we've given America teddy bears, *Jaws,* and most of the Christmas songs.

That first bite might be as good as it gets, though. My problem with cheat days is never the first bite, or even the first sandwich; it's that I keep eating. It's the tacos later in the day, with the nachos as a side. (You can talk yourself into nachos as a side, despite the fact that they're just the deconstructed ingredients of, like, five crunchy tacos.) The clock keeps ticking. At midnight you turn into a pumpkin. Pumpkins can't go to the ice cream shop; how would they hold the cone? You keep eating, you keep eating, and you don't even have the storage space that you'd normally have because you've been eating healthy! The spirit is willing, but the flesh is not sure if it's going to burp or barf.

I'm dumb as hell, but I'm smart enough to know this isn't the best way to be managing my eating habits. I know this system I've created for myself is a trap that probably just exacerbates my toxic relationship with food. I know the proper model for healthy eating is to be mindful all the time. If I want a cookie, I shouldn't give it all this power, I should just have a cookie. But . . . what if . . . *I always want a cookie?* I start off with the best of intentions when I'm eating intuitively, but eventually my intuition is warped by the gravity of processed sugar, salt, and fat. One cookie turns into two cookies turns into too many cookies for Corduroy and the whole day is shot and then the cycle continues—unless I jam a stick in the spokes. It's not a good system, but it's the best one I've found so far.

I think what attracts me to the cheat-day dynamic is how little I have to think about it. It might be incompatible in the long run, but in the short term it's worked for me and it's been sustainable because of its rigid binary. It's "set it and forget it."

I know that there are healthier ways to approach eating, but when people tell me that I should just be gently mindful about eating all the time, I feel like I'm seven years old and I'm being told to ride a bike without training wheels. The first time I rode a bike without training wheels for real, my dad took me to the top of the cul-de-sac, gave me a gentle push down the slope of the asphalt, and watched me career into the cherry tree in our front yard. Maybe that's why I'm nervous right now.

This is all making me think about theory versus reality, though. It seems to me like the conventional wisdom around fat, health, and weight loss is anything but conventional. It's always changing. In my lifetime alone, the nutritional reputation of eggs has ping-ponged back and forth faster than I can track. They're the culinary equivalent of skinny jeans. That's just a micro example. I don't remember hearing about intermittent fasting at the Weight Watchers appointments I attended when I was ten years old, and now that shit is like Nalgene bottles in the 1990s—it's everywhere. I know in my core that cheat days aren't a long-term solution. I know that they continue to warp my relationship to food. I know they keep me in a state of mind that is informed by the toxic effects of diet culture. I know all of that is true in theory, but is it possible for diet culture to be bad for me in theory, but right for me in practice?

What I'm saying is, if cheat days work for me, can they still be so wrong? Aren't we all, to some extent, single-person experiments just trying to do the best we can to get through as long of a life as possible?

My issue with taking off the training wheels is the fear that I keep confronting at the end of every cheat day. I stand in front of the freezer, tossing ice cream into a hole that I've never been able to fill, and I'm faced with an idea so obvious that it's terrifying. I want to be mindful, but what if my mind is broken?

As I think about my relationship to eating, I keep returning to the same thought. When I was fat, I thought that losing weight would fix all the significant troubles in my life. Every problem I suffered, whether it was with my romantic relationships, my health, or my career, was refracted and magnified through the lens of my obesity. I thought that cracking that lens would solve those problems. It turns out losing weight didn't fix anything. It didn't really even fix being fat. My physical health is better. I don't have to go to a special store to buy clothes. Yet I'm still the same person. My brain still works the same. The synapse chains are still telling me to load a structurally unsound amount of guacamole onto each tortilla chip. I'm the same me who got fat in the first place. I've pulled myself from the burning wreckage of my catastrophically poor health, but I'm still the same guy who crashed the car in the first place. Despite everything I've been through, here I am, still calling it a problem to be fat. Still framing my body as a character flaw. I can't help but think that it's all connected. The insecurity, the mania, the depression, the terror, the resentment, the self-soothing and the fallout therefrom: It's all part of my big fat brain. The cheat days are the flower; the brain is the root.

I guess it's progress just knowing that my cheat-day system isn't the healthiest path forward. This is kind of my pattern. I go from "I didn't know this was bad for me" to "I know this is bad for me, but I'm doing it anyway" to "I don't do that thing that's bad for me anymore!" That's progress in the real world. What I'm saying is, watch out for our next book, *Five Reasons to Get Stoked About Spelt.*

CHUNKY.

I am not peanut butter. I am not Diane Keaton's cable-knit sweater. I am not the third act of *The Goonies*. I am not "chunky."

CHAPTER 13

Late Late Weight Weight

For more than eight years, I was a writer on *The Late Late Show with James Corden*. The first time I met James was for a job interview six months before the show launched. He was sitting alone in the back corner of the Soho House in West Hollywood. I wasn't nervous because this was still back when I thought I was hot shit and also because nobody in America really knew who Corden was at that point. Everything I knew about James I had learned from his IMDb bio and from a conversation with John Oliver's equally British manager, who called James "a bit laddy." I immediately googled "laddy." It's British for "bro-ey." I think it was an attempt to scare me off, but it only made me more excited. I, too, am a lad. I have shoplifted beef jerky. I have not won a Tony Award, which James had just done, so after failing to square his "laddy" reputation with his impressive résumé, I went into the meeting ready for anything. I wasn't nervous, but I was prepared. We sat down, we exchanged pleasantries, James explained his vision for his iteration of *The Late Late Show*, and then I started excitedly ticking through the ideas I'd written down in my notebook. He earnestly laughed at some of them; I realized some of them were shit even as they were leaving my mouth, and he laughed at those, too, though less earnestly. Already a skilled talk show host.

After about half an hour, the brainstorm ran its course, and we just sat there for a moment with nothing else to say about the direction of the show. Then, like a switch flipping, we fell into a spirited bullshit session that would last the better part of a decade. Throughout the rest of that meeting and over the next eight years, I got to know James and helped shape the future of *The Late Late Show*. This was easy, because I saw so much of myself in him and so much of him in me. We were both fat kids who grew up trying to make people laugh because it was that or fighting—and we all know that comedians can't fight; we've seen it on the Oscars. We learned to make the joke before the bully could. We developed an overcompensating charm. We heard the people making fun of us, and we imagined the people who weren't. We carried that pain into adulthood, and our (wildly varying levels of) success did nothing to dampen it. We shared the constant need for validation and affirmation that lures someone into show business, and especially comedy, in the first place.

As the show grew, we would leverage our pain for that validation. I say "we," but James bore the brunt of it. He was the front line; I was just one of a handful of people feeding him jokes. And feed him jokes I did, especially jokes about feeding. I'd litter monologues with self-deprecating fat jokes because I knew they worked, and he told them because he knew the same. In the early days of the show, Oreo would release a bacon-flavored cookie, and he'd stand up there and tell a variety of jokes about these ridiculous, disgusting cookies, but it would always end on a joke about him eating an entire package anyway. We wrote sketches that hinged on his body: A commercial for a service that offered "Before" models. A send-up of cologne advertisements where a nearly nude Corden pulled poses next to a befuddled David Beckham.

It's not that the sketches weren't funny, they were fine, but they were . . . well, they were fucking fat jokes! Through his considerable talent, Corden was always able to eke out some dignity in these sketches. He has such a command of his comedic tools that, even if a joke's entire premise hinges on belittling him, he's never going to come off as a total schmuck.

To me, all this almost made the fat jokes worse. James Corden is one of those rare entertainers who is capable of nearly anything. I apologize for the continued hagiography, but I swear it's serving a larger point. James can sing, dance, sell a joke. He can do pretty much every kind of acting—pure late-night ham, network sitcom Bazinga-core, prestige television where during the press cycle you do one of those actors' roundtables and wear a scarf, serious Broadway, musical Broadway, and whatever the hell is happening in commercials. I've seen him handle it all capably. And yet we still returned to the fat jokes. Even as we grew away from them, they'd creep back in, and when they did, the laughs they'd get from the studio audience were explosive. They were tension-relief laughs, the kind you only get when something unspoken is hanging over the room and somebody finally acknowledges it. No matter what you do, no matter what you become capable of, you're always the fat kid. John Candy, Chris Farley, it doesn't matter, you're always the fat kid. You know, unless it's time to get serious, then the fat kid will almost always be played by a skinnier actor in a fat suit.

I felt bad writing the jokes that hinged on James's weight, because they sort of hinged on mine, too. I'd make fun of myself in the scripts and know that James could go up there and make it about him because we'd shared this foundational experience in our lives. I don't think James liked telling the fat jokes either. It stings to make fun of yourself; it just stings less than bombing.

I get an uneasy feeling looking back on it. You know that you can make those jokes as personal as you like, but you're still trading on a system that affects fat people everywhere. There's a razor-thin line between self-deprecation and furthering harmful stereotypes, and that line is different from person to person, and especially from generation to generation. We were on network television and had a big following on YouTube; there were a lot of opportunities for that line to be crossed. It's easy to look back now and say this, of course. At the time, it wasn't at the front of my mind. James and I weren't having conversations like "Bro, what are the long-term consequences of making fun of how you're chubby?" Maybe we should have had those talks, but I've been fat my entire life and it didn't occur to me at the time. All I could think about was getting to the next show. It's terrifying making a new episode of TV every single day. You're sprinting a marathon. So sometimes it's a Tuesday and it isn't an election year and no silly studies have come out recently, so you just write a fat joke for your friend to tell about himself because you need to get to Wednesday because maybe there'll be better stuff to joke about then.

At least when we were doing it some fat people were in on the fat jokes. In 2016, right around the time I started at *The Late Late Show*, I auditioned for a tiny part in a single episode of the Showtime series *I'm Dying Up Here*, a fictionalized retelling of the rise of the Los Angeles stand-up comedy scene in the late 1970s. I got the email from my agent asking me to audition and right there in the body of that email it said the character's name was "Tubbs the Obese Comedian" and maybe you're thinking it had to be satire. Tubbs the Obese Comedian is up there with Jabba the Hutt and Fat Bastard in terms of subtlety. This was a TV show about a bygone era of stand-up comedy. Having a character named Tubbs the Obese Comedian had to be a way to skewer the bombastic self-immolation fat comedians often practice onstage, walking hand in hand with a grinning entertainment industry as it leads them to an early grave.

I don't remember thinking that, though. I just remember seeing the words "Tubbs the Obese Comedian" and thinking I knew what they were looking for and I was ready to give it to them. I memorized my lines for the audition, something about how Tubbs the Obese Comedian was so fat that when he stepped off a bus, the bus caught on fire. The joke, I think, was supposed to be bad, but the script did a bad job of writing a bad joke. It was dreck on dreck. I'm still haunted by how little sense the joke made. To me, it was proof that they didn't have any actual fat people in the writers' room. A fat person would have made a better fat joke. Maybe the entire project was a meta takedown of bad prestige television, I don't know. When I got to the audition, I chortled through the joke, shaking my jowls and double chin at every available opportunity. I gave them enough Tubbs the Obese Comedian to choke on. I hoped I'd get the part, and I hoped that I'd have an opportunity to make the character more self-aware than it appeared on the page. I got the part, but I don't think I managed to make it more than a caricature.

The show was filmed in a shockingly detailed reproduction of the Comedy Store that they built in a warehouse. I stepped onto the stage of that fake comedy club and delivered my terrible joke about a bus catching on fire. Then I did it again. Then I did it one more time for safety. Then they had me do it about a dozen more times while the camera focused on two of the show's other characters standing by the fake bar of that fake comedy club. They were too far away for me to hear what they were saying. When you've got a small part on a show, you have no idea how your part is going to fit into that episode, and since this was a brand-new show, I didn't even know what tone the program was hoping to achieve. I didn't know until I saw the episode. In the end, Tubbs the Obese Comedian wasn't any kind of satirical barb aimed at a shallow industry; he was just a shitty fat comedian. The two main characters weren't talking about how Tubbs was actually pretty funny when you talked to him, and it's a pity that he feels like he has to belittle himself for laughs because he could easily be getting big reactions from his material about the Carter administration. They were talking about how he was just a shitty fat comedian. I wish I could tell you I was upset at that moment. I wish I could say I was outraged or shocked. I wish I was furious that I had been misled, either directly or by my own misplaced goodwill, but the truth is, I didn't feel anything. I didn't even feel excited that I was on television.

Most notably, I didn't feel ashamed. I think I should have felt ashamed. I wasn't Mike Myers in prosthetics to play Fat Bastard; I wasn't the giant slug puppet used to bring Jabba the Hutt to life; I wasn't a skinny guy in a booth voicing Eric Cartman. I was a fat person playing a horrible, carelessly conceived cartoon version of another fat person for no other purpose than to get a lazy laugh. It was me doing it, the same me who "Get in my belly'd" his way through Pop Warner Football practice just so other kids wouldn't do it.

I don't think very many fat kids are going to see me in *I'm Dying Up Here.* I don't think very many fat adults are going to see it either, because fat adults are people, and one good thing about *I'm Dying Up Here* is that people didn't watch it. It's like I suicide-bombed myself in the middle of the Mojave Desert. It still stung, though. Just like writing those fat jokes for the show stung. It still felt like I was selling myself out to get ahead in the rat race. It felt like I was selling my community out. It hurt. Just not enough to stop me from doing it. It's a complicated thing. I was so aware that fat people were underrepresented in media, especially in a positive light. When I got a foothold in the industry, though, I kept repeating the old, harmful tropes because I knew they worked. I traded the whole positive-light thing for more of the representation-in-media thing. At the time, I looked at it like "Fuck it . . . everybody is already laughing at me, I guess I might as well be in on it, too." It was comforting working alongside James, who I know wrestled with these same feelings.

I think this is why when we were finally presented with an opportunity to use our platform to actually say something constructive about being fat, we jumped on it the way James Corden would jump on an entire package of bacon-flavored Oreos. Sorry, old habits. In 2019, Bill Maher used his television show to go on a rant about how we should bring back fat-shaming. Here's a quote just to give you a taste of the whole thing:

"We've gone to this weird place where fat is good," said Maher. "It's pointing out that fat is unhealthy, that's what's bad. Fat-shame? We fit-shame."

Fit-shame! Billy, you've done it again. Do you get it? Because fat sounds like fit. Fat, fit, the difference is merely a letter, and he noticed it. *His mind.* If there's one thing Bill Maher loves to do, it's make a long, terrible point while looking like a business-casual Nosferatu. He sank his teeth in here. Maher called for fat-shaming to make a *return* to society, which is like calling for roast beef to make a return to the menu at Arby's. Anyway, this clip started making the rounds on the internet immediately after it aired, and I saw it right away because I was hopelessly addicted to Twitter. I was incensed. Honestly, it still makes me angry. I don't want to relitigate his entire video point by point, but what he did sucked so bad. First of all, fat-shaming didn't stop at any point, anywhere in the country. I know Bill Maher has been living in a Hollywood bubble for the last few decades, but I'm in that bubble, too, and this isn't the Fat Fuck Utopia he'd have you believe it is.

What pissed me off more was that he delivered his bullying in the guise of wanting to help fat people out. It was tough love, it was the hard truth that we needed to hear, it was . . . a joke about how fat people can't see their penises. Goddamnit! If you're going to be a smug prick, be a smug prick, don't hide behind some sorry story about wanting to save our lives. I understand it's a comedy show. I understand you need laughs. I was the head writer of a late-night show, I wrote fat jokes, I understand all of that as well as anyone, but I also understand what it feels like to be fat, and I understand how helpless it can feel. I was hoping someone would come along and help me figure out a way to get to a healthier weight. I wanted someone to say, "Hey, you can't keep living like this; let's figure something out." I didn't want the person saying that to be a lifelong skinny dude making fun of how I couldn't see my own dick because my gut was too big. We made fun of James's weight, but we never did it with such venom, we never did it while we were pretending to help.

When I talked to James about the Maher clip, we had the same idea. He could use his platform to refute the harmful message that fat-shaming needed to make a comeback. He was one of the few fat people on television and pretty much the only one with a daily talk show where the format would allow him to respond. James wanted me to take the lead on writing the response, which was good, because I was frothing at the keyboard. I wanted to write the late-night version of "Hit 'Em Up." James is an actual famous person and an adult with children, so he urged me to take a more measured approach with Bill Maher, which was smart, because we shared a studio building with him. If I went too hard, and he found out I wrote it, he might pull out a stepladder, climb to the top of it, jump, and punch me in the face. *I kid because I love, Bill!*

Over the course of a couple of days, we put the piece together. James and I shaped it; other writers pitched jokes; it felt great. We were proud of the piece. James was proud of the anti-bullying message. I was proud of the joke I wrote about Bill Maher's sense of self-satisfaction burning 35,000 calories a day. Over the years we had struggled to find our show's voice on serious issues. James had strong personal convictions, but it never felt like John Oliver–esqe deep dives were our strong suit, even as the late-night landscape proved that people were hungry for this kind of content. With this fat-shaming piece, it finally felt like we had something James could really stand on. He took what I wrote and infused it with his own personal experiences. It was like the negative image of the fat jokes we'd conspired to deliver. Here was a fat man, on television, standing up to a bully and doing it with humor and empathy and intelligence. Here was someone saying, "Hey, this doesn't work, because fat people exist and we're shamed every day of our lives." Here was a fat kid putting on for the fat kids. I'm pretty skeptical of late-night television's ability to do anything other than make people laugh, and don't get me wrong, that's a lot on its own. I know this, though—when I was a chubby little kid, laughing off fat jokes because I didn't want to let people think they were getting to me, I would have loved the piece we wrote. I would have loved to see a fat guy on television standing up for other fat people. I would have loved to see somebody calling the bully a dick for cracking a joke about how I couldn't see mine.

There is the matter of the medicine mixed in with Maher's dog shit, though. Being too fat can be bad for you. I don't think the answer to that health problem is fat-shaming people. I think that's like trying to get an insomniac to sleep by hitting them over the head with a sledgehammer. I do think that sometimes the conversations around fat get stuck in a pattern of harming and soothing. The world bullies you for being fat and then the people who love you try to comfort you. That can mean that the people who love you the most are never in a position to have a frank conversation with you about your health. I'm not certain that it's even helpful if someone you love tries to have that kind of conversation with you. It raises a question, though: If fat-shaming isn't helpful in any kind of meaningful way (and it isn't), then . . . what is helpful?

WELL-UPHOLSTERED.

I actually like this one. Feel free to call me this. No complaints.

CHAPTER 14

Body Positivity

When I played football, we would end every practice with a round of wind sprints. After two hours of slamming into one another like elephant seals on a shallow beach, it was the coach's way of wringing every last drop of vitality out of our bodies, just in case we'd kept any in reserve for ridiculous pursuits like homework or posting Taking Back Sunday lyrics on AOL Instant Messenger. Wind sprints suck whole ass. Running at full speed only makes sense when the alternative is a wolf eating you. There were no wolves. There was only the vague sense of wanting to impress the coaches with *how bad you wanted it* (I did not want it) and the embarrassment of falling behind the pack (I always fell behind the pack). The wind sprints were retribution for my effortless gigantism. I was big for free, so when it came time to be fleet and indefatigable, the whole bill came due at once. Every session went the same way. For a few legs I'd stay, more or less, flush with the ranks of lithe and limber Kyles and Brandons. I was like Wile E. Coyote floating a few feet past the edge of the cliff, a moment of thinking that maybe, somehow, it'll be different this time, just before the bottom inevitably dropped out. I'd fall a few lengths behind the pack with each sprint. The gap would grow longer, my legs would grow heavier, and honestly, that whole routine, in and of itself, didn't bother me that much. That's just physics. Big is hard to move. There's a reason nobody is out there winning Le Mans in a sprinter van. Falling behind didn't suck any more than the sprints themselves sucked. It's what happened when I fell behind that slid between my ribs. First the coaches, and then the other players, would uncork a choir of encouragement so resounding that you'd think that none of them were bullies.

It's weird to complain about encouragement. Every single person cheering me on had the best of intentions. They were mentors and colleagues who respected my abilities and valued my contributions. We'd shake hands and mean it. We made eye contact with each other. We stole beer from grocery stores together. These people liked me, I liked them, and yet every single "You got this, Karmel!" felt like an insult. It made the wind sprints harder than they already were. It felt like I was running with my own fat body lugged over my shoulder in a fireman's carry. They'd yell out their completely sincere locker-room platitudes. I'd hate it. They'd keep going. I'd hate it more. They'd clap and bray like a bunch of jackasses who only wanted the best for me. I'd seethe. Oftentimes, as a retort to these lovely people trying to put wind in my sails, I'd shout, "Shut the fuck up!" but I'd be so out of breath that nobody could make out what I was saying. Or they were so into the role they were playing as "supportive guy who gets it" that they didn't really care how I felt.

Sometimes, when I encounter "body positivity," I feel like I'm back in those wind-sprint lines, drowning in encouragement. "Body positivity" is a massive term, though, and I don't think you can paint all of it with some broad brush. In my life I've encountered three distinct kinds of body positivity that have informed the way I've seen myself, the way I've seen the world, and the way the world has seen me. Those three forms are corporate body positivity, relational body positivity, and personal body positivity: the way companies see fat people and how they can commodify and make money off them, the way my friends and family see me and interact with me, and finally, the way I see and treat myself.

We've got to start somewhere, so let's start with corporate body positivity, the most nakedly craven. Every Nike/Under Armour/Lululemon/Powerade commercial proceeds as follows—fit person doing battle ropes, fit person hopping off a mountain bike, fat person slowly doing yoga. They'll let us be in their sports commercials, but only if we're doing a workout that doesn't make us jiggle. I can't believe it took the sports companies this long to realize they could sell round after round of workout clothes to the "diet starts tomorrow" demographic. Buying new gym clothes releases the exact same endorphins as completing a spin class. I'm not sure that's *true* true, but it certainly feels true, and they'll make a mint off that feeling. It's plain that their body positivity is driven by profit, and I hesitate to even call it body positivity because it's still shackled, in part anyways, to the weight-loss industrial complex, but it's at least a small win. They're conceding that our very presence in a commercial won't scare off the normies. You know, as long as they're selling us clothes we can wear while we're doing yoga.

This trend of marketing to fat customers doesn't seem to have caught on in other circles. If you walk into an Olive Garden, you're going to see some fat people, because everyone goes to Olive Garden, and fat people are part of everyone. If you happen upon an Olive Garden commercial, though, you're going to see a lot of people who look like they don't even indulge in carbohydrates on a vacation to Rome. Inside the restaurant, never-ending breadsticks. Inside the commercial, never-ending bullshit. The fatter the customer base, the less you'll know it from the advertisements. I spent years buying my clothes at Big and Tall stores. All the guys in those print ads looked like Paul Bunyan: more big than they were fat, really. Even a store that sold 8XL T-shirts with a graphic of a cheeseburger on them was trying to throw someone off the scent. I think that someone was us. I don't know how to explain why a store that sells exclusively to fat people would try to disassociate itself from fat people. In either their perception or our reality, or very likely some combination of both, fat people don't want to go somewhere that's earmarked for fat people because if we go there, then we're fat people who have to go somewhere for fat people. No matter what's being sold—pasta or pants—the dissonance between product and presentation is dizzying.

I'm not saying this is fat people's fault at all. The feelings of self-loathing are fertilized by the sense that we're the other in society, and there's a flaw inherent in being an outsider. Maybe if we saw fat people more often, everywhere, we wouldn't feel such intense shame. Maybe if skinnier people saw fat people more often, they wouldn't utter the occasional negative remarks that we, in our vulnerable state, turn into the perception of an unceasing whisper campaign about how disgusting we are. Maybe if I'd grown up seeing fat people in commercials selling me yoga pants, I wouldn't be so suspicious when I see them now.

I can feel myself rapidly sliding out of my depth. This feels like an excellent place to introduce my younger sister, Dr. Alisa Karmel. She's an expert on this kind of thing. She's an expert on all kinds of things pertaining to fat, actually, not just the concept of body positivity. She's got a doctorate in psychology, she counsels fat kids, and she's got something that might be even more valuable than an education—experience. Like me, my sister was a fat kid. Like me, she was a fat adult. Like me, she lost a bunch of weight, put a bit back on, lost that, put it back on, and is now seeking a state of mental, physical, and emotional health. You can't buy that kind of wisdom, and thank god you can't, because she's already about $200,000 deep on student loans from the doctorate. My sister and I are going to talk back and forth a bit about body positivity and then I'm going to turn the book over to her capable hands. Hands that have spent plenty of time in downward dog and the lotus position. What I'm saying is, Alisa, you're a fat woman who's done yoga—how do you feel when you see billion-dollar corporations put fat people in advertisements?

I FEEL TORN. Thank you, corporations, for seeing my size and not encouraging me to lose weight. It's a nice change, though I do prefer and feel more comfortable engaging in other forms of movement such as hiking, walking, weight lifting, Lagree, and basketball. Why not invite me to one of those photo shoots? Fatness is only acceptable when it's kept within the confines of society's comfort zone. I feel more uncomfortable attending a yoga class than heavy lifting at the gym or conquering a new hike in Mother Nature. Why fat women are featured in yoga advertisements is a paradox to me: I've gotten more fat-shaming looks from Lululemon-wearing skinny regulars at yoga studios than anywhere else I have gone to exercise. Plus, yoga is hard for me, and from my experience, it isn't the *most* accessible form of movement when you're carrying more weight. Why has the corporate body-positive movement chosen yoga as the representative exercise for fat people? Yoga has never made me feel body-positive.

Condescension is one of my biggest issues with body positivity. Who are these forces granting the body positivity? I'm not sure I ever gave them the right to tell me my body was good, bad, or otherwise in the first place. If they can grant it, they can take it away again. They're trying to fix a fundamentally broken system by doubling down on it. It feels like they're building with a brick they just used to bludgeon me. I don't know who I mean exactly when I say "they": Apparel giants, sure. Prevailing trends on social media, I suppose. Academia, I imagine. Publishing, HR departments, bullies, friends, family—I mean, I could go on. I feel a little bit like a madman raving about unseen forces working in clandestine concert to regulate my self-esteem like the pH levels in a pool. Even if it's more coincidence than collaboration, it feels coordinated. It feels omnipresent. I hear someone telling me it's okay to be fat, and I want to yell back, "Shut the fuck up, I didn't ask you." I don't want to hear about my body from anyone.

I want things to be better for future fat kids, but I keep slamming into an uncomfortable thought, and maybe I just need to go back to therapy, but I can't shake it. Body positivity wouldn't have made me fit into that roller coaster. When I weighed 400 pounds, body positivity wouldn't have made me any more fun to sit next to on a crowded airplane. They could make the seats bigger, but then they'd be more expensive because fewer people would fit on airplanes, and then they'd blame fat people for the higher prices and the baggy seats. We could talk in circles about how capitalism is dehumanizing, but I'm pretty sure North Korea doesn't have roller coasters for fat kids either.

You know what would have helped me in those situations? Being less fat. When you're prone to eating your feelings, it certainly doesn't help to live in a society that loves to whack around fat people like piñatas. There are a million other caveats I could drop here, so many "wells" and "buts" and "excepts"; they're all valid, and they're all important. The fundamental truth remains the same: I caused myself untold amounts of pain by staying fat and unhealthy for as long as I did. It's my truth and perhaps my most personal one. I would never want to force it onto another fat person. Their life is their business, and I don't think it works like that anyway. It is true for me, though. I'm fast approaching forty years old, and I look at the shit I've put my body through, and I worry so much. I worry about my heart, my literal heart, and the state of my arteries, the toll of high blood pressure on my eyes, my nerves. I hope it's not too late.

I look back on how unhealthy I was and I wonder . . . Why didn't anyone try to stop me? If I had been an alcoholic, there would have been an intervention. If I had been a drug addict, I would have been sent to rehab. My best friends brought me buffalo wings. My mom made me lasagna. My dad took me to dim sum restaurants. These are the people who love me the most in the world. These are the people who celebrated with me when things were good and soothed me when things were bad. Usually, we used food for both types of occasions. None of these people ever made me feel bad about being fat—quite the opposite, actually; they made me feel better about it. Most accurately, they gave me time and space where I didn't have to feel anything about it at all. This is relational body positivity: the people around you loving and accepting you for who you are. I wonder, though, does that mean accepting harmful behavior? Does that mean watching someone you love slowly kill themselves because you don't want to hurt their feelings? My unhealthy weight was the main culprit in so many of my issues. The people around me dashed about for years, helping me sort out all these tiny problems, many of them caused by this massive elephant in the room. Why didn't anyone try to do anything about this fucking elephant?

I know why nobody said anything. How could they? Problem drinking is a pretty obvious problem. Being fat is just, like, more you. Literally, there's just more of you around. Being fat doesn't immediately change the person they love the way drugs and alcohol do; it just physically expands them. It takes its toll over time, though. I know my parents worried about my weight. I know they fretted over it. I know they saw, up close, the way it tormented me. They were aware, but honestly, when is the right time to say something? You know how in spy movies there's a room full of crisscrossing laser beams moving around, constantly shifting patterns, unpredictable, impossible to navigate, but then some techno music starts playing and somebody in a leather jumpsuit capoeiras through it and steals the diamond? That's how it must feel to find the right time to talk to a fat person about their health. The world is heavy enough. You don't want to be another blow. You don't want to send someone you love into a shame spiral because you cared about them in a way that they weren't ready to receive. Their

birthday is coming up, and you don't want to bum them out before their birthday, even if it means fewer total birthdays in the
long run. I realize that I'm being particularly down on body positivity right now, but what is its real value when your life is on the
line? What does love really mean when you're eating yourself to
death?

Alisa, we were both fat, but I was very fat. I was worryingly fat.
I didn't drink often, but when I drank I got "cut off at a karaoke
bar" drunk, even around the family. Especially around family! You
all saw me tipping the scales at 400 pounds, going back for a third
piece of lasagna, ghosts of recently vanquished charcuterie boards
floating in the periphery. Did you ever talk about me with our
parents? Did the family ever worry behind my back? Was there
ever a plan? I spent years suspecting that maybe I was a mutant,
impervious to the physical tolls of being extremely fat. Was everyone joining me in that delusion, or was it all just too much to talk
about?

YOU SAID IT earlier, Ian: "I don't want to hear about my body from
anyone." How would your family be any different? People don't
change when they are told to change. Changes can only occur when
someone is *really* ready for change. Of course the family wanted
your future to exist and wanted wind sprints at football practice to
suck less for you, but actually telling you, "It's time to be less fat,"
telling *me* it's time to be less fat—what was it going to do for us?
Miraculously increase our motivation to be less fat? Probably not.
Mom did her best to support us in dieting when she would join us
in weight-loss competitions, but do you remember how long those
lasted and how effective they were? Our family supported you, and
me, because we received enough hate from society.

I remember flying to Florida with you to visit our grandparents.
You had to lift up the armrest between our seats so you could fit.
Body positivity wasn't going to make that seat bigger, but body positivity might have stopped our well-intentioned grandparents from
fat-shaming us. The effects of body positivity might have lessened

the blow when they fired off weight-based comments at our innocent fat bodies as we sat around the table indulging in copious
amounts of delicious Jewish American cuisine, which they insisted
we eat even as they worried about how fat we were. Body positivity
is a form of protection against the excessive scrutiny fat people face.
It reminds us that we are still acceptable, lovable, and functional
human beings, even when our bodies seem unacceptable, unlova-
ble, and dysfunctional according to cultural expectations of thin
ideals.

For things to be better for fat kids in the future, it is important for
those of us who were fat kids to address the challenges we faced
and use whatever platforms we have access to in order to carve out
a different reality for them. Being fat doesn't always translate to staring death in the face. When you weighed 400 pounds, body positivity wasn't going to change your roller-coaster eligibility, and it won't
for a fat kid today; however, it might change the way they feel when
they're denied entrance. It might prevent the fat kid from internalizing the rejection and turning it into a core belief like "Because I am
fat, I can't do anything." This happens a lot. Our brains will take even
just one piece of evidence and create a rule about ourselves. If that
rule is not disrupted, it can quickly take over our view of ourselves
and result in ruminative depressing thoughts, even if they aren't
backed by facts.

Because you were both fat and unhealthy for such a long time,
you have a lot of regret and angst about the choices you made to
maintain such poor health. You are surprised that for decades you
were able to withstand this level of health, but it terrifies you to
consider the long-term impact it had on your heart, your joints, and
the rest of your body. This regret and angst turned into health anxiety that motivated you to eventually reclaim your health and now
somewhat obsess over it. It's not that no one tried to stop you before. Making the caliber of changes you made is very rare, but not
because of body positivity. Fatness isn't common because there is
"too much acceptance for fat people." The changes you made required an immense amount of hard work that you will have to

choose to remain committed to for the rest of your life, which can be a super-lonely experience.

Our family opted to write a different script. They helped you feel better by giving you time and space to not feel shitty about being fat. While some might call this avoidant parenting, others might see it as body positivity. How does a parent handle raising a fat kid? Sending them to fat camp every summer or making them a serial dieter doesn't relay a super-supportive message.

I try to remember that our parents had their own complicated relationships with their bodies. Dad was always fixated on staying "in shape," and Mom always thought she was fat, despite all reality-based evidence to the contrary. In addition to how they addressed their own insecurities with their bodies, they had to figure out how to co-parent two fat children because our siblings didn't have weight issues. I explicitly remember Dad being more direct with us than Mom, which stung a bit. He encouraged us to remain active and even coached some of our sports, making us work harder than our teammates. Despite his good intentions, several fat-shaming comments slipped out over the years, which taught me that my fatness was not acceptable to him. Mom's approach was much different, though equally painful. She would love us, feed us, and soothe our hurt feelings when people insulted our weight, but she never really addressed the root of the problem.

Here are some suggestions from the latest research on how to talk to children about weight:[1]

1. Use everyday examples of fatness to reduce the power of fatphobia. For example, start a conversation with your children and normalize words like "fat" without making a negative association to promote body positivity.

   I don't think this was ever done in our household.

---

1. S. J. Pont et al., "Stigma Experienced by Children and Adolescents with Obesity," *Pediatrics* 140, no. 6 (2017), https://doi.org/10.1542/peds.2017 -3034.

2. Talk about weight stigma when children hear examples of it, and normalize all body sizes.

   All body sizes were never acknowledged for us. We were the fat ones, which everyone knew, but no one talked about all body sizes with us directly.

3. Discuss and challenge the overgeneralizations that are made about fat people, such as "Fat people are lazy" or "Fat people don't know good nutrition."

   I remember this happening sometimes, but it was almost always done defensively to protect our feelings when we were fat-shamed by a peer or a peer's parent, like in the stands of Ian's football games.

4. Address the profit that is made off people hating their bodies in multiple ways, not just because of fatness. Discuss the dangers of some diets.

   We constantly dieted and contributed to the profit, which was never discussed.

5. Model body acceptance and the changing relationship with an evolving body.

   I don't remember either of our parents communicating that they accepted their own bodies or ours.

6. If a fatphobic comment is made by a child, stay calm and engage in a dialogue.

   Whenever a fatphobic comment was made by someone near us but not necessarily directed at us, Mom would whisper an insult about their behavior to lessen the blow.

7. If a child is fat-shamed, provide an affirmation about their body that doesn't dispute their weight status.

   Nope. Never happened. We were often fat-shamed, and it was rarely followed by a non-weight-related affirmation.

8. If a child's weight gain is becoming unhealthy, ask them about their relationship with their weight and body, and how, if at all, you can collaborate about changes that can be made as a household. These changes can include conversations about body positivity; introducing a more balanced menu with vegetables, proteins, and exploration of new foods; increased family activity levels; reduced screen time; improved mental health awareness; increased social engagement; and anything else that seems to be impacting their health.

It was always about dieting in our household, but in a restrictive way rather than a more "balanced" way. Screen time wasn't much of an issue for us in the 1990s, and mental health was definitely not addressed.

I list these support strategies because *all* parents will face fatphobia. It is critical to use these strategies to promote body acceptance, particularly if your child is fat, while supporting engagement in healthy behaviors. No, Ian, body positivity does not mean watching someone you love slowly kill themselves because you don't want to hurt their feelings. I disagree with you—the culprit was not your unhealthy weight. The culprit was that people didn't know how to discuss fatness in a more supportive way when we were children. You can be body-positive and support healthy living. The culprit was the belief that these concepts were mutually exclusive. There is no perfect opportunity to tell a fat person how you are concerned about their health, especially when they are a child. Use every day to express love, to educate on body acceptance, and to support engaging in healthy behaviors. We'll have the opportunity to move the needle forward when we become parents, too. Are you ready?

No! I'm definitely not ready! I'm horrified! I'm plagued by visions of a baby holding up a 3XL Big Dogs T-shirt and yelling, "I learned it from watching you!" I was a fat kid. If I have kids, I feel like it's pretty good odds that they'll be fat kids, too. If that happens, I'm not certain I'll handle it correctly, even with everything I've learned, because of everything that I've been through. You know how you drive for the first few months after you've been in a car wreck? Wincing at intersections, stopping at green lights because you think they're about to turn yellow, being so overly cautious that you're actually being less safe than before your accident? I'm worried that I'm going to do that with my kids. I'm worried that I already do that with myself.

I'm worried that I'm still too angry. I'm mad at everyone. I'm mad at the media that mocked fat people when I needed to feel normal, and I'm mad at them for trying to correct those mistakes now, partly out of suspicion, partly out of jealousy.

I'm mad at my family for not pulling me aside and telling me to lose weight. I'm angry that nobody sat me down and said, "If you keep this up, you will die." When I was a little fat kid, we visited our aunt and uncle in New Jersey. I feel like I must have been eight or nine years old. I remember being down in their basement. My aunt pulled me aside and said, "Aren't you worried about how big you are? It's going to hurt." I told her that the body compensated for carrying all that weight by developing extra muscle, so I was actually able to carry the weight pretty well. I thought she was worried about my knees. I was naïve. She clarified that she meant that it was going to hurt me emotionally. Other kids would tease me for being so fat. She added that it would hurt my health in the long run. It was a scary conversation for me. She was a terrifying person no matter the situation; she could make brunch feel ominous. More than that, though, it was the first time a trusted adult had talked about my weight like that. After Mom was done with her, it was the last time a trusted adult spoke about my weight like that, too. Any kind of useful information in my aunt's thoughtlessly delivered words was shredded by Mom's instinct to protect her children from any kind of immediate danger, emotional or otherwise. I'm left wondering if there was some kind of in-between, but even as I wonder, despite all my anger, I know it's impossible.

The conversations that I wish someone had taken the time to have with me are conversations that I could only ever have had with myself. The person who I'm the most angry with is me. I am the common denominator in all my unhealthy relationships with body positivity, in all my unhealthy relationships with fat. I set out here to talk about how much body positivity pisses me off, but now I'm sitting here in a pile of broken toys, and I can only be angry with myself. All this anger I'm feeling for other people is because my cup runneth over. I've got too much dip for one chip to hold. I'm fucked off past capacity and we're rioting in the streets.

This is personal body positivity: the way we feel about ourselves, the way we treat ourselves, the relationship we have with our own fat bodies, the delusions we let ourselves believe. I can't claim that I had a healthy relationship with my body—I think that's clear by now. I look back on my life, though, and I can't tell you my relationship to my body was entirely unhealthy. I've done cool stuff and had fun doing it. I've had a wonderful life. I didn't fit in the roller coaster, but I was at the amusement park. People scowled at me as I squeezed into the airplane seat next to them, but that plane eventually landed, I hopped off, and I was on vacation just like everyone else, just like that scowling prick who acted like sitting next to me was dental surgery on tax day. I lived my life. I dated; I danced at weddings; I collapsed to my knees in the throes of heartbreak and doused the pain with pints of ice cream. It was, perhaps, less of an anomaly for me to be pounding pints of ice cream, but that doesn't mean it didn't feel like the second act of a rom-com. I pursued a career. I joked about being a fat piece of shit, and I joked about people who treated me like a piece of shit because I was fat. I'm a broken person, and the bone may have healed wrong, but I walked on it anyway. There was too much lasagna on the dinner table at home on a random Wednesday, but my family sat around that table and laughed and gave each other shit and processed the world together. We loved each other. We love each other. We gave each other a space in the world where we didn't have to be fat, or not fat, or even anything at all. We could stop justifying our own existence to the world; we could stop telling everyone that we were okay, okay? Yes, we're fat, but you don't have to worry about it; we're good. Great, actually. Better than you, in fact. We could be quiet, we could be nothing, and even that was okay. I have already lived a better life than anyone could ask for and it isn't even over yet, so what am I so angry about?

I'm angry because I knew. I knew how unhealthy it was. The whole time, I knew. When the roller-coaster bar wouldn't close, it broke my heart, but there was also a part of me that thought, "Well, I can't let this go on for much longer." It kept going for decades. Every pint of ice cream, therapeutic or not, came with a mental caveat—"Okay, I'll eat the ice cream this time, but tomorrow, we're going to straighten up and fly right." For years I did this. Ages, epochs, massive swaths of my life that are as gone as gone gets, all procrastinated into oblivion. Yes, I continued to live my happy life in the intervening periods, but I spent so much time and energy trying to not define myself by my fat that I let myself ignore my health—mental, spiritual, and physical.

I knew. I knew that the steaming pile of Panda Express wasn't a great everyday dinner idea. I knew that I wasn't some chosen one whose body was impervious to sodium and cholesterol. In high school, my friends and I would try to bankrupt Chinese food buffets. I'd eat so much that I'd puke in the parking lot. My seventeen-year-old body would fall into a food coma on benches they built for septuagenarian mall walkers. This was my body at its prime, God's perfect creation glowing in the magic hour, millennia of evolution and luck, working in concert to manage an orange chicken insulin spike. As my chest heaved with labored breathing, blinking like corn syrup, I knew that this wasn't any kind of way to live.

I knew. I knew I wasn't normal. I knew I couldn't just will my-self to have a light salad for dinner because I had a pastrami Reu-ben and a bowl of matzo ball soup for lunch. I had feeding frenzies that lasted for months. I hit rock bottom so many times that I started keeping toiletries down there. I knew I needed help, real help, and I didn't ask for it. I didn't want to admit I was different, but I am different. I'm angry that I went so long at such an un-healthy weight. At the root of it is the anger that I went so long trying to tell myself that I wasn't different. I'm angry that I went so long thinking that different meant worse.

Here is body positivity, real body positivity, real because it's honest. The other stuff matters, too. It's inextricable from our lives. Every expression of body positivity is in a relationship with every other form. It's a web of forces, good and bad, but we can't control it the way we can control ourselves. The media is going to do what the media is going to do, and if it's arcing in a direction of empathy, that's wonderful. Your friends and your family are who they are, and if they're operating with love, even if it some-times feels like the wrong kind of love, you're one of the lucky ones. Put pressure on these forces. Be an activist in the world and an advocate for yourself. But be honest. Be honest with yourself. I lived through Fat Bastard and gout. Gout hurts worse. I kept put-ting my health off until tomorrow. I'm lucky that I didn't run out of tomorrows. I'm angry that I walked so close to that ledge. I'm angry, but I'm even more happy. Happy just to be here. Here's to many more birthdays, and a little less cake.

What Now?

IAN AND I have spent countless hours discussing our opinions and experiences of living life as fat siblings, side by side, in this weight-focused world. Being fat has significantly influenced the person I am today, more than most of my other attributes. And I believe that if you are reading our book, fatness has impacted your life, too. Fatness silenced me through much of my childhood and early adulthood. My size held me hostage. It left me feeling unworthy of love and success. After years of silently suffering alone, I've finally had enough. Fat people deserve more. I deserve more. My personal and professional goal is to change the contemporary narrative around fatness. Because as it turns out, silence will do nothing to change this paradigm that we've all accepted for too long. So now I break the silence.

My approach for this book is to think of it as something akin to a guide. I am here to get at the why behind Ian's how, and to offer support. In the following pages, my intention, through personal and professional stories, as well as important research, is to instill hope. Your story might be unique and your body one of a kind, but please understand, my reader, regardless of how isolated you may have felt for most of your life, you are not alone anymore. I encourage you to keep reading to feel the warm embrace of the T-Shirt Swim Club.

CHAPTER 1A

Is the Joke on Us?

EVERY CHILD DESERVES to experience joy and freedom regardless of their weight. If the T-Shirt Swim Club is one of the few places, or maybe the only place, where joy and freedom are found, then embrace that water, kid. Because once a giggling and blissfully unaware child realizes that they are fat, their purity shatters and their swimsuit is tossed onto the Goodwill pile.

Fat kids deal with constant scrutiny from everyone: family, peers, teachers, coaches, healthcare providers, community, and social media—you name it. A fat kid's appearance is unacceptable everywhere they go, which means *they* are unacceptable. The relentless judgment takes a huge toll, leaving most children feeling anxious and depressed, especially because their social ranking is determined by their looks. Unresolved anxiety and depression can evolve into feeling shame about their body. Shame about fatness results in lower self-esteem, body-image dissatisfaction, even more anxiety and depression, and problematic eating. Cortisol levels increase, which stimulates appetite, reduces the full feeling, and challenges self-control around food. All these outcomes quickly equate to more weight gain, depression, and anxiety. It's a relentless cycle that traps so many children (and adults)! This cycle trapped me during my childhood. It trapped me into constantly overeating in response to perceived judgment and resulting anxiety about my body.

Body anxiety is common in adolescence; more than half (57 percent) of participants in one study said they considered going on a diet to reduce their body dissatisfaction.[1] Boys report wishing they had more muscular bodies, while girls prefer thinner ones. Kids learn about the importance of their appearance and develop attitudes about their weight when they absorb dominant sociocultural messaging. When this messaging idealizes a smaller body type than theirs, they develop a belief that they are fat and that being fat is bad. Many children who think they are fat attempt to avoid scrutiny, which sometimes includes ditching school, opting out of extracurricular activities, and isolating instead of hanging out with friends at social gatherings. Some kids skip out on exercising—particularly swimming because of the revealing bathing suits. They won't wear trendy clothing because it could reveal their "abnormal" size and ruin their reputation. These behaviors can begin at any age; a child's environment and how it impacts neurological development determine when.

With instant access to all forms of media, comparison of appearance and weight occurs before most children have the tools to challenge the negative internal messages that come with it. According to a 2000 study in the *Journal of the American Dietetic Association*, 34 to 65 percent of girls age five had thoughts about dieting,[2] and 40 to 60 percent of girls ages six to twelve were concerned about get-

1. Be Real, "Somebody Like Me: A Report Investigating the Impact of Body Image Anxiety on Young People in the UK," 2017, https://www.bereal campaign.co.uk/research/somebody-like-me.

2. B. A. Abramovitz and L. L. Birch, "Five-Year-Old Girls' Ideas About Dieting Are Predicted by Their Mothers' Dieting," *Journal of the American Dietetic Association* 100, no. 10 (2000): 1157–63, https://doi.org/10.1016/S0002-8223(00)00339-4.

ting too fat.[3] According to research completed by Common Sense Media, more than 50 percent of girls and 33 percent of boys ages six to eight think they should weigh less.[4] If you think these numbers are hard to digest, Jennifer Harriger, PhD, who is a professor of psychology at Pepperdine University in Malibu, California, and studies body-image issues in children, found that children as young as three are already beginning to express and internalize stereotypes about body size.[5]

When I ask my patients to think about their earliest memories of feeling fat-shamed, most recall an experience that occurred at home before they even started interacting with peers. This indicates that body anxiety starts early and the source is people whom the child trusts: parents, siblings, or other caregivers, for example. When body-shaming is taught by such influential people at the most impressionable time, it makes sense that children develop a preference for people who aren't fat before they're even aware of it. While the trajectory of children's attitudes toward weight throughout their development is still not understood, kids who show greater negative attitudes toward people who weigh more also experience higher levels of depression and anxiety, lower self-esteem, body-image dissatisfaction, and disordered eating. Children who keep these thoughts to themselves and don't speak about them at home are more likely to report these same consequences regardless of their own weight and shape.

3. L. Smolak, "Body Image Development in Childhood," in *Body Image: A Handbook of Science, Practice, and Prevention,* 2nd ed., ed. T. F. Cash and L. Smolak (New York: Guilford, 2011), 67–75.

4. Common Sense Media, *Children, Teens, Media, and Body Image,* 2015, https://www.commonsensemedia.org/sites/default/files/research/report/csm -body-image-report-012615-interactive.pdf.

5. J. A. Harriger and J. K. Thompson, "Psychological Consequences of Obesity: Weight Bias and Body Image in Overweight and Obese Youth," *International Review of Psychiatry* 24, no. 3 (2012): 247–53, https://doi.org/10 .3109/09540261.2012.678817.

This information tells us that children might be developing weight- and body-based opinions about themselves and others around them without saying a word. To promote the development of a healthy body-image relationship, it is critical for influential people in a child's life to start having open and neutral conversations that are centered around their appearance and weight attitudes early on, even if it doesn't seem relevant. Otherwise, children may learn from others that they are fat, develop shame about being fat, treat others poorly for being fat, and internalize all negative feelings and thoughts associated with being fat.

Children are likely to experience food behaviors that are confusing and difficult to manage on their own if discussions of appearance and weight attitudes are ignored early on. Kids overeat for a variety of reasons, including actual physical hunger; emotional hunger evoked by loneliness, fear, sadness, or boredom; cultural influence; limited access to food on a regular basis; insufficient awareness of their fullness cues; genetics; and the simple joy of eating. Overeating doesn't always lead to fatness, but it can when repeated over time without support, especially when the child is genetically vulnerable.

The prevalence of childhood obesity has increased exponentially over the last few decades. I'm sure you've seen plenty of lists detailing its "causes." Most of the reasons haven't changed or improved, but here is an up-to-date version:

1. **Money.** Families with less money have reduced access to resources such as healthcare and nutritional education. The caregivers in these families might be working several demanding jobs, which limits how much attention they can devote to their child's nutritional needs. Families with limited funds are incentivized to compromise quality for quantity, which typically means buying food laden with preservatives, refined sugar, and unhealthy fats for the household. Once their taste buds establish preference and

neuropathways develop, a child might become "picky" and reject a healthier alternative.

2. **Childhood anxiety or depression.** Children who experience chronic stress are subject to frequent surges of the stress hormone cortisol, leading to increased appetite and other hunger-related consequences. Additionally, unmanaged chronic stress can cause mental health issues, including anxiety or depression, which can result in overeating or unhealthy food choices while attempting to cope.

3. **Inactivity paired with sedentary entertainment choices.** A child who spends a lot of time watching TV, playing video games, or using their cellphone is less likely to move their body. Because these activities can also be isolating, the child doesn't engage with their peers and avoids body scrutiny. A cycle of eating, inactivity, and avoiding social interaction is perpetuated.

4. **Ancestry and genetics.** Children with fat parents are significantly more likely to be fat themselves. This is due to both nature and nurture.

Most of these causes are beyond the control of a child. Children who are not supported might overeat, gain weight, and eventually become fat. If that happens to your child, is it all over? Have you screwed up as a parent? How do parents raise a fat kid?

Above all, love your child regardless of their weight. Pretending that fat bodies don't exist or shouldn't be respected sends a message to children that they aren't lovable as they are. Countless studies show that putting kids on a diet is the number one risk for developing an eating disorder in adolescence and adulthood. While well-intentioned, these decisions communicate that your child is not accepted because of their appearance and weight. The rejection does not encourage them to be healthier or less fat; instead, it increases body shame, which is likely already at an all-time high because of messages they receive everywhere they go. Ragen Chastain, a fat activist and researcher, put it best when she spoke of "trying to raise, essentially, a fat positive kid in a fat negative world."[6]

It's hard to be a parent. The moment you think you finally understand your child and provide good parenting, things change. Parents who support a fat kid often feel as if there's nothing they can do to prevent an unhealthy future for their child, filled with bullying, judgment, and self-hatred. Fortunately, researchers have joined forces to identify strategies to challenge the stigma of fatness and support kids toward a more freeing and joyful life. Here are a few ways to promote body love in a fat child:

1. Regular discussions with a child about how to build and maintain healthy lifestyle habits *as a family* will have a more positive impact than focusing on weight and dieting alone. Emphasize movement, sleep, stress management, social interaction, and a balanced diet. These family discussions will prevent alarms from going off in their brain indicating something is wrong with them and their appearance. Many parents have noted struggles when their child dishes up larger portion sizes or habitually skips vegetables and opts for a dessert instead. Teach children to engage in health behaviors that will promote good emotional and physical health, like listening to hunger and fullness cues. Oh, and don't bash on dessert; just remember to celebrate the nutrients found in vegetables, too!

2. Avoid falling into the trap of expressing dissatisfaction with your own body. Instead, provide children with an

6. M. W. Moyer, "How to Raise Fat-Positive Kids," November 9, 2021, https://melindawmoyer.substack.com/p/how-to-raise-fat-positive-kids.

example of living in a body unapologetically. This demonstrates both body comfort and the beauty of imperfection. It will also initiate natural conversations about how a child feels in their body. These conversations can be powerful.

3. Remind children that everyone's body is different because individual bodies don't use and store energy in the same way, which is why there are so many shapes and sizes. When a child asks questions about being fat or sees someone who is fat, do not feel the need to reassure them otherwise. The stigma of fatness may not have taken root in their young mind yet, and now is the opportunity to define fatness in a way that is not negative. If an older child identifies as fat and feels shame associated with it, be empathetic and seek a better understanding of how their opinion was formed and who influenced it.

4. If weight loss is necessary for a child's health, follow a family-based behavioral treatment program that is monitored by a medical team and requires participation by both parent and child. Program styles vary, though they all require family involvement and most include lifestyle modifications. You know, making good old diet, exercise, sleep, and stress management changes.

Despite a parent's best efforts, a fat child might still feel shame. Fat-shaming often occurs in places outside a parent's control, such as school, where weight-based teasing and bullying occur at recess, in hallways, in classrooms, during gym class, and in the cafeteria. Teasing based on weight is one of the most common reasons for bullying children. Outcomes associated with exposure to bullying include depression, anxiety, low self-esteem, body dissatisfaction, suicidal ideation and completion, lower engagement with physical activity, and disordered eating such as restricting, bingeing, and compensatory behaviors (e.g., self-induced vomiting and excessive exercise). Kids don't seem to be able to avoid these outcomes.

There are mixed opinions about the best ways to address the shame associated with fatness for younger audiences. Engage in body-positive conversations to let them know it's okay and totally normal to have inconsistent or conflicting thoughts about their appearance. It's important for them to learn how bodies evolve in a weight-focused and noninclusive world, and to engage in mindful movement that supports body function and drives self-compassion. If possible, provide opportunities for them to discuss body image with peers in a supervised space.

While these strategies sound great, and in theory should reduce body-shaming, the reality is that they are seldom applied. Most children who experience fatness won't have access to this support because it requires a venue, a facilitator, and funding, all of which are not prioritized in most places frequented by young people. Even those parents with some knowledge of these skills may not feel comfortable teaching them to their child.

Providing basic nutrition and body-acceptance education to all children might be a great place to start. I taught this to small groups of children in middle and high schools. I noticed that when no individual was targeted by me, every student appeared engaged in learning how to navigate and accept their body. I also noticed that each student experienced their own insecurities and appreciated the opportunity to think and talk about them when provided with a safe space. This wasn't an experience offered to me during my upbringing, and it isn't standard for most young people today. The only learning opportunities that came close were my health and PE classes, both of which emphasized health goals only from a standardized lens, never offering me a moment to feel heard or seen in my nonstandard body type and negative self-view.

Ultimately, we can all agree that children should experience joy and freedom regardless of their size. It is our responsibility as their parents, as supportive adults, and as those who have been fat and survived the pain of living in a fat-shaming world to provide a safe space where children can thrive. Being on defense all the time takes its toll. As Ian said, adding up all the fat-based comments from your childhood may not equate to everything ever said about you, but they cut deep, and the scars can last a lifetime. Let's step up, acknowledge the impact of fat-shaming, and support our fledgling members of the T-Shirt Swim Club.

Media Gains from Fat Shames

CHOOSE ANY ENTERTAINMENT platform and you can instantly find a fat person who is being ridiculed. I can't think of a fat character who I related to when I was a little girl. The young girls who were cast were never fat and always seemed to have it all: good grades, a strong group of best friends, and a handsome, smart boyfriend. The lack of fat representation made me think I was the only fat girl and I needed to change, especially since fat characters were never respected. This was true in the 1990s and remains true in the twenty-first century.

Fatness continues to be shamed through a comedic lens on the big screen because it is more comfortable that way for all viewers. It allows people to think they are hiding their fat-shaming behind humor, when in reality they are allowing their discomfort and fear to have more control over their fatphobic thoughts. Because we live in a weight-centric world, the fear of fatness is instilled in us before we even realize it. This world popularized "fattertainment," which is media that makes fun of fat people and leads to constant exposure to weight bias. Communicated through both obvious and more ob-scure messaging in advertisements, scripts, and character develop-ment, weight bias is damaging both emotionally and physically. It causes moods to plummet and can shatter any preexisting motiva-tion to get healthier.

Fatphobia and fattertainment aren't naturally occurring concepts of nature; they're cultural constructs conceived by humans. We ar-rived at this fatphobic reality by mindlessly participating in anti-fat thoughts and activities, such as laughing at a person on television simply because they are fat, even when we, the viewers, are fat our-selves. To reject these cultural norms, we can begin by challenging our acceptance of the hatred of fatness. While it appears that the media is to blame for marginalizing fat people through jokes and name-calling, it is just as much the viewers' responsibility to radi-cally change our judgment of this population.

Media has expanded its reach beyond television, which allows each person to subscribe to their preferred type of entertainment. Weight bias has become even more invasive since the develop-ment of social media. It's inescapable because its ubiquitous na-ture allows people to instantly share their raw thoughts with anyone at any time. Currently, more than 3.6 billion people engage with social media worldwide.[1] This number is projected to grow even more in the next decade. Weight discrimination has also in-creased substantially in the United States, by as much as 66 per-cent from 1995 to 2006.[2] Weight discrimination and bias are experienced across all forms of entertainment, but there is grow-

1. M. Yuen, "Social Media Users in the World (2021–2025)," *Insider Intelligence,* May 17, 2022, https://www.insiderintelligence.com/charts/social -media-users-worldwide-pernetwork/#:~:text=There%20will%20be%20 nearly%203.6,dramatically%20since%20the%20pandemic%20peak.

2. T. Andreyeva, R. M. Puhl, and K. D. Brownell, "Changes in Perceived Weight Discrimination Among Americans: 1995–1996 Through 2004–2006," *Obesity (Silver Spring)* 16, no. 5 (2008): 1129–34, https://doi.org/10.1038 /oby/2008.35.

ing acknowledgment of the role that social media plays in their promotion.

On social media apps, such as TikTok, Snapchat, and X, the platform formerly known as Twitter, weight-biased content can be made visible anonymously to hundreds of people within seconds. Thankfully, due to the interactive nature of social media, other participants can shame the abusive content creator just as quickly, which can lead to removal of the content by either the creator or even the app itself. Even with this censorship, hateful content can still make it through. Imperfect and biased algorithms on social media platforms can filter posts based on clicks from a user, who may identify as part of a stigmatized group, and as a result, the user gets exposed to a high degree of painful content that perpetuates harmful messaging. The invasive algorithms play a critical role in shaping beliefs of social media users, which can lead to internalization of weight stigma, especially with daily engagement.

Two researchers recently analyzed how the term "obesity" was represented on YouTube and found that highly negative depictions of fat people were common.[3] In another YouTube analysis, researchers explored the platform by using the search term "fat," which revealed popular videos that included content devaluing fat people.[4] In these YouTube videos, men were the target for fat stigmatization twice as often as women. Those who engaged in the shaming or vilification of fat people were also overwhelmingly men.

Do phone apps offer a potentially less-weight-biased entertainment option? Unfortunately, many apps aren't safe and represent fat people as ugly, greedy, and lazy, needing encouragement to engage in weight-loss activities. Apps such as Fatty—Make Funny Fat

3. J. H. Yoo and J. Kim, "Obesity in the New Media: A Content Analysis of Obesity Videos on YouTube," *Health Communication* 27, no. 1 (2012): 86–97, https://doi.org/10.1080/10410236.2011.569003.

4. M. Hussin, S. Frazier, and J. K. Thompson, "Fat Stigmatization on YouTube: A Content Analysis," *Body Image* 8, no. 1 (2011): 90–92, https://doi.org/10.1016/j.bodyim.2010.10.003.

Face Pictures, Fat You!, FatBooth, and Fatify—Get Fat are for creating fat versions of submitted photos. Another genre of fatphobic apps uses questionable approaches to shame subscribers into controlling their diet and losing weight: CARROT Hunger—Talking Calorie Counter is just one example.

While weight bias is damaging to everyone, it affects the younger population most; according to a survey completed in 2016, about 94 percent of teenage girls reported feeling body-shamed on their social media account.[5] The high prevalence of weight stigma and bias that kids deal with is well-documented, and evidence suggests that children who experience weight-based teasing, especially from the media, are more likely to binge eat, decrease their physical activity, and isolate. As a result of these behaviors, young people are at a higher risk of gaining weight and experiencing poorer mental health outcomes.

Another harmful aspect of social media is cyberbullying that targets fat youngsters. The increased anonymity, lack of real consequences for the bully, and widespread reach result in exponentially higher rates of body-shaming. Young people who are cyberbullied can experience body dissatisfaction, desire for the thin ideal, and internalized negative thinking about themselves and the world. When they internalize their thoughts, they don't feel comfortable asking for help, which can lead to social isolation and anxiety, as well as feeling judged by others and, ultimately, deterioration of their self-value. Today's young people have unmonitored, uncensored, and unlimited access to global news that exposes them to potentially triggering and traumatizing content about politics, tragedies, and celebrities, which can leave them feeling unsafe and inadequate.

Some parents choose to limit their children's phone use in the hope of controlling the amount of harmful content they see. While

5. The Child Advocacy Center of Lapeer County, *Social Media: Cyberbullying, Body Shaming, and Trauma*, https://caclapeer.org/social-media-cyberbullying -body-shaming-and-trauma/.

this approach filters some of the toxic matter, television continues to be a source of weight discrimination. Many children's shows and movies communicate negative messaging about being fat and what being fat entails. Fat cartoon characters are often portrayed as unattractive, dumb, unhappy, and evil. In 40 percent of children's movies, fat characters are disliked by the protagonist, and in 50 percent of those same movies, the fat character is shown regularly thinking about or eating food.[6]

As infuriating as it must be for parents to raise their child in a fat-shaming world, there is hope. Despite the abundance of one-sided fat-shaming scripts in the early days of TV and the internet, fat activists are beginning to reclaim their power within "the Fatosphere" by using social media as a positive change agent. These content creators are finally joining the conversations and demanding overdue respect by challenging the long-standing and relentless fatphobic messages that have remained undefeated for too long. The advocacy is occurring through formal groups such as the Body Positive Alliance and Health at Every Size, and less formally through social media, where users are replying to Reddit posts, challenging hateful tweets, responding live on TikTok, and even communicating directly with show writers. Social media is becoming the main hub for social movement groups whose aim is to raise awareness of weight bias; to encourage body positivity, self-compassion, and advocacy; and to promote acceptance of all body sizes by providing people with a safe space to express their needs and formulate their identities.

To support our young people and the efforts being made on social media, television can play an important role in educating the public, too. According to a survey of U.S. viewers conducted by the Centers for Disease Control, 50 percent of those who watch TV at least two times per week believe the health information presented

6. J. B. Howard et al., "Obesogenic Behavior and Weight-Based Stigma in Popular Children's Movies, 2012 to 2015," *Pediatrics* 140, no. 6 (2017): e20172126, https://doi.org/10.1542/peds.2017-2126.

on their shows.[7] This statistic tells us that we can challenge weight discrimination by including intentional messaging on nightly programming. Providing more positive portrayals of fat actors could also help to reduce weight stigmatization.

Pediatricians were recently ranked as the "most trusted" source of health information by mothers.[8] Healthcare professionals who discuss body-related issues with patients are encouraged to engage with compassion and use social media as a tool to promote healthier, less-stigmatizing conversations. Government entities are encouraged to explore legislative solutions to support anti–weight discrimination policies with dedicated weight-bias training while interrogating bias in existing social media algorithms. Researchers can explore how weight bias is entrenched across the various forms of media and how to reduce or eliminate it.

Ian and I experienced weight discrimination as children when we innocently engaged with pop culture. The same is true for today's fat kids. There is no perfect cure for the impact of weight bias. Challenging weight discrimination is going to require a concerted effort from every stakeholder, including the entertainment industry, all viewers of entertainment, social media users, the government, healthcare providers, parents, and, of course, readers of this book, like you, because more voices will equate to more progress. Fat kids will continue to watch TV shows in their pj's, use their parents' phones at family gatherings, and go to their local theater for popcorn and laughs. Donkeylips shouldn't be the only character they relate to. It is our responsibility to create an entertainment world where they will learn that it's okay to be fat.

---

7. National Center for Health Statistics, *Healthy People 2000 Final Review* (Hyattsville, Md.: Public Health Service, 2001).

8. M. Bailey, *Marketing to Moms Coalition and Current Lifestyle Marketing* (non-peer-reviewed research report), September 18, 2008. Brought to you by the Marketing and Communication Strategy Branch in the Division of Health Communication and Marketing, National Center for Health Marketing, Centers for Disease Control and Prevention (CDC).

The Beacon of Hope for Fat Adolescents

MIDDLE SCHOOL IS a petri dish of uncertainty. Adolescents desperately search for clues to help them build an identity during the most vulnerable time of their development. They suffer as they search for those clues while attempting to understand science and maintain super-important yet superficial relationships. The circumstance of this social experiment dissuades teens from caring about their health because everyone is uncomfortable regardless of their nutrition and activity level.

Because of the limited control adolescents feel they have over their own lives, they are uncomfortable in their bodies, thoughts, relationships, expectations, hopes, dreams, and realities. Very few teens feel secure. Even when they do, each day is another opportunity for their environment to attack their already-crumbling self-worth. Ian's refuge was *Ultima Online,* and mine was hiding in my bedroom while studying every subject that piqued my interest, specifically human rights, health, psychology, political science, and law. Both of us were searching for an identity that felt more within our control, one that wasn't compromised by how fat we looked.

Being fat and going through puberty in middle school can be a death sentence for a teen's emotional health. Depressive symptoms increase with puberty in adolescents who don't have weight issues and skyrocket for adolescents who are fat. Generally, young people who go through puberty earlier are more likely to become fatter. Adolescent girls who experience early puberty are at a higher risk of psychological problems, risk-taking behavior, and other health problems such as eating disorders. When those girls are fatter, they are more vulnerable to developing chronic health conditions such as polycystic ovary syndrome (PCOS). Fatness during puberty can also increase the risk of future insulin resistance and lifelong difficulty with weight-related diseases. When a fat teen deals with the emotional turbulence of puberty, they are likely to become highly susceptible to bullying.[1] This is because puberty hits without warning during an already sensitive and disorganized time.

While most teens typically are teased for some aspect of their appearance or behavior, being fat is a fast pass to unlimited and constant weight-based bullying. Though some bullying from peers is to be expected, bullying from adults, the people who are supposedly protectors, is torture. Teens might experience physical bullying, verbal teasing, cyberbullying, and relational victimization from peers and teachers alike. Researchers at the University of Connecticut found that weight-based bullying is one of the most common forms of bullying reported by adolescents and that some teachers have lower expectations for their fatter students compared to their less-fat students.[2] There have also been well-documented stereotypical assumptions made by teachers that

1. M. S. Golub et al., "Public Health Implications of Altered Puberty Timing," *Pediatrics* 121, no. S3 (2008): S218–30, https://doi.org/10.1542/peds.2007 -1813G.

2. R. M. Puhl, J. Luedicke, and K. M. King, "Combating Weight-Based Bullying in Schools: Is There Public Support for the Use of Litigation?," *Journal of School Health* 85, no. 6 (2015): 372–81, https://doi.org/10.1111/josh.12264.

students who weigh more are lazy, unsuccessful, and unintelligent; they have no willpower, exercise poor self-control, and are self-indulgent.[3] Weight bias by educators may contribute to gaps in educational achievement for fatter students. That fat kid–decent adult treaty that Ian felt protected by is short-lived for most fat adolescents.

Teachers aren't the only ones judging. Adolescents are often critiqued about paying attention to their health and are body-shamed by loving and well-intentioned family members. Adolescents weigh more if one parent discusses weight with them; weight only increases if adolescents have two parents who engage in weight-related conversations with them. Fathers are more likely to engage in pressure-to-eat behaviors, such as telling their son, "Finish your plate, you need to bulk up for basketball!" And boys are more likely than girls to be on the receiving end of this pressure.[4]

In a 2003 study of 4,700 adolescents, researchers found that of those who responded, 30 percent of girls and 25 percent of boys reported getting teased about their weight by similar-aged peers.[5] Additionally, 47 percent of girls and 34 percent of boys were teased about their body weight by family members. Approximately 15 percent of girls and 10 percent of boys reported body-weight teasing from both peers and family. Weight-based teasing and bullying can also come from adults who are part of an adolescent's healthcare team. When discussing body weight and health-related behaviors,

3. L. M. Lessard and R. M. Puhl, "Reducing Educators' Weight Bias: The Role of School-Based Anti-Bullying Policies," *Journal of School Health* 91, no. 10 (2021): 796–801, https://doi.org/10.1111/josh.13068.

4. L. Dahill et al., "Prevalence of Parental Comments on Weight/Shape/Eating Amongst Sons and Daughters in an Adolescent Sample," *Nutrients* 13, no. 1 (2021): 158, https://doi.org/10.3390/nu13010158.

5. M. E. Eisenberg, D. Neumark-Sztainer, and M. Story, "Associations of Weight-Based Teasing and Emotional Well-Being Among Adolescents," *Archives of Pediatrics & Adolescent Medicine* 157, no. 8 (2003): 733–38, https://doi.org/10.1001/archpedi.157.8.733.

physicians and other members of the healthcare team can harm their adolescent patients if they use scrutinizing language that communicates weight bias.

Adolescent weight-based teasing and bullying, especially when it comes from influential adults, has consistently been associated with lower body satisfaction, lower self-esteem, higher depressive symptoms, suicide ideation, and suicide completion.[6] Researchers have also learned that bullying from two adult sources (for example, one parent and one coach) was associated with worse emotional health outcomes than teasing from only one influential adult. Now that your head is spinning from these concerning statistics, here are some ways for parents, teachers, and healthcare providers to support fat adolescents:

Parents: Start an open conversation with fat adolescents. Directly ask them if they have been teased or bullied, and if so, ask what the focus of the teasing or bullying was. If it was about their body, ask how they are feeling and identify the impact of the interaction. Explore different approaches with them that might help resolve any body-based discomfort they are feeling, including strategies to repair their damaged self-esteem or body image. Unless the adolescent expresses concern about their weight, it is recommended that parents stay clear of their own weight-related worries and instead focus on the promotion of healthy behaviors.[7]

1. Encourage moderation and emphasize healthful food choices rather than restrictive eating patterns.

6. R. M. Puhl et al., "Cross-National Perspectives About Weight-Based Bullying in Youth: Nature, Extent and Remedies," *Pediatric Obesity* 11, no. 4 (2016): 241–50, https://doi.org/10.1111/ijpo.12051.

7. UConn Rudd Center for Food Policy and Obesity, *How to Talk to Your Child About Weight Bias,* https://uconnruddcenter.org/wp-content/uploads /sites/2909/2020/07/Parents-How-to-Talk-to-Your-Child.pdf.

2. Engage in changes as a family instead of narrowing in on changes for the adolescent.

3. Choose language wisely; avoid referring to "fat" as "bad."

4. Avoid criticizing your own body.

5. Avoid use of "should" statements, especially surrounding food.

6. Support the development of their self-esteem and teach them that self-esteem includes more than appearance.

7. When emotion-based eating is noticed, talk to the adolescent to see if they are aware of their behavior and explore other ways of coping with their emotion.

8. Be their support, not another source of judgment.

Teachers: Many teachers acknowledge the severity and impact of weight stigmatization in school settings. A national sample of teachers agreed that weight-based bullying has been identified as the "most problematic" form of bullying in schools. According to a 2016 study, more than 90 percent of middle school educators reported being in support of modifying anti-bullying policies to strengthen the protection of fat adolescents from peers and weight-biased teachers.[8] While educators believe these policies could help, it is not known whether they will actually reduce educator weight bias.

8. Puhl et al., "Cross-National Perspectives About Weight-Based Bullying in Youth: Nature, Extent and Remedies."

To further support educators in supporting adolescents, a multi-pronged approach is recommended:[9]

1. School policymakers can engage with teachers to develop and implement policies against weight bias.

2. Professional development curricula for teachers should address weight bias.

3. Teachers can learn strategies to support fat adolescents when they witness their peers or students engaging in weight-based teasing or bullying.

Healthcare providers: Health-centered conversations are a necessary part of the role of a healthcare provider in an adolescent's life. For an adolescent to feel respected and hear helpful guidance, establishing a strong rapport first is crucial. While time is often limited, be creative and cautious, and find a way. Get to know the adolescent by talking with them about their lifestyle, emotional experience, and body relationship. This might open the door to safe and effective communications surrounding their body and health goals. When coordinating with other healthcare providers, take responsibility to ensure everyone knows the adolescent's comfort and health behaviors, especially when discussing anything related to body and weight. When the topic of weight is broached, use the following techniques:[10]

9. R. M. Puhl, Y. Suh, and X. Li, "Improving Anti-Bullying Laws and Policies to Protect Youth from Weight-Based Victimization: Parental Support for Action," *Pediatric Obesity* 12, no. 2 (2017): e14–19, https://doi.org/10.1111/ijpo.12129.

10. Holland Bloorview Kids Rehabilitation Hospital, *Fostering Positive Weight-Related Conversations,* https://research.hollandbloorview.ca/sites/default/files/2019-10/WeightRelatedConversationsKTCasebook.pdf.

1. Be sensitive to the adolescent's cultural influences and genetic history.

2. Plan to weave medical advice throughout several visits to avoid overwhelming the adolescent.

3. Prioritize health behavior engagement and avoid conversations focused on weight loss. There's no need to use words such as "overweight," "obese," or "fat" with the adolescent.

4. Reduce the power imbalance by creating a trusting and relaxed environment.

5. Use a strength-based approach when discussing topics related to health and weight. This includes celebration of success and avoidance of scare tactics.

There is little concern about going overboard when it comes to helping fat adolescents. Teens face very confusing and constantly changing expectations in their social worlds, and because of that, any consistent and positive support goes a long way. Many adolescents spend most of their time hiding from the confusion of it all while doing their best to blend in and avoid awkwardness, just as Ian and I did decades ago. There will always be cruel adults and judgmental peers who clap when the fat kid does something impressive, thinking that they are encouraging them. Those actions will never feel good to a fat adolescent. Those attempts at validation and support are embarrassing.

Some parents believe that supporting their child means giving in to every indulgence while avoiding conversations about health and body image because of their own discomfort. Other parents believe that providing emotional support to a fat adolescent means they are supporting their adolescent's fat status along with all the behaviors and consequences associated with it. Both of these beliefs are not true.

Fat adolescents need all the emotional support and love they can get, which does not include feeding insecurities or avoiding discomfort. Fat teens deal with far more judgment and hate in their everyday lives than all the possible support they could get if every parent, teacher, and healthcare provider combined followed the suggestions listed earlier in this chapter. There is no such thing as "too much support." Ultimately, any positively framed conversation about health or body image that is sourced from an influential adult in a fat adolescent's life will be powerful. There's never a bad time to show up for any adolescent, especially a teen who is experiencing the negative worldviews of a weight-biased person.

Acceptance Through Identity Development

THE HARDEST PART of being a fat teen varies, and it depends on what the teen values. For Ian, the fear of rejection seemed to be the hardest part of being fat. And it was for me, too. Despite his concern, Ian found authentic moments of joy even when he wasn't being his authentic self. In contrast, I spent most of my time desperately searching for acceptance, hoping my weight wouldn't limit me. I wanted teachers, coaches, sales associates at clothing stores, boys, parents, my siblings, popular kids, bullies, acquaintances, friends, best friends, celebrities, and even random strangers to express appreciation for my existence, including my size. High school was just as miserable for me as middle school was until I identified the strengths of my body, but that wasn't until my senior year. To this day, whenever someone appears to be scanning my body size, I tense up because I remember the rejection that followed me for so much of my adolescence.

Ian and I were both desperate to be accepted, and that is not unusual for most teens. We are social creatures. Finding our pack and developing cherished connections within it is necessary for survival. A plethora of research has demonstrated that social connection has a strong influence on us in multiple ways, including improved ability to regulate our emotions, increased self-worth, more empathy for others, and improved physical health. This tells us that we are essentially wired to be social, that our bodies and brains crave connection.

Our identities are forming every moment we interact with our surroundings, and because of that, our environments heavily impact how we think and feel about the world and our relationships. The environments of middle and high school are minefields. Despite feeling exhausted from years of avoiding social traps and decoding expectations of acceptance in middle school, most teens somehow find a way to reset and prepare for the arduous experiment of high school.

Teens do whatever it takes to maintain their premature middle school identity, or they ditch it because what they liked in middle school might cramp the style of their new high school clique. As Ian said, teens investigate the various archetypes around them and then attempt to mimic the template that seems to be the coolest. Sometimes mimicking the new template requires abandoning authentic personal qualities because fitting in feels so important, even at the expense of acting like someone they are not.

All teens, fat ones included, want to make it through their high school career and enjoy it. Enjoying it relies on finding their people, the ones whom they can laugh with in between classes and sneak off campus with at lunch. When a teen has difficulty connecting with their peers on a regular basis, social anxiety develops and can quickly transform into social rejection. Every high schooler is subject to scrutiny, just as they were in middle school, except now there's more on the line. Dating becomes more common, grades come with far-reaching consequences, and it seems like your friends are the only ones who can come close to understanding. With all this at stake, acceptance by peers seems more important than ever before, and being fat adds another complication to an already complicated situation.

Though all teens are eager to find acceptance in high school, fat teens have added barriers because weight stigma inhibits social acceptance. According to a recent study, many fat teens engage in strategies to either minimize their exposure to negative attention or increase their social acceptance. To be invisible, they don't participate in class, they engage in less conversation with peers, and despite feeling physically uncomfortable (not fitting in a desk, for instance), they won't complain the way other students might. To increase social acceptance, they pretend to be confident or act out to gain rapport with their peers. The strategies can have a variety of results.

Fat teens who are labeled as "loners" become targets of teasing. In contrast, some fat teens build a wide circle of friends to reduce their vulnerability to teasing. One teen stated, "People rarely bullied me because I was probably friends with one of their friends. I was in a safe zone." Another common identity for fat teens is being "naughty," which is how teens describe themselves when they become the class clown. One student linked his class clown role to his insecurity about his weight, stating it worked as armor to keep other kids from teasing him. Another student said her naughty behavior in the classroom was about finding a place to fit in so that she wasn't alone at school: "To fit in with the popular kids you have to be skinny and pretty, and I wasn't."[1] Fitting in with the mischievous group allowed her to develop confidence to thrive in other social interactions, which was crucial for her social survival. Ian quickly learned that whatever stigma he felt from being fat could be mitigated by his ability to make people laugh and the protection provided by his place on the football team.

Socializing requires confidence and curiosity. These qualities are

1. R. Langford et al., "Links Between Obesity, Weight Stigma and Learning in Adolescence: A Qualitative Study," *BMC Public Health* 22, no. 1 (2022): 109, https://doi.org/10.1186/s12889-022-12538-w.

rare among all teens, and circumstances can make them even more rare among fat teenagers. Many of the adolescent patients I've worked with have expressed feeling timid and insecure about their appearance. They reported feeling this way because of having a negative evaluation of themselves that convinced them that they must conform to the thin ideal to be accepted by everyone— something that was impossible to achieve. Many vulnerable teens subscribe to this doctrine because it feeds on impressionable minds that are hopelessly seeking acceptance. As Ian said, fat teens deserve to transcend the bullshit that other people put on them and that they put on themselves. Fat adolescents deserve to experience euphoria while engaging in teen shenanigans.

When teens learn that their acceptance is jeopardized by their fatness, their purity shatters. My purity shattered when I learned this in high school. Every promotion of thinness that unknowingly seeped into my high school brain hit me like an avalanche. I knew I was fat—I had learned that sometime in middle school—but I never thought being fat would prevent me from being accepted; that is, until the fat-shaming comments started pouring in and impacting my relationships. At that point, every negative weight-focused message directed at me was louder than ever. My social worth was based solely on my weight. My likability was dependent on my pant size.

The adolescent patients I work with who are fat and hurting because of how society treats them often describe their identity through painful thoughts and emotions that are centered around their appearance. A common statement I hear is "I know I am fat because of how people treat me," which leads to a host of reported emotions, including shame, loneliness, and worthlessness. When we discuss their needs further, they identify that they are searching for a community, for belonging, just as I was in middle and high school. When I explore the roots of these thoughts and the emotions associated with them, teens tend to automatically translate them into their core beliefs.

A post on Reddit asked users to name the worst part of being fat; a variety of answers poured in: "I feel uncomfortable all the time," "People assume I'm lazy," "Nobody will ever fall in love with me," "Bullying sucked during childhood," "I'm lethargic all the time," "I feel guilty whenever I eat my favorite foods," "I hate the way I look," "Being called 'big guy,'" "Discomfort in clothing because of rubbing and chafing," "Noticing how much space I take in a room," "Feeling different than how I see myself physically," "When people treat me differently because I'm down 20 pounds," "Being mistreated by everyone in public," "Hurting when I try to move," "Being invited to anything social."[2] The list of heartbreaking comments goes on and on. Being fat impacts people socially, physically, and emotionally, and it impacts everyone differently. As values shift, the impact of being fat shifts. High schoolers value appearance over everything and because of that their social acceptance is conditional. When a teen looks different from the standard mold, they are treated differently.

Being fat in high school is hard! It adds difficulty to all the other already difficult things about being a teenager. Teachers have less faith in your academic pursuits; fewer peers express interest in seeking a friendship with you; clothes aren't made for your fatter body; healthcare providers blame every medical concern on your size; parents unintentionally harm you when they try to prevent you from becoming fatter; and the entire world body-shames you because fatness is hard for people to accept.

Fat teens can feel more connected in high school by hitting their stride: excelling academically, finding a group of people with whom they vibe, joining an extracurricular activity that highlights strengths of their identity, securing a job that gives a taste of financial freedom, or joining a sports team. Ian and I hit our strides on the field. He became popular because of his leg-breaking tackling skills, and

2. "What Is the Worst Part About Being a Fat Person?," r/AskReddit, Reddit, May 20, 2022, https://www.reddit.com/r/AskReddit/comments/uu3utw/what _is_the_worst_part_about_being_a_fat_person/.

it was rumored that I was a lesbian because I was a fat teenage girl who played rugby, and I was good at it. Rugby was my ticket to surviving and enjoying the arduous social experiment, and football was Ian's. We secured social acceptance by finding our roles in the game of high school.

Excelling When You Are XXLing

YOU'VE DONE IT! You are graduating from your first set of social experiments and it's your turn to level up. It's the first time in your life when you have complete freedom: freedom to spend your time how you like, freedom to choose whichever relationships you want, and freedom to develop a new identity, one that won't be based solely on your appearance but on some conglomeration of everything you have ever liked about yourself and others. While refreshing, the autonomy can be overwhelming.

Even though Ian acknowledged that being a fat kid was part of his identity, he was able to distract himself and everyone else with his status as a popular varsity football player. The distraction was all he needed to be accepted in middle and high school. When our mom drove Ian to Ashland to start college, he had no idea who he was anymore. His high school identity—playing football and eating lasagna at team dinners hosted by Saint Sue—had run its course.

He no longer had a role to play and no guidance in choosing a new one. Plus, he was stripped of his resources. His team, his coaches, his friends (both real and superficial), his annoying little sister and other siblings, his fans, his stability, and his parents were all back in Beaverton. He was isolated, and it was entirely up to him to figure out who he wanted to be and how he wanted to spend his time. This metamorphosis revealed all his insecurities: disgust with being fat, uncertainty for his future, loneliness, longing for love, and the anxiety of being viewed as a fearful, confused, and lazy fat person. These insecurities made him think that he needed to justify his fatness to people.

Almost one in three American college students reported being fat, with nearly half of them describing their weight as being "more" than they wanted.[1] Fat students on college campuses anticipated experiencing the same harmful weight stigmatization that they endured in middle and high school. They reported feeling both hypervisible, because everyone sees and scrutinizes them, and invisible, because no one views them with respect and their opinion is ignored.[2]

Regardless of weight status before entering college, many students during their first year experience a weight gain popularly referred to as the Freshman 15. Research suggests this weight gain is due to increased agency paired with decreased confidence.[3] Once an adolescent leaves their home, they become responsible for meal planning, food purchasing, cooking, and budgeting, which can lead to poor food choices and unhealthy portion sizes. These behaviors, coupled with high stress and hectic schedules, result in frequent

1. "Almost 1 in Every 3 College-Age Americans Are Now Obese," *U.S. News,* Nov. 23, 2021, https://www.usnews.com/news/health-news/articles/2021-11 -23/almost-1-in-every-3-college-age-americans-are-now-obese.

2. C. Stevens, "Fat on Campus: Fat College Students and Hyper(in)visible Stigma," *Sociological Focus* 51, no. 2 (2018): 130–49, https://doi.org/10.1080 /00380237.2017.1368839.

3. Rachel A. Vella-Zarb and Frank J. Elgar, "The 'Freshman 5': A Meta-Analysis of Weight Gain in the Freshman Year of College," *Journal of American College Health* 58, no. 2 (2009): 161–66, http://doi.org/10.1080/0744848090 3221392.

emotion-based eating, increased consumption of alcohol, and reduced engagement in physical activity.

After exploring all sorts of unhealthy substances and finishing
his first year of college, Ian realized that any chance he had of figuring out who he was going to be in life required moving back to
Portland. When he returned home, he resumed his studies. He was
incredibly lucky to stumble on a career path a few years before
graduation that tapped into a set of skills he had mastered throughout his childhood: coping with being a fat kid while making people
laugh.

While Ian dealt with being fat by becoming a stand-up comedian,
my career path took a few more turns. I believed it was important to
work toward a career that meant something to me, one that was
rooted in my personal values, one that didn't involve making my
friends come to open mic nights. Being fat consumed my existence,
though, so identifying any personal values beyond my appearance
didn't seem possible. Many of my career aspirations were based on
my desire to help people feel less shitty about being fat.

At first, I thought teaching elementary school was the answer.
After I completed my teaching degree, however, I pursued a master's in counseling for children to offer a more individualized and
less fat-shaming lens for them. With little understanding of food to
help with the weight-loss process, I pursued a master's degree in
nutrition. My primary goal remained the same throughout my academic pursuits: to support people through the mud, emotional baggage, countless challenges, and complicated diet and exercise
behavioral changes to achieve and maintain a healthier lifestyle
consistent with personal values.

I came to this realization because this type of comprehensive
and authentic support didn't exist. I found weight-loss clinics that
hired naturopathic doctors and nutritionists; medical weight-
loss centers with staff dietitians; weight-loss surgery centers with
medical teams; therapists who addressed mood, trauma, or eating
disorders; and certified health coaches, but I never found a pro-

fessional who provided every aspect of support that seemed necessary to me.

As a result, my final academic venture was to earn a doctorate in
psychology with a health emphasis. I believe this would have been
the ideal type of provider to help me and my brother improve our
health, lose weight, and maintain a healthy lifestyle. We needed
more than a dietary protocol to change food habits. Our fatness was
complicated. It included an unrelenting need to eat, whether in response to hunger cues, emotional distress, insecurity, need for belonging, or simply just because. But it encompassed more than that:
a need to address other core pieces of our unhealthy habits and
identities. Improving my own health, Ian's health, and the health of
my patients isn't only about the food: There is much more surrounding our plates. It's harder for fat people to find acceptance,
identity, and success. This really resonated with me.

Researchers have identified that in general fat people are less
likely to be successful. When a fat person applies to a university or
for a job, their appearance prevents them from passing go. Researchers have also found that being fat can limit people's chances
of success in undergraduate and graduate programs, as well as on
the job, because of weight bias and discrimination from professors
and managers. In a 1998 study of college women, those who perceived themselves as fat were more likely to have low self-esteem
and higher levels of anxiety and depression than women who didn't
identify as fat, which made them believe they weren't qualified for
college or careers. Fewer fat women apply to college programs to
avoid the stigma and disappointment.[4]

Stereotypes lead employers to not hire fat people. In a 2009
study, most employers reported a preference for healthy workers
with positive attitudes and social likability; supposedly, fat people
don't possess these qualities. Fat people also reportedly earn less

---

4. D. M. Quinn and J. Crocker, "Vulnerability to the Affective Consequences
of the Stigma of Overweight," in *Prejudice: The Target's Perspective*, ed. J. K.
Swim and C. Stangor (San Diego: Academic Press, 1998), 127–48.

money, are hired less often, and are more likely to remain unemployed because of weight stigma.[5] In a 2019 study, a difference in employment experiences between men and women was identified. Fat women were found to have lower monthly wages and lower job-quality features, such as permanence status, bonus provision, and labor union presence. However, for men, fatness was associated with higher monthly wages and a higher likelihood of having professional jobs and enjoying other high-quality features such as being part of a labor union.[6] While both fat men and fat women are discriminated against, it's not equal.

Despite the odds, Ian—a fat kid from Beaverton—has made a name for himself. And his sister can't be prouder. He continues to give other fat people hope to overcome our weight-biased world of employment. He also encourages others to challenge their stereotypical thinking and give the fat guy a chance.

5. E. Han, E. C. Norton, and S. C. Stearns, "Weight and Wages: Fat Versus Lean Paychecks," *Health Economics* 18, no. 5 (2009): 535–48, https://doi.org/10.1002/hec.1386.

6. H. Lee et al., "Impact of Obesity on Employment and Wages Among Young Adults: Observational Study with Panel Data," *International Journal of Environmental Research and Public Health* 16, no. 1 (2019): 139, https://doi.org/10.3390/ijerph16010139.

CHAPTER 6A

But First, Love Yourself

WE ALL WANT IT. We want connection, loyalty, attraction, and touch. It feels good, and research shows that engagement in healthy intimate relationships results in a longer and more fulfilling life. But it's difficult to find love. During an era of body positivity, size diversity in love exists, but significant evidence shows that dating continues to be more difficult for fat people because weight stigma can interfere with the early stages of interpersonal attraction.[1] (Tell us something we don't know, science.) In many recent studies about dating, both men and women reported experiencing rejection due to their weight.[2] Fat people are still rarely cast on dating shows. While everyone wants love, fat people aren't given a fair chance to find it.

1. A. Schmidt et al., "Couples Losing Kinship: A Systemic Review of Weight Stigma in Romantic Relationships," *Journal of Social Issues* 79 (2022): 196–231, https://doi.org/10.1111/josi.12542.

2. A. Blodorn et al., "Unpacking the Psychological Weight of Weight Stigma: A Rejection-Expectation Pathway," *Journal of Experimental Social Psychology* 63 (2016): 69–76, https://doi.org/10.1016/j.jesp.2015.12.003.

Everyone is naïve and inexperienced when they start looking for love, fat or not, and my brother and I were no exception; however, our fat bodies didn't help the process. We quickly learned that if we wanted to find someone, we had to identify ways to compensate for the inconvenience of our fatness. I captivated people with my hazel eyes, high IQ, and modesty while Ian showed off . . . I'm not sure what people see in him. I'm sure there's something. I'm kidding— he's very smart, funny, and handsome. The point is, both of us did whatever it took to hide the fat elephant in the room because we felt like we had to. Unfortunately, we were probably right.

Despite Ian's positive qualities, he believed that no one could be sexually attracted to him because he was fat. Some research actually backs this up. According to a study done in 1990, fat people were perceived as less attractive, less deserving of an attractive partner, and less likely to be dating.[3] More recent research found earlier beliefs to remain true today. A fat person is viewed as less desirable for a potential dating partner and is still perceived as less sexually attractive. The study that identified this disappointing update asked research participants to rank drawings based on characteristics they would most and least prefer their sexual partner to have. Below each drawing was a written description of the following characteristics: fat, in a wheelchair, missing an arm, history of suicide attempts, history of curable STDs, and healthy. The most preferred category was healthy, and the least preferred category was fat. The researchers noted that another compelling finding was that men were more likely to choose sexual partners based on weight than women. Assuming most of the sample had heterosexual preferences, then this potentially illustrates that when dating, the fat stigma affects women more than men.[4]

3. M. B. Harris, "Is Love Seen as Different for the Obese?," *Journal of Applied Social Psychology* 20, no. 15 (1990): 1209–24, https://doi.org/10.1111/j.1559 -1816.1990.tb01469.x.

4. E. Y. Chen and M. Brown, "Obesity Stigma in Sexual Relationships," *Obesity Research* 13, no. 8 (2005): 1393–97, https://doi.org/10.1038/oby .2005.168.

Ultimately, all fat people experience weight stigma, and that stigma is emphasized when we date. Ian's blanket apology for his bundle of problems in relationships comes from a good place, but I'm not sure it's necessary. It's good to be aware of your faults, and being fat doesn't exempt you from being a jerk. When you're fat, though, you also need to have empathy for yourself, for how you behave in the face of a world that hates you.

Sure, my brother lacked self-confidence, felt a driving need for validation, experienced constant self-hate, and engaged in some self-harm, but what do we expect? He was growing, learning, feeling, engaging, and attempting to find acceptance and love as a fat person in a fatphobic world. Fatness causes a reaction for everyone, and the evidence is clear: Fat people are less desirable, even to other fat people.

The fatphobia and self-hate that brewed within Ian for decades convinced him to avoid dating and engaging in intimacy with another fat person because of what he claimed were pragmatic problems; however, the real reason was that dating another fat person reminded him of his own insecurity about his fat appearance. Dating another fat person would tell the world that he was only able to attract another fat person, which would only harden the blow of being fat. It would give fat haters another thing to hate on. Instead of addressing the heartache from a life of weight-based scrutiny, he ignored his unmet emotional needs and decided to pursue good-looking women with chaotic lives. From my perspective, he dated skinny women with too many red flags to count. From his perspective, these women were a reward. I was a concerned sister who didn't understand his attraction, and he thought I was aloof for missing their beauty.

Ian was trying to distract himself. He wanted to ignore the indigestible truth that he hated his appearance. He hated his weight and insecurities. He couldn't see the goodness in himself, that he was and still is hardworking, funny, smart, and attractive, someone who has a lot to offer. Most fat people don't see their positive attributes because they are so used to feeling ashamed about their weight.

As Ian said, most people spend their lives wishing they were more attractive, skinnier, funnier, smarter, richer, stronger, and more popular. Likely this is because these attributes would allow for more partner options. In a 2005 study, women with higher BMIs were less selective in their speed-dating decisions, whereas men who varied from the BMI norm in an upward or downward direction were less selective in their speed-dating decisions.[5] This evidence suggests that weight bias influences who we think we are good enough to date. Many of my weight-management patients have asked me, "Am I worthy of dating someone who is more attractive than me?" When we further explore their doubt, more questions surface. They wonder if they can date someone who is in better health, who is richer or more successful. Most fat people date whoever they can get and think they can't be picky because of the limited options of mates who are *willing* to date a fat person.

Ian always shared with me that he felt incapable of being loved by someone he perceived was better than him. When he was in a relationship, he seemed as if he felt unworthy of his partner's respect because of his size and, as he said, paralyzed by fear that they would reject him if he made the wrong move. He frequently asked me for communication advice to reduce the chance of insulting or misreading the confusing cues they provided. He thought that he suffocated them with his unrealistic and unjustified needs. In contrast, I always reminded him that it was okay to have expectations within his relationships, even while being a fat person. Since he fiercely believed that no one could be attracted to him because of his fatness, he usually ended romances and opted for the friend zone, a place where he felt he could better manage.

He would say he would do better with the next relationship and apply what he learned, though he never appeared to address his root problems. He never examined how his mental health was rup-

5. R. Kurzban and J. Weeden, "HurryDate: Mate Preferences in Action," *Evolution and Human Behavior* 26, no. 3 (2005): 227–44, https://doi.org /10.1016/j.evolhumbehav.2004.08.012.

tured by these painful interactions and, more important, how he treated himself because of his weight. He wasn't ready to love himself enough. As a result, he mimicked previous behaviors with future relationships. It always struck me that he wasn't sure how to navigate dating as a fat person because he wasn't sure how to give himself the respect he deserved. Neither was I. We both, like he said, constantly made some attempt at balancing our social value, which was always at a deficit due to our insecurity from being fat. It was hard to let ourselves get to know people without thinking we had something to prove.

So how do you date as a fat person? We aren't entitled to anything, yet it *is* harder for us to find love than it is for people who aren't fat. We can't give up because what will that do? Leave us alone forever? That sounds horrible to me. Some people like being alone, and that's okay, but for those of us who want companionship and are fat, there's a way. The most important suggestion I have, and this is coming from someone who isn't a dating expert but has talked with a lot of patients about the heartache of trying to find love while being plus-size, is that losing weight won't make love happen. Even if you lose weight, if you become less fat, there's no guarantee that you'll attract the right person. You might attract more people and you might attract great people, but they won't necessarily be your person. While getting healthier can lead to weight loss, weight loss doesn't always lead to getting healthier. When my patients lose weight with drastic and unsustainable measures and then immediately try to find love, they don't usually succeed. This isn't because of any one thing. Love is complicated regardless of size.

When emotional health is ignored, especially with regard to the impact of living life as a fat person in our society, it is very difficult to show up in a relationship with ourselves, let alone with someone else. Research in 2018 illustrated that more than 60 percent of Americans reported weight-bias internalization, viewing the self negatively because of their fatness and applying negative weight stereotypes to what they believed they deserved in a partner.[6] This means that when we ignore our own well-being and hold ourselves in low esteem, we can't show up and engage in a healthy and meaningful way. When dating, women are more concerned about their weight than about the connection they make with a potential partner, and men are not very comfortable going out with an overweight potential partner.[7]

This data shows that connection requires more than physical attraction. As Ian stated, we become more attractive as we gain more confidence in who we are. When we can love ourselves in an authentic way, we become more available to love others and to take part in healthy intimate relationships.

6. R. M. Puhl, M. S. Himmelstein, and D. M. Quinn, "Internalizing Weight Stigma: Prevalence and Sociodemographic Considerations in US Adults," *Obesity (Silver Spring)* 26, no. 1 (2018): 167–75, https://doi.org/10.1002/oby.22029.

7. M. S. Aruguete, J. L. Edman, and A. Yates, "Romantic Interest in Obese College Students," *Eating Behaviors* 10, no. 3 (2009): 143–45, https://doi.org/10.1016/j.eatbeh.2009.03.004.

CHAPTER 7A

Weighing the Value of a Doctor Visit

EVEN THOUGH FATNESS, or obesity (the medical term healthcare providers use to refer to it), is a risk factor for many diseases, the strong and hurtful stigma around weight does not actually help prevent or reduce it. It does the opposite. Weight stigma is harmful to health and *more* related to death and chronic health conditions than obesity itself. Obesity is not a popular status, we all know that, and yet almost one billion people in the world are obese.[1] One of many reasons for this is that weight is part of health, and health can be scary to face. Health is especially scary to face when you are fat.

Throughout our lives, we all experience varying levels of concern about our health for different reasons. Perhaps you have faced a chronic health condition like obesity for years and are exhausted, hopeless for better days ahead, and somewhat numb to the prob-

---

1. World Obesity Federation, *World Obesity Atlas 2023*, https://www.world obesityday.org/assets/downloads/World_Obesity_Atlas_2023_Report.pdf.

lems related to it. When you go to a doctor, the entire appointment is focused on how fat you are; you hear the fear in the medical assistant's voice when they take your blood pressure and tell you it's really high; you're told to make changes to your diet even though you won't maintain those rigid and unrealistic changes for long; or you feel overall shame because of your size. You are reminded of your chronic health condition every moment of every day, whether you are alone or navigating the seemingly cruel world around you. And those relentless reminders can't be turned off without turning off all your senses, which is why you become numb.

Or perhaps you feel invincible, as if the forces of fate will not find you, especially if you have successfully avoided dealing with your health and have yet to visit your doctor, if you even have one. You check out the latest diet fads *in private* on your cellphone as you scroll through your different social media platforms. You might even secretly try one to see if you notice any changes within yourself. You shop online when you notice your go-to pants or T-shirt doesn't fit anymore. You don't generally complain to anyone about your health concerns or inquire about anyone else's well-being. You coast. You throw caution to the wind. You only think about your health for a moment when you see a health insurance deduction from your paycheck.

Ideally, we'd all remain engaged in our healthcare and become fighters who advocate for our needs every day, speaking up when our providers mistreat us and believing that it is important to complete those end-of-visit surveys because we feel our voices need to be heard. We'd know that seeking healthcare is important because we want to be the healthiest version of ourselves. We'd hear our doctors' recommendations, and even though some might sting, we'd avidly take detailed notes, hoping to discover some nuggets of wisdom hidden within the pain. And we'd compassionately let our providers know that there are kinder ways to deliver the news.

Even though I am a healthcare provider myself, I know none of the above is easy. And for most of my life, I identified as part of the exhausted and hopeless group. I did my best to blend in; I avoided making eye contact with healthcare providers and allowed them to mispronounce my name as "Alissssa" instead of "uh-lee-zuh" throughout my appointments, even when I was in the most vulnerable position—during a pap smear or when having an IUD inserted—so long as I escaped without being fat-shamed.

Eventually, the unbearable discomfort I experienced from relentless weight stigma led me to completely avoid healthcare. I was tired of calling my mother after each appointment to rattle off all the insults and subtle fat-shaming comments I received to make sure I wasn't being "too sensitive." She always validated me and insisted that I "report them," because "no provider should treat someone like that." And I followed her instructions most of the time, but calling a clinic to report a provider took more emotional energy resources than I usually had to give. Surviving the appointment was hard enough. Recounting the painful interaction to someone who didn't understand the life of a fat person was another challenge. It took the minuscule amount of emotional energy I had left. Half the time my complaint wasn't resolved. Maybe the provider got a slap on the wrist, but there was no way for me to know. Even if they were disciplined, nothing about my report to the clinic helped me feel better. I still had to sit in the aftermath of being fat-shamed by someone who "cared." After a while, I stopped choosing a primary care provider, I skipped annual checkups, and I cruised on autopilot while I lived the unhealthiest time of my life because I knew I would be fat-shamed.

I still feel anxious when I go to a medical appointment, despite being educated and comfortable talking with providers. I have come a long way toward developing a healthier relationship with my body and appreciation for it, yet I continue to worry, even though I know that it's not okay to be stigmatized. That's how powerful weight stigma (any stigma, really) is within the medical system. That's how powerless stigma can make someone feel. But now I'm able to manage the anxiety better and not let it get in the way of my health. I am more unbounded and fed up with weight stigma and the mistreatment that comes with it when a healthcare provider fat-shames me.

I speak up. I speak up about my medical needs, especially the ones that aren't weight-related, even though my weight always seems to be the number one topic. When a medical assistant greets me in the waiting room by calling me "Alissssa Kar-mole," I correct them: "My name is actually 'Uh-lee-zuh Car-mehl.'" When they walk me toward the examining room and stop by the scale to get my weight, even though the appointment has nothing to do with weight—it's for fibroids, knee pain, headaches, hemorrhoids, a mammogram, an ingrown toenail, a rash on my hand, lower back pain, hip pain, or whatever else is going on with me—I say, "You don't need my weight; my weight has nothing to do with my primary concern today." At this point, they usually appear to be uncomfortable and quietly mumble, "Okay," then take me to the examining room. Owning my space as a patient is something I've only recently started feeling comfortable about.

If weight-centric conversation continues to be the focus of the visit, and the provider doesn't adjust their approach, I end the appointment and search for a new healthcare professional. I know that there is a shortage of medical providers in some areas; if that is the situation in your case, do your best to let your provider know what does and does not make you feel comfortable, although I recognize that this is easier said than done.

Weight is not a necessary metric for your provider to determine your health, unless your appointment is related to obesity, concerns medication, is an annual physical wellness visit, or involves your experiencing a high-risk pregnancy. Getting on the scale only grants permission to the provider to discuss your weight, which likely detracts from the reason you scheduled the appointment in the first place.

Invincibility is the privilege of ignorance. What we don't know about our health doesn't kill us, at least not today. After years of working in clinics, I've seen the terror on patients' faces after they've met with their primary care provider. Even if providers are empathetic, they are often messengers of shitty news that feels completely out of the blue for some, and inevitable for others. I worked as a behavioral health consultant, or BHC, at a primary care clinic. BHCs provide mental health support as part of your doctor's team, ideally more than your doctor has time to give. A BHC is sometimes requested at the end of a visit to address any mental health concerns that were brought up.

When I entered an examining room, the patient typically appeared overwhelmed. I was usually consulted for three reasons: The patient was informed of a new medical condition; a screening tool they completed revealed a mood-related concern; or they needed support with adjusting a health behavior. In addition, sometimes a patient felt discriminated against for some aspect of their identity. I'd found that when the focus of the appointment was weight, patients shut down. From the time they stepped on the scale to the uncomfortable discussion they had with their doctor about their BMI, they likely experienced shame, powerlessness, and weight stigma. Above all, they were eager to escape a space they perceived as judgmental and unsafe. Most patients didn't want to stick around to meet with me because they anticipated more humiliation.

This is the current state of our medical system, particularly in the eyes of people who are fat. To reiterate what my brother said, not all fat people are unhealthy and not all doctors are assholes to fat people. However, most doctors consider fat people to be unhealthy, and some mistreat their fat patients. According to recent research, physicians, nurses, medical assistants, dietitians, and medical students are most guilty of stigmatizing weight in medical settings.[2] Some medical providers believe that stigmatizing obesity and applying pressure to support weight-loss efforts improves

2. S. M. Phelan et al., "Implicit and Explicit Weight Bias in a National Sample of 4,732 Medical Students: The Medical Student CHANGES Study," *Obesity (Silver Spring)* 22, no. 4 (2014): 1201–8 https://doi.org/10.1002/oby.20687.

health because it increases motivation. However, the latest research suggests that weight stigma can result in physiological damage and behaviors that worsen metabolic health and self-esteem.[3]

Specifically, several studies have demonstrated that when people experience weight stigma they eat more and are less able to self-regulate their behavior; their cortisol levels increase, which is a direct effect of stress, resulting in weight gain.[4] This is just the physical impact. Weight stigma also has a significant negative effect on mental health. Some studies have shown that individuals who perceive treatment by a healthcare provider as weight-based and discriminatory are 2.5 times more likely to experience mood or anxiety disorders. Weight stigma increases the risk of depression and suicide, and it can exacerbate someone's already-established eating disorder.[5] More research is piling up about the harmful effects of weight stigma on mental health.

Weight stigma occurs in healthcare every day. Healthcare providers' weight bias, the negative stereotypes they hold about patients with high BMIs, and a lack of medical training with higher-BMI patients all contribute to make fat-shaming tragically pervasive. Healthcare providers spend less direct time with higher-BMI patients and provide a lower quality of care; some completely avoid

3. R. Puhl and Y. Suh, "Health Consequences of Weight Stigma: Implications for Obesity Prevention and Treatment," *Current Obesity Reports* 4, no. 2 (2015): 182–90, https://doi.org/10.1007/s13679-015-0153-z.

4. B. Major et al., "The Ironic Effects of Weight Stigma," *Journal of Experimental Social Psychology* 51 (2014): 74–80, https://doi.org/10.1016/j.jesp.2013.11.009.

5. M. L. Hatzenbuehler, K. M. Keyes, and D. S. Hasin, "Associations Between Perceived Weight Discrimination and the Prevalence of Psychiatric Disorders in the General Population," *Obesity (Silver Spring)* 17, no. 11 (2009): 2033–39, https://doi.org/10.1038/oby.2009.131.

treating high-BMI patients.[6] Fat patients are receiving the message that they are unwanted and untouchable. When individuals decide to make an appointment despite these challenges, they might feel ignored, mistreated, and discriminated against during their visit; that is, if they even show up. Like Ian, many patients with a higher BMI avoid seeking healthcare to skip the trouble, putting off treatment until it might be too late.

How do we change this paradigm? We know that being fat can cause certain health conditions, but for others there's no correlation. It's important for healthcare providers to make this distinction and support patients in their efforts to improve their health. Importantly, weight should be discussed only if the patient gives consent and believes that improving their health is related to their weight. When better health includes addressing their weight, the steps likely require reducing the impact of weight bias, providing mental health support, increasing body acceptance, changing health behaviors, and sometimes the option of using medication or pursuing surgery. The order of this list of interventions is intentional. The implications of weight stigma on mental health can become extreme obstacles even when someone successfully changes their health behaviors, uses medication, or pursues surgery. Setting aside interventions, sometimes the individual doesn't want to lose weight because they are content and happy with their body. Two questions should be posed at every medical appointment when weight is discussed: "Are you happy with your body and weight?" and "How can I make your appointment comfortable today?"

Perhaps the patient accepts and loves their weight just as it is. Or they feel uncomfortable due to recent weight stigma or shame. Maybe they have a complicated relationship with their body, or they are currently between toxic diets, or they are desperate for support because of a past trauma. To be clear, they may need mental health

6. S. M. Phelan et al., "Impact of Weight Bias and Stigma on Quality of Care and Outcomes for Patients with Obesity," *Obesity Reviews* 16, no. 4 (2015): 319–26, https://doi.org/10.1111/obr.12266.

support instead of weight-management support. It's possible that the person is unaware of the potential problems caused by their weight. A person at a healthy weight could have an unhealthy blood sugar or cholesterol level. A person who is fat or "obese" can be healthy, because being fat does not automatically translate into being unhealthy.

The important point is that healthcare providers need to find a way to authentically open a dialogue between them and their fat patients leading with compassion and curiosity instead of judgment and agendas. Unfortunately, my brother's story isn't uncommon. Most people who are fat know they are fat. They know this because they face society every day and may be fat-shamed everywhere they go. Most people who are fat are aware of the chance that they might die because of some weight-related disease. Most people who are fat fear the complications of being fat, whether subconsciously or not, and likely don't talk about it with anyone. Your body is your choice, not your doctor's choice. However, doctors are extensively trained to understand health at a level beyond a layperson's comprehension. Each doctor has a different specialty. Perhaps your appointment is with a doctor who is less familiar with body image, weight stigma, and obesity. This has happened to me more times than not. Their lack of knowledge doesn't equate to lack of care; their intentions are likely good. You can take this opportunity to educate them, if you like, though it's not your responsibility.

Some doctors I've consulted immediately recommended weight-loss surgery after reviewing my weight on my chart, even before asking me about my health behaviors. Others made judgmental facial expressions or sounds when seeing me for the first time, as if I were some kind of anomaly because I am a fat person. For most of my young adult life, I chose to be on birth control to prevent unwanted pregnancies. When I arrived for a visit to get a refill, my doctor encouraged me to try a different type of birth control, one that didn't cause weight gain *because of my current weight*. This unsolicited recommendation indicated to me that my provider had a problem with my weight. It was my first visit with the doctor, and they didn't ask me for my opinion of my weight or my experience with the birth control itself. Instead, the doctor assumed that my recent 10-pound weight gain was directly caused by my birth control and may have wanted to offer support by giving me another option. While their intentions may have been great and their diagnosis correct, the problem lay with their assumption. The doctor didn't take a moment to interview me to identify the presence of any current stressors, changes in lifestyle, or health updates.

This process needs to change, and we need to promote a more inclusive space for patients of all weights and sizes. It is argued that the most effective approach is to address the behaviors and beliefs of the healthcare providers rather than poke and prod more at the patients. In other words, weight stigma is a systemic problem, and we need to get to the core of it. One study suggests that medical training for healthcare providers should include education on weight bias: how it's perpetuated, how to address it, and the implications it has on patient care.[7] Another study suggests that providing a weight-inclusive experience instead of a weight-centric one could result in appointments where well-being is the focus instead of weight management.[8]

Some higher-BMI patients have shared experiences of having their care exclusively focused on weight-loss efforts instead of exploring other labs and exams, and as a result, a serious illness such as cancer was overlooked. The bottom line is that weight stigma impacts health. Challenging weight stigma could result in more people seeking healthcare when they need it, whether for gout like my

7. A. J. Goff, Y. Lee, and K. W. Tham, "Weight Bias and Stigma in Healthcare Professionals: A Narrative Review with a Singapore Lens," *Singapore Medical Journal* 64, no. 3 (2023): 155–62, https://doi.org/10.4103/singaporemedj.SMJ -2022-229.

8. L. Bacon and L. Aphramor, "Weight Science: Evaluating the Evidence for a Paradigm Shift," *Nutrition Journal* 10 (2011): 9, https://doi.org/10.1186/1475 -2891-10-9.

brother experienced or for any other diseases that can co-occur with being fat. Making this adjustment could improve overall health and the quality of life for many, and possibly reduce healthcare costs.

While this issue impacts all genders, women are especially stigmatized due to their weight across multiple sectors, including health. Very little research has considered weight stigma in the context of pregnancy, which is strange since weight gain is a healthy and important part of the process of growing a baby. More women with higher BMIs are pursuing pregnancy than ever before and are likely facing discrimination at prenatal appointments. The lack of attention in the research is concerning because, as I've mentioned throughout this chapter, weight stigma impacts mental, physical, and behavioral health, which could be harmful to maternal and fetal health. Fortunately, researchers have recently turned some attention to this population, and the results of the limited findings aren't surprising. Even those who began their pregnancies at what is considered a "healthy" BMI experienced weight stigma from healthcare providers. When weight stigma was experienced, the patient had higher rates of depression, unhealthy eating behaviors, emotional eating, stress, and postpartum weight retention.[9]

Going through my own pregnancy as a high-BMI/fat/obese woman has highlighted these concerns for me. I was told I likely wouldn't be able to get pregnant because I had a high BMI, large fibroids in my uterus, and the *BRCA* (breast cancer) gene mutation. My age was also a factor. For context, I was thirty-three when I expressed an interest in getting pregnant to my doctor. I left my appointment experiencing weight and age stigma, fear, hopelessness, and anger. Weight stigma because for the millionth time, a doctor told me my weight was a problem. Age stigma and fear because my

9. A. C. Incollingo Rodriguez et al., "The Psychological Burden of Baby Weight: Pregnancy, Weight Stigma, and Maternal Health," *Social Science & Medicine* 235 (2019): 112401, https://www.sciencedirect.com/science/article/pii/S0277953619303879.

doctor's opinion caused me to worry that I had waited too long to get pregnant even though it was important for me to accomplish my career goals before pursuing motherhood. Hopelessness because the list of my medical concerns suddenly seemed like a huge red light telling me "You can't get pregnant," despite my intentional health management. And anger, because I was sick of being discriminated against in the context of my weight, my body, and now my age.

At that first pre-conception appointment, my doctor encouraged me to lose weight. This encouragement came *after* very clear language from me, the patient, to my doctor directly, that I was aware of my health and was practicing good health behaviors; that I had recently and intentionally lost 75 pounds through addressing my mental health, my relationship with my body, and changing my nutrition and fitness behaviors; that I was a licensed professional counselor with nutritional expertise and completing my doctoral internship to become a psychologist with a health emphasis; and that I was motivated to enter this work to support people who have been discriminated against by healthcare providers because of their weight and want to reclaim their body and their power. Let me say that again. My doctor heard all of this about me, from me with confidence, and then proceeded to encourage me to lose weight if I wanted to get pregnant. I was completely dumbfounded and yet despite my anger, she still managed to get to me. I felt fearful, hopeless, and discriminated against because of my weight despite identifying as an assertive and educated woman who works in the medical system.

When I left that appointment, despite my career, values, and current health, I said to my husband, "I need to lose weight before I can get pregnant." Astounded, my husband responded with compassion, "No, you don't. You are healthy." At first, I was defensive and bothered *by him*. Of course he was wrong; my doctor knew what was best for me. Before he let me obsess over restructuring our healthy and well-balanced meal plan and rescheduling my next month with more workouts than I had already planned, he asked me to sit with my thoughts for a couple of days, and we could revisit it. Thankfully, I married a genius. Not even hours later, his support combined with my thought process allowed me to remember all my knowledge and experiences. Suddenly, my anger strengthened and obliterated the other emotions. This experience was unacceptable. I was fat-shamed yet again by another doctor, and I didn't even realize it because while it seemed so obvious, it was very subtle. She wasn't the first doctor to tell me to lose weight, but she was certainly going to be the last.

To pause my rant for a moment: It is suggested at the Mayo Clinic and National Institutes of Health websites that trying to conceive at a higher weight could result in a higher risk for difficulty with fertility, miscarriage, high blood pressure, venous thromboembolism, preeclampsia, blood clotting problems, gestational diabetes, heart problems, sleep apnea, and laboring challenges. When you review the literature about obesity and pregnancy, there are endless articles detailing these risks. Being an obese pregnant person doesn't directly equate to being at higher risk for every one of these concerns. The risk associated with many of them is higher in obese people; however, it is not *significantly* higher for *every* concern, but it is *higher*, which is why medical providers consider them all a risk when you are obese. These important distinctions should be discussed with each patient and tailored to their pre-conception health issues based on genetic and family history. The data should be used not to spread fear and weight stigma, but rather to provide knowledge and support to allow the individual to make an informed decision.

More generally, I apply this same concept to global health for fat people. Not all of us are always at risk for every fat-related disease or condition or death just because we are fat. My brother may have been at high risk for a heart attack because he had very recently cleaned up his health behaviors after years of engaging in a "I don't give a fuck, I'll eat however many chicken wings and fried pickles as I want" diet, some occasional illicit drug use, and consumption of fraternity-house amounts of alcohol on the regular, all while having high blood pressure, engaging in zero exercise, and not addressing his mental or physical health with a healthcare provider. Going from months of very focused and attentive dieting and exercise, which resulted in rapid weight loss, to a sudden and intense burst of loosey-goosey health behaviors, even if just for a short period of time, caught his body off guard, and resulted in a terrifying moment when he thought he was dying and typed 911 into his phone.

Ian's frightening experience upsets me because I wish I had been there for him in that critical time, to provide love, assurance, and maybe some *guidance to call for help*. He absolutely should have pressed "call" when he dialed 911 into his phone. Like every human, he deserves to have a care team, whether he is fat or not, whom he feels comfortable with and trusts to provide personalized medical opinions to guide him toward a high quality of life and longevity. Unfortunately, he believed that he would die from being fat (many fat people believe this); he also believed that he couldn't achieve anything but being fat—until he did—as if his destiny were predetermined: fat until death. Then after a traumatizing, life-threatening but life-renewing moment, his opinion changed. Not because a healthcare provider convinced him using a popular and easy-to-access fat-shaming approach. Ian decided to make the very difficult changes that were required for *him* to get healthy, which resulted in losing weight, when he decided it was *his* time to change.

When I meet with my patients, they seem very eager to change. They are sick of being fat-shamed, are tired of feeling exhausted, have tried *everything* to improve their health, may have recently been discriminated against or humiliated by someone on their healthcare team, and don't know what else to do or who else to turn to. Some of the most common emotions they express are shame, hopelessness, and desperation. Motivation is strong when you are scared, but it might be short-lived. Fear incited by a medical provider's warnings can be incredibly persuasive, but only for a limited time. Eventually, after the height of the emotion fades, the motivation wanes and people retreat to where they were before their scary moment, in a state of denial. For Ian, though, his fear of dying was enough. Before this moment, he ignored his health. He convinced himself that going to the doctor would disrupt his fantasy world where everything was okay just the way it was, even though he knew deep down that his health was declining rapidly. When you are rooted in your own lies, it can feel impossible to start making the tiny changes that are necessary to have a big impact.

These changes require more than just telling your healthcare provider, "Yes, I will start eating salads and running five miles every day," after they fat-shame you. Because . . . will you? Really? These changes require a daily commitment to yourself to show up for every decision that impacts your health, especially the hardest ones. Ian stated it accurately: "It's the hardest thing I've ever done in my entire life." Maintaining health is one of the most difficult, and yet most gratifying, challenges of life. It can feel inaccessible, unsustainable, and not for you when someone else is telling you it's time. That feeling might be hard to kick. Most of the patients I work with feel this way. And yet they reach out to me, which tells me there is a glimmer of hope.

The glimmer of hope is important because it can grow. Hope can grow with every step you take in the direction of health, even when each step looks different. Even when you take a step that feels imperfect, that doesn't mean it's wrong. Each moment is an opportunity to grow and learn something new or different. The ignore-it-all approach that many fat people choose, and Ian adopted, leads to disconnect. On autopilot, we fall out of tune with our bodies and only pay attention to what's immediately in front of us on our latest feed instead of examining our needs within. As a result, we might miss a clear signal from our bodies indicating something is wrong that needs immediate attention. We neglect our health and avoid seeking care because of constant fear.

Having a strong and supportive, compassionate and creative, patient and personable, connected and collaborative, educated and experienced healthcare team is essential for pursuing and maintaining a healthier life. That team should include all aspects of health that are important to you, and it may change as you evolve.

It takes time to carve out a quality healthcare team who provides safe and supportive care and encourages you to call for help when you need it. It can be difficult to create a team like this when you are fat, especially when you are fat and have limited resources, such as shaky finances, no reliable transportation, and little social support. However, it is important to prioritize your health even when it feels nearly impossible because that's probably when you need it most. As Ian said, he found the right doctor. It wasn't immediate, it wasn't easy, and he still did it. It all starts with finding one good healthcare provider.

For everyone, especially our fat readers, confronting the belief that you don't deserve care is crucial in all of this. Teach every healthcare provider how to treat you. There are caring providers who are eager to treat you with every ounce of respect that you deserve. Once you confront the reality that you want and deserve help, you'll be able to address your needs and feel better, more capable, and happier! Life is short, so you might as well enjoy a quality life, one that is filled with people who genuinely care about your health and well-being, which needs to start with you.

CHAPTER 8A

Aspirations Can Hinder Inspiration

TRYING TO MANAGE a constantly changing relationship with an ever-evolving body can be exhausting. We've all decided, as a society, that you need to cover that ever-evolving body with something, and so we add clothing to the equation, and that makes things even more complicated. Clothing choices tap into the psychology of culture, body image, sexuality, influence, neurocognition, and so many other aspects of the human experience.

After selecting an outfit for the day, we stand in front of the mirror to analyze our choice. That's when our neurocognitive wiring automatically identifies the imperfections staring back at us. Sometimes those imperfections overwhelm us to the point of forfeiting the entire look and frantically going through everything we own to find something, *anything,* that feels right. We might even cancel whichever social plan we were preparing for because we can't remember if we already wore the only outfit that feels and looks good during the last visit we had with that person. Clothing significantly impacts the way we view and think about ourselves, as well as the way we evaluate and are being evaluated by others. Clothing, and how it affects our appearance, is one of the currencies of attraction.

The emotional effect of not finding something that works for your size is damaging. It feels crappy on all levels. As Ian said, it's hard not to take the entire fashion industry personally when you are fat because you are limited to very few choices. And those few choices are rarely your first, second, or even tenth favorite. I remember times when I purchased something new *only* because it fit, and not for any other reason. During the 1990s, designers seemed to assume that fat young girls loved wearing floral print shirts, which I believed only attracted more attention to my fat abdomen. I guess it could have worked as camouflage, but unfortunately, my grade school didn't contain a single rose garden. Every new floral item that my mom bought changed its address from the store's shelf to a hanger in my closet to a rack at Goodwill, never spending a second on my body.

The entire clothing experience is difficult, and it is made worse when you are fat. You notice that what you are wearing doesn't fit anymore, so you need to buy something new. This realization is packaged with shame: You've done it again; you've become even fatter. Buying something new not because you want to but because you have to ditch a beloved piece of clothing frustrates you. You are disappointed in yourself. You feel anxious about going to the mall because shopping for clothes is an unpleasant experience when you aren't fat, and it's even worse when you are fat. You anticipate a limited inventory, or nothing at all. You know you will be judged by at least a few store employees for wasting their time. If you find something that does fit, you throw yourself a little party in the tiny fitting room and purchase the overpriced clothing. It doesn't matter if it's ugly; you can't wait to get the hell out of there and return to the safety of your nonjudgmental car. That is, if you comfortably fit into your car: Auto designers, like their fashion counterparts, usually don't consider fat customers when they create their vehicles.

The clothing experience sucks even more for a fat kid. Being fat isn't the ideal version of a youthful body, so it's a reminder to the kid that their body betrayed them. At least that's what fat kids are told by their peers, TV shows, pediatricians, coaches, and just about everybody they talk to. When fat kids can't wear clothes they enjoy, they lose the ability to express their identity. This loss can be monumental for a kid because appearance defines status. Fat kids are then forced to find alternative ways to display their identity, like wearing trendy shoes, which Ian enjoyed, or exploring funky hairstyles. Some fat kids prefer not to be noticed and opt to blend in with their peers who aren't fat because they don't want their identity to *be* fatness. I was one of those kids. My personality and body were big, but I prioritized a subtle appearance to avoid scrutiny.

Like Ian, I always kept aspirational clothing, though . . . just in case. Denim skirts that *almost* buttoned, Abercrombie jeans I couldn't *quite* squeeze my hips into, and stylish T-shirts that *nearly* allowed my shoulders to slip through. There were periods of my life when these clothes consumed half or more of my closet real estate. In my bedroom, I'd try on these "almost clothes," just in case I somehow lost a bunch of weight without noticing, just in case they fit. They never did.

You'll find lots of aspirational clothing in fat people's closets. Every patient I've worked with on weight-management goals has some spot in their house for these clothes. I know of only a few patients who remained committed to lifestyle changes for a significant period and used goal clothing to reach their target. Buying that clothing was a positive experience for them. It acted as short-term motivation to achieve their already-in-process long-term goals. Rewards can be very effective when used correctly.

More of the patients I see form well-intended plans attached to unrealistic goals, only to have their strategies backfire. When they don't achieve their unrealistic goals, they retreat to familiar unhealthy patterns that take them further away from the body that the aspirational outfit requires. Then they feel bad, as if they have failed again. The failure annihilates their motivation, gives new life to preexisting body shame, and reactivates emotion-based food behaviors; that is, until they become fed up *again,* find a new or recycled source of motivation, and choose a new aspirational outfit. This cycle repeats indefinitely, sometimes for a lifetime.

Even for those who remain committed to their lifestyle changes and lose weight, there is no guarantee of fitting into aspirational clothing. Bodies change in ways that aren't predictable. When the number on the scale drops, weight distribution, muscle mass, and body circumference can change, too—and likely do. There is no way to anticipate how a body will look 20, 50, 100, or 300 pounds lighter. Many of the patients I work with who undergo weight-loss surgery have to assemble entirely new wardrobes with more different styles than they ever imagined because their significant weight loss is accompanied with even more significant body changes.

When bodies go through such drastic changes, it's crucial to consider how the brain might work differently, too. Some people might feel and think in unpredictable ways. When an old friend exclaims, "Wow, you look great!" one individual might be flattered while another feels disconnected from their changed body. Some people feel exactly the same way about themselves, while others perceive themselves as a different person.

Clothing options may continue to seem limited after a significant weight loss. Anxiety sets in because uncertainty and low confidence make people question when the appropriate time is to let go of clothes that are, for once, too big, and to stop holding on to the associated fear that they will regain the weight. During this unique time, my patient and I discuss their fears and review the behavioral changes they've already made and remain committed to. If they still seem uncertain, we explore the impact of cognitive dissonance and identify small cognitive changes they can make toward accepting their improved health.

If unresolved, cognitive dissonance can result in poorer mental and physical health outcomes, sometimes leading to obsessive behaviors, including binge eating, fasting, overexercising, vomiting, and taking laxatives, to maintain the changes. The unavoidable co-occurring changes of body and mind impact the way we feel about our appearance and how we dress. There's no escaping the social meaning of it all, which adds pressure to the already highly stressful clothing experience.

Here's a heads-up for those of us who don't lose weight and never fit into goal clothing: You'll probably always have a pile of aspirational clothes that you move from one closet to another as you transition through life's various phases because that's what humans do. We hang on to hope, we dream, and we set goals, even when we may never adopt the behaviors that are associated with our hopes, dreams, and goals.

Whether we stay fat because we choose to, or we stay fat because we have difficulty committing to the lifestyle changes necessary for weight loss, maintaining a wardrobe we like can be draining. We slowly learn the brands that welcome and reject us, sizes that are usually safe, and styles to avoid even if they seem good for other bodies. Accepting our bodies today and celebrating what we look good in now is difficult yet necessary for emotional well-being. Even so, it's still possible to get stuck in negative thought traps. When that happens, a healthy response is to acknowledge the source of the emotion, validate the frustration, remember that there is significant variation in clothing, and maybe even ditch the aspirational clothing because it's probably cramping your vibe. It's okay to toss the palm tree pants, too. Even if they fit.

CHAPTER 9A

Diets Fail, Not People

ACHIEVING A HEALTHIER weight has been my life's focus, both personally and professionally. As Ian said, fat people know how to lose weight. We know how to lose weight better than any other group of people. It's not the knowing, though, it's the doing, and the doing is significantly more challenging than the knowing. The lack of doing is not because fat people are chronically lazy, despite what the rumors say. We may have our moments, but I can confidently say that laziness is not what causes us to be or remain fat. I can also assure you that I am far from lazy—Ian is closer, but still far from it—and every patient who takes time out of their busy lives to seek out my weight-management psychotherapy services is certainly not lazy. We are discouraged because of how difficult weight management is. We are exhausted from the constant battle associated with being a fat person. We are infuriated by the expensive lifestyle that accompanies being fat and trying to become less fat.

Every year, between forty billion and one hundred billion dollars is spent on diets.[1] These numbers illustrate people's desperation to achieve healthier weights. Why do we go to such expensive measures to change what we take into our bodies? Because diets are appealing. We all have good intentions to be healthier than today's version of ourselves. Every fat person I talk with has a different specific reason for losing weight, yet a similar general reason; that is, they want to enjoy their life more. They want to avoid death; reduce their dependence on medication; improve the quality of their sleep; eliminate their chronic pain; decrease their blood pressure, cholesterol, or A1C level; enjoy nonrestrictive eating; fit comfortably and attractively into their clothing; find true love; feel respected by society; be attractive; fit into airplanes to travel the world; be able to ride on roller coasters; enjoy a television show without feeling scrutinized; improve their credit; not have to wear a T-shirt to swim; and simply be free from the weight of the world. Okay, maybe not the credit thing, but the rest of them.

Approximately 47 percent of men and 75 percent of women in the United States diet at some point during their lifetime to achieve these experiences, and usually because someone influential in their life told them to do it.[2] This statistic tells us that a significant number of people want to achieve a more enjoyable life, one that most believe requires changing their diet. So how does focusing on diet impact food decision-making? The complexity of food decision-making goes beyond someone's willpower; it is impacted by social, affective, cognitive, and environmental variables, too. For this reason alone, most diets don't address the multitude of root causes that result in difficulty with weight.

Diets are alluring because they present as a golden ticket. As Ian

1. D. Cutler, E. Glaeser, and J. Shapiro, "Why Have Americans Become More Obese?," *Journal of Economic Perspectives* 17, no. 3 (2003): 93–118, https://www.aeaweb.org/articles?id=10.1257/089533003769204371.

2. R. W. Jeffery, S. A. Adlis, and J. L. Forster, "Prevalence of Dieting Among Working Men and Women: The Healthy Worker Project," *Health Psychology* 10, no. 4 (1991): 274–81, https://doi.org/10.1037/0278-6133.10.4.274.

mentioned, the diet industry is a monster that feeds on intimida-
tion. People think that they can't lose weight, be healthier, and
enjoy life more without dieting, without miracle products, without
the juice cleanse, or whatever else the schemers scheme about. The
issue is, people vary widely in how they respond to dieting, and
every diet was made with a specific population in mind, though
most companies don't take the time to educate potential consum-
ers about this up front. Instead, they dangle the carrot with the
promise of a skinnier, healthier, and longer life. Some people will
thrive on low-carb diets; other bodies will require fasting. And that's
just the nutritional part of dieting.

Most diets fail. One reason is that they require more than "just
change your food," though that's how they initially present their secret recipe to success. Most secret recipes require an "all in" mentality: "If the dieter fully commits, then the inches will burn right
off!" Any plan that starts with all-or-nothing thinking is nothing. It
will always end. While humans are drawn to routine and find comfort in it, there are few people who remain 100 percent committed
to a restrictive way of eating for the rest of their lives, regardless of
the benefits they may reap from it.

When an individual wants to change their eating behavior, care-
ful and thoughtful steps are critical as they learn what motivates
them and maintains that motivation, especially when faced with ad-
versity or unpredicted social environmental changes or pressures
that can lead to emotional eating in response to sadness, boredom,
or stress.[3] When someone can understand these aspects about
themselves, they are better able to overcome obstacles and remain
committed to their dietary plan. The study of health psychology,
which is what I've pursued a career in, has carefully examined what
it takes for people to change and remain committed to health behaviors.

3. M. P. Kelly and M. Barker, "Why Is Changing Health-Related Behaviour
So Difficult?," *Public Health* 136 (2016): 109–16, https://doi.org/10.1016/j
.puhe.2016.03.030.

For example, health psychologists have explored the effective-ness of choice architecture in improving people's commitment to dieting. Choice architecture is an intervention that involves altering small-scale physical and social environments to cue healthier be-haviors for an individual.[4] This could include moving the fruit bas-ket from a corner in the kitchen to a more accessible location. This location change will ideally promote increased fruit consumption and decreased cracker grazing. The problem with most dietary pro-tocols is that people go from maintaining one lifestyle for years that is familiar and comfortable to attempting a drastic change that is unfamiliar and very uncomfortable. When smaller-scale, more real-istic, and sustainable changes are gradually and intentionally made by someone, they are more likely to stick.

When Ian tried the all-juice reboot, his body went from consum-ing bottomless chicken wings to bottom-opening vegetable and fruit juice. While the diet suggested a commitment of sixty days, Ian was able to put in a solid three weeks. His energy improved, he ex-perienced cramps, and he lost a bit of weight. But then, after three weeks he threw in the towel, found the lost weight, added a bit more to top it off, and felt completely deprived. The deprivation he experienced from three weeks of restriction changed his relation-ship with food in a dangerous way. It reinforced binaries for him: healthy and unhealthy foods, succeeding and failing. This was the very same mentality that had fueled his earlier beliefs and would continue to destroy his future attempts at developing a healthier relationship with food.

Most diets fail. It is not that people lack an understanding of what is supposedly good for them, but that knowledge alone does

4. T. Marteau, M. Kelly, and G. Hollands, "Changing Population Behavior and Reducing Health Disparities: Exploring the Potential of 'Choice Architecture' Interventions," in *Population Health: Behavioral and Social Science Insights*, ed. R. M. Kaplan, M. Spittel, and D. H. David (Bethesda, Md.: National Institutes of Health/Agency for Healthcare Research and Quality, 2015), 105–26.

not drive a change in behavior. If it did, people would smoke less and drive drunk less, and doughnuts would no longer exist. Ian knew that vegetables and fruit were good for him even before his juice cleanse, and he probably believed that including fruits and vegetables in his diet would be beneficial. Eating them exclusively, however, is not realistic. In addition, we don't always act rationally even if cold hard facts are staring us in the face. Sometimes we act altruistically, selflessly, or out of love, jealousy, fear, or fun. It is not always about the profit and loss of calories, or awareness that something is right or wrong. We calculate our intake sometimes, and there is also an automatic system that responds to environmental and social cues in a way that requires very little conscious awareness of our dietary choices. The idea that simply providing people with information will make them understand how to eat, and that once they have the facts they will change, is foolish.

Most diets fail. Some people can decide that they are no longer going to consume a particular food or group of foods and then take appropriate actions to remain committed to that decision onward. It's simple for them. However, for others, the decision to eat or not eat something requires a much more laborious decision-making process. Those who struggle more with eating decisions are considered restrained eaters. Dietary restraint is the perpetual, cognitively mediated effort that an individual makes to combat the urge to eat.[5] When someone is a restrained eater, they are concerned with their weight and use dieting in an attempt, most often unsuccessfully, to maintain a weight that they have identified as a goal. This is because when people feel restrained, they likely deal with competing values or goals regularly: "I want to stay away from pizza because it's unhealthy and I want to lose weight. Oh no! I was invited to my granddaughter's birthday party at a pizza place. I can't miss her day. I will

5. M. G. Bublitz, L. A. Peracchio, and L. G. Block, "Why Did I Eat That? Perspectives on Food Decision Making and Dietary Restraint," *Journal of Consumer Psychology* 20, no. 3 (2010): 239–58, https://doi.org/10.1016/j.jcps.2010.06.008.

go off my diet for the party, just for one day." Diets aren't usually sustainable, and as Ian mentioned, people don't stay fat because getting healthier seems hard; they stay fat because getting to a healthier weight seems impossible. Missing a grandchild's birthday party is not an option. Yet seconds later, the guilt sets in; days later, the regret sets in; and a week later, the anger sets in because it's terrifying, confusing, and more difficult than imaginable to remain committed to a diet that feels restrictive.

Most diets fail. If changing behavior were simple, and all that people had to do was make easy changes in support of better health, wouldn't more people be doing it? It does not matter whether the language is simple or obscure; change is difficult and requires sustained motivation and support. This kind of thinking ignores the reality of human behavior.[6] There is a very busy and confusing intersection where habits, automatic responses, conscious choices, social pressure, and goals come together in an instant. Those moments of truth occur for dieters more frequently than most are prepared for.

Most diets fail and every fat person has tried most diets. Some might work for those who commit to doing the diet perfectly, or close to perfectly, but those are the individuals who hurt the diet industry's bottom line. The diet industry thrives when we fail, and because of that, the diet industry preys on the fat and vulnerable. So long as there are fat people, there will always be "the 10 newest ways to lose 10 pounds!" It's a cause-and-effect relationship. Anytime a fat person feels insecure about their weight, with *very* little effort they can sign up for the latest and greatest soul-sucking intervention at a weight-loss center nearest them, or even right there on their phone. Whenever we walk past our "diet and results" reminders, we feel horrible. All our insecurities flood our minds and leave us feeling self-hate and disappointment. This is what the industry

6. Kelly and Barker, "Why Is Changing Health-Related Behaviour So Difficult?"

wants. It wants you to feel flustered and alone when you walk past those boxes reminding you of failure.

Don't let the diet industry isolate you. There are professionals who actually do want to help! There are a lot of people like my brother's trainer Jason out there. There are also people who have attempted weight loss and succeeded who want to offer their guidance and support. There are fellow fat people who will advise you. They will tell you the truth about what it took to make their changes and what it might require for you to make your own sustainable changes, ones that feel good and align with your values. These people will affirm you when you feel discouraged by diet culture. Eventually, you might even become the person offering support to someone else (like Ian and I hope to do with this book!).

CHAPTER 10A

It's Not So Simple

IAN CURATED A lifestyle that worked for him and eventually achieved a healthier weight. Keep in mind, he didn't get there overnight. He tried many bad apples (none that were bad per se, but just not for him) and eventually identified three simple and yet difficult behaviors that he could both sustain and enjoy: eating less food, eating better food, and working out. I appreciate that Ian didn't tell us what to do; instead, he told us what actually worked for him, and that's an important distinction.

Ian's approach is promising because it is consistent with findings from the U.S. National Weight Control Registry, which is the largest prospective study of long-term successful weight loss. By tracking the weight-loss stories of more than ten thousand people, researchers identified six factors contributing to success: (1) consuming a low-calorie diet, (2) consuming a low-fat diet, (3) engaging in high levels of physical activity, (4) eating breakfast every day, (5) self-weighing at least once a week, and (6) limiting television time.[1]

1. V. A. Catenacci et al., "Physical Activity Patterns in the National Weight Control Registry," *Obesity (Silver Spring)* 16, no. 1 (2008): 153–61, https://doi .org/10.1038/oby.2007.6.

While Ian is right about the simplicity of his weight-loss experience, every person has their own set of complicating variables, and because of that, everyone responds differently to different diets. This is the reason for the maddening number of approaches. None are outright wrong; it's just that some diets have very specific target populations, yet most diet companies don't advertise this caveat. As a result, most diets fail.

Some populations thrive on low-carbohydrate diets, and others do best with low-fat diets. Gluten-free makes a huge difference for some people, and paleo is a game changer for others. Fasting works for a lot of metabolisms, Ian's included, and ketogenic diets have shown great results. There is an endless menu of weight-loss plans, but as you can tell from Ian's story, it's not just about what you are eating; it's also about how much you are eating and moving, along with several other variables. It's the full package, and many diets don't make that clear. Due to the lack of clarity, people tend not to understand which diet will work best for their needs and why. As a result, they agonizingly try one diet after another, often without medical supervision, and end up feeling lost and discouraged, while making no progress with weight loss.

The Obesity Society is a professional group composed of doctors and scientists who are "dedicated to improving people's lives by advancing the science-based understanding of the causes, consequences, prevention and treatment of obesity." At a symposium in 2018, two leading scientists presented their findings on two high-profile diets: low-fat and low-carbohydrate. Dr. Christopher Gardner, a professor of medicine at Stanford, found that after a year of healthy low-fat or healthy low-carbohydrate diets with the same number of calories, patients in both groups experienced similar weight loss.[2] Dr. David Ludwig of Boston Children's Hospital found

2. C. D. Gardner et al., "Effect of Low-Fat vs Low-Carbohydrate Diet on 12-Month Weight Loss in Overweight Adults and the Association with Genotype Pattern or Insulin Secretion: The DIETFITS Randomized Clinical Trial," *JAMA* 319, no. 7 (2018): 667–79, https://doi.org/10.1001/jama .2018.0245.

that a low-carbohydrate diet was better than a high-carbohydrate diet in helping patients keep weight off after dieting to lose 12 percent of their initial weight. He also found that the low-carbohydrate diet supported patients in burning 200 extra calories per day.[3] These results left everyone wondering which approach works best for weight loss. A moderator and other professionals hashed it out at the symposium and reportedly—not surprisingly—landed on no consensus. Fantastic.

People should know that dieting for better health is not necessarily the same as dieting to lose weight. Put differently, any protocol that reduces the number of calories you eat will result in weight loss; however, some diets are not healthy for your body's system even if you are losing weight. When a diet emphasizes consumption of fruits, vegetables, and all the other good stuff we know about, it can promote better health. There are also diseases that benefit from specific menus, such as diabetes, which improves with low consumption of carbohydrates. What we don't know is why people have such varying responses to diets. Many researchers who have explored genetics have been unable to find diets that respond in certain ways to specific genes. While this doesn't mean genes aren't involved in the interaction between diets and weight loss, it has been hard for researchers to find a definitive answer.

The *best* diet for everyone does not exist. There is nothing new in the diet industry that we don't already know. Some diets have been around for a while, such as the low-carbohydrate diet that was introduced by William Banting in 1863.[4] Since then, modern diet companies have emerged and offered new (and empty) promises to people, as if they have found *the* answer. All they really did was make one or two modifications to an already existing and untailored diet to increase profit, not to improve people's health. I always

3. C. B. Ebbeling et al., "Effects of a Low Carbohydrate Diet on Energy Expenditure During Weight Loss Maintenance: Randomized Trial," *BMJ* 363: k4583, https://doi.org/10.1136/bmj.k4583.

4. W. C. Roberts, "Facts and Ideas from Anywhere," *Proceedings (Baylor University Medical Center)* 13, no. 3 (2000): 303–11.

remind my patients to listen to their instincts when a diet protocol guarantees results that seem unrealistic.

Because few dietary protocols undergo a peer review process, when results are guaranteed, they are generally not backed up by evidence. Most progress is short-term, and it's nearly impossible for researchers to know if participants truly follow a given protocol. Further, due to insufficient funding, participants often cannot be followed long enough to confirm sustained success. When researchers can gain some insight from their findings, it is usually accompanied with limitations, along with even more questions. And finally, when studies are conducted to explore the effectiveness of a protocol, they don't usually address potential obstacles that people may experience when dieting because it would be nearly impossible to consider every potential concern. Ultimately, dieters are left to fend for themselves, both when it's time to choose the approach that seems right for them and when they begin to struggle with adherence because obstacles come with every diet. No diet is without its problems. Unfortunately, most company representatives will read off a general script to support you: "Just use willpower and discipline; being skinny will make everything okay!"

When I start working with a new patient, we create a tailored plan together to continue their health journey with me. This plan includes identifying their current habits, obstacles, and goals. Through this exploration, we can prepare them for potential solutions and then focus on specific strategies for them to practice before making any significant changes to their actual lifestyle. Here are some of the questions I ask my patients to consider: Which diet will work best for my life? What is my relationship with food? Do I have the time to dedicate to these changes right now? Does the thought of taking ten thousand steps each day terrify me? Am I able to commit to any amount of movement? How many attempts have I already made in an effort to live a healthier life? Does this all seem manageable? Affordable? Wait, am I crying?

The goal of all lifestyle changes and diets is to get healthier. For most fat people, healthier means losing weight. Losing weight is achieved by following a simple calculation of calories in and calories out. Importantly, it is also a complicated algorithm of quite a few other variables. Ian identified one of the variables: overcoming everything in society, which seems a bit challenging to me, even with the body-positivity movement. Rising above billions of years of genetic evolution based on the concept of scarcity is another challenging and debated variable, but this one seems to be out of our control, which is strangely refreshing and one less thing to worry about. Ian's last step, not eating after 8:00 P.M., is also debatable, although recent findings suggest that eating later (noon to 11:00 P.M.) compared to eating earlier (8:00 A.M. to 7:00 P.M.) resulted in increased weight. Researchers found that for participants who ate earlier, the hormone ghrelin (appetite-stimulating hormone) peaked during the day, and the hormone leptin (appetite-suppressing/full-feeling hormone) peaked later, which suggests that eating earlier may help in preventing overeating in the evening and at night.[5] It should be considered that this study asked participants to sleep between 11:00 P.M. and 9:00 A.M., and not everyone has this sleep schedule, these eating habits, or such a controlled environment. In short, don't base all your health behavior on a comedian's joke, because he probably hasn't done any research.

Aside from changing your food, increasing your fitness, acknowledging the impact of societal and generational stress, and stopping caloric intake at 8:00 P.M., there is another very crucial part of the weight-loss process, and that is actively building awareness of your *why.* Why is achieving a healthier weight through a different lifestyle important to you? If you have little intrinsic motivation (internal, natural desire) to change and you're primarily relying on extrinsic motivation (consequences and rewards outside of your control), changing your lifestyle can be significantly harder. Another variable

5. N. Goel et al., "0064 Delayed Eating Adversely Impacts Weight and Metabolism Compared with Daytime Eating in Normal Weight Adults," *Sleep* 40, no. S1 (2017): A24–25, https://doi.org/10.1093/sleepj/zsx050.063.

is challenging automatic thinking, which is hard to do. Most of us have self-deprecating thoughts on replay that have been around since childhood. These thoughts can cause us to engage in the infamous "fuck it" mentality, as many of my patients call it. Once that mentality is activated, most goal behavior is out the window. Challenging those familiar negative thoughts involves resetting brain pathways and takes daily practice.

Implementing any of these behavioral changes takes quite a bit of time and focus. Ian took about a year through trial and error to identify the lifestyle he wanted, the behaviors required for that lifestyle, and why the lifestyle was important to him. Once he formed new healthy habits that were manageable and enjoyable, he committed to them and lost weight as he regained his health for the first time in his life. The diet industry should know that dietary needs and environmental circumstances vary significantly from person to person, yet the rigid protocols don't portray such an understanding. For that reason alone, Ian's approach appears more effective than most of the diets available.

His simple approach is general enough. It allows personalization with some guidance. It's broken down into three simple steps that can be modified and stretched out over someone's lifetime even when important events occur, and we all know that they always will. Eating less is an ever-changing marker that is flexible but rather self-explanatory. Most of us eat more than we need because we want to and can, so try eating less; it'll make a difference. Eating better is harder to implement. Many people aren't aware of the quality of their current food choices. Defining better depends on where you start. This is the hardest part about diets. They give you a menu of the allowed foods or their products, and you are expected to convert to their doctrine overnight. If you meet your goal, they throw you back into the ocean of unknown, assuming you'll figure it out. Eating better is the most subjective and gray of the three steps because there's a lot of room for error. Most of us know what is healthy, but how much healthy food do we need to be a healthy person?

Working out is clear. Move more. Get that heart rate up. Give new physical activities a try. Try them again if they weren't great the first time. Find someone to move with or find a way to enjoy it alone. Adopt a dog—they'll get you outside. Just move!

So, are you ready to tie it all together with a nice, healthy bow? To find a way to eat less, eat better, and work out? To find a way to challenge those negative thoughts because otherwise they will stick around forever? To find a way to frequently check in with yourself about what motivates you and keeps you focused on your health because you are the only person who will reliably and consistently care? Weight loss might be an outcome of these actions, but it also might not be. You may achieve happiness, health, and longevity. Ultimately, there is no "one size fits all" strategy for successful weight loss. Some people may have to work harder than others, but in the end, speaking as someone who fits into this category, what else do we have to live for?

To Live Happily Ever After After the Weight Loss

HEALTH AND WEIGHT LOSS are about how people internalize thoughts within the context of food and their bodies. This includes how people think about interacting with food, how people view and treat their bodies, and how people spend their time and energy when not eating. When new patients seek my support, their primary reason for referral is often to lose weight, not to maintain their weight loss. Shortly after we begin our work together, the iceberg beneath the fatness emerges. The fatberg, if you will. The process usually requires significant vulnerability, committed digging through societal and familial bullshit, and trust in the sometimes painful exploration, because fatness sticks with all of us in different ways.

After Ian dedicated attention to his own fatberg, he lost a significant amount of weight, but then he didn't know who he was anymore. Being a fat person sticks with us because it is all-consuming. He will find a new way to connect with himself, a way that will both include his past fat self and acknowledge his new identity, which is less fat. This has been and will continue to be a part of his own sometimes painful exploration. He might see the same person in the mirror now, and he might always, but that could change as he evolves into a newer version of himself, one that he and the world will inevitably treat differently. And this is all part of Ian's maintenance phase.

How do we know when it's time to enter the maintenance phase? I'm talking about the actual one related to body weight, not the existential one. The maintenance phase follows successful weight loss. Successful weight loss is voluntarily decreasing body weight by 10 percent or more and keeping it off for a year.[1] Only a small number of people can do this because thermogenesis adapts to the lower body weight and further efforts are required if negative energy balance is to be maintained.[2]

Our body is always seeking "homeostasis," which is a scientific word for stability. Once our bodies adapt to a lower body weight, we are required to work *even harder* to achieve the same outcome: run faster or longer to burn the same number of calories as before, eat less food than before to be at a new deficit, sleep longer than before to continue to lose weight, watch even less television than we already do, and so on. This adaptive reduction in thermogenesis can contribute to plateauing, which is when we experience stalls in our weight loss. While discouraging at times, it's always important to respect the process and, as Ian said, listen to our bodies.

Data was collected from approximately three thousand households about weight loss and weight-loss maintenance. Among the adults who participated and reported weight loss, 31 percent were successful at both losing weight and maintaining it. In a review of twenty-nine long-term weight-loss studies, more than half of the

1. R. R. Wing and J. O. Hill, "Successful Weight Loss Maintenance," *Annual Review of Nutrition* 21 (2001): 323–41, https://doi.org/10.1146/annurev.nutr.21.1.323.

2. E. C. Weiss et al., "Weight Regain in U.S. Adults Who Experienced Substantial Weight Loss, 1999–2002," *American Journal of Preventive Medicine* 33, no. 1 (2007): 34–40, https://doi.org/10.1016/j.amepre.2007.02.040.

lost weight was regained within two years, and more than 80 percent by five years. Behavioral strategies mentioned in this study for maintenance of weight loss included frequent self-weighing, reduced caloric intake, smaller/more frequent meals throughout the day, increased physical activity, consistently eating breakfast, more frequent at-home meals compared to dining out, reduced screen time, and portion-controlled meals.[3]

Ian's maintenance phase has included continued commitment to eating less, eating better, and working out, as well as finding out who he is free of weight-defining attributes, acknowledging the fear he experiences now because of ignoring his health conditions for many years, and importantly, continuing to pay attention to all the micro daily behaviors that got him to this point in the first place. Specifically, Ian has prioritized weighing himself, listening to his body, developing "boring habits," and no longer pretending that everything was okay with his health.

Ian weighs himself, and he treats the number on the scale as data, a part of his complete health picture. He doesn't ruminate or self-deprecate about the number; instead, he allows himself to have a natural reaction (which is understandable!) and then responds with a different behavior. Self-weighing is one of the top factors for long-term maintenance.[4] Ian chooses not to prioritize the number on the scale, and he doesn't ignore it either. He interacts with the data instead of sticking his head back into the sand. Sometimes enjoying food a little more than usual is important to him depending on his social environment, and during those times, enjoyment involves a slice of cake. He engages with food intentionally and keeps

3. J. Kruger, H. M. Blanck, and C. Gillespie, "Dietary and Physical Activity Behaviors Among Adults Successful at Weight Loss Maintenance," *International Journal of Behavioral Nutrition and Physical Activity* 3 (2006): 17, https://ijbnpa.biomedcentral.com/articles/10.1186/1479-5868-3-17.

4. K. D. Hall and S. Kahan, "Maintenance of Lost Weight and Long-Term Management of Obesity," *Medical Clinics of North America* 102, no. 1 (2018): 183–97, https://doi.org/10.1016/j.mcna.2017.08.012.

track of his choices. As part of successful weight-loss maintenance, mindfully allowing indulgences when deemed appropriate reduces chances of overindulging on a regular basis. Keep it up, brother.

Ian listens to his body. He acknowledged this is a difficult practice because of the amount of noise surrounding life. We live in a distracting world. As a result of the distractions, we tend to listen only when something is wrong, and sometimes it's too late. Research shows that the more attuned we become to our bodies, the better we manage our health conditions and the greater chance we have of living a higher-quality life. As Ian said, he has learned that his body knows exactly what it needs to feel good; he just needs to listen, which is something he managed to avoid for the first thirty-five years of his life.

He developed boring habits. Some may call Ian's health behaviors boring; others may call them essential. Researchers consider Ian's habits as relapse prevention. Ian proactively develops plans and practices strategies for managing his days in a way that keeps him feeling in control. For him, that includes preparing his meals in advance and walking a lot. Okay, these are boring, but maybe they're boring *and* essential.

Ian has a few other "boring habits," and I know about them because I'm his sister. As mentioned a few chapters ago, he interacts regularly with healthcare providers, which sometimes includes testing or shifting a medication. He engages in non-food coping mechanisms—hobbies that minimize his counterproductive stress eating, such as opting to spend time outside tending to his garden or inside watering his plants instead of spending hours on his Xbox. He frequently finds new books to read, plays with his cats, organizes his massive and impressive (and frankly, ridiculous) sneaker collection, writes comedy bits, reads up on new ways to grill/smoke meat on his epic grill, and plans trips with his equally curious wife. He tries to check in with himself to ensure he is steering clear of cycles of negative thoughts and coping patterns, especially when he notices a slight increase on the scale or when he has had one too many bites of his wife's delicious baked goods. He has worked hard at developing cognitive flexibility, which has reduced some of his tendency to engage in all-or-nothing thinking during his interactions with food.

He stopped pretending like nothing was wrong. This reiterates the importance of Ian keeping his head out of the sand. Even when it feels hard to hear, information helps people understand a health condition more and potentially improve it, or at least make informed decisions about navigating it. Being fat is now considered a chronic health condition, which means it requires regular self-management. Due to the stigma surrounding obesity, combined with the uncertainty of the effects of it and daily discomfort from it, it is easy to ignore any attempts the body makes at communicating.

Becoming knowledgeable about what it means to be fat, coming to terms with the reality of fatness, and adjusting to what it means to accept it are associated with less emotional distress; reduced symptomatology; reduced anxiety, depression, and body dysmorphic thoughts; and less-severe disordered eating tendencies and suicide ideation, as well as better health, vitality, physical and social functioning, and general well-being. Now that Ian has participated in therapy and might prioritize it again in the future, he has a dedicated space to process his experience with being fat. He learned how to manage the negative thoughts and respond to them with "boring habits." He also practices meditation now, and it goes without saying that this will help in unlimited ways as he continues to manage his anxiety and maintain his new health habits.

What we know, thanks to research, is that most people don't maintain the weight loss they work so hard to achieve. Relatively few adults can maintain their weight over ten years (28.6 percent of women vs. 23.0 percent of men). Women who exercise are successful with weight maintenance, but the following factors are associated with weight gain: having two or more children, frequent use of sweet drinks, irregular eating, a history of dieting (intentional weight loss), and low life satisfaction. Among men, higher baseline weight and higher education were associated with successful weight maintenance, whereas irregular eating, a history of dieting, and smoking were associated with weight gain.[5]

For most of our lives, Ian and I struggled to lose weight and achieve a healthy lifestyle, but after figuring out our bodies' unique needs, we have arrived. Weight used to consume our existences, and now, while being fat will always be part of our stories, there's much more to focus on. As I continue to develop more understanding of the psychology of fatness, through my personal weight story, Ian's weight story, and those of my patients, I have learned that my primary career and life goal remains the same. I will continue to support people of all ages through the mud, emotional baggage, countless challenges, and complicated dietary and exercise behaviors that are necessary to achieve and, importantly, maintain a lifestyle that is consistent with personal values.

Once Ian was able to process the "catastrophic" burden on his health that he created and sustained, he let go and moved forward. He couldn't outsmart his body's natural reaction to the self-destructive behavior he was engaging in before, nor can anyone else. After he started treating his body with the love and respect it deserved, his body returned the favor. While Ian and I both hesitate to give specific strategies to maintain weight loss, especially since everyone gains weight, loses weight, and maintains their weight loss differently, the research is clear. There are effective approaches to make it happen. And, as Ian said, we are all a work in progress. The maintenance phase is the rest of our lives.

5. U. Kärkkäinen et al., "Successful Weight Maintainers Among Young Adults—a Ten-Year Prospective Population Study," *Eating Behaviors* 29 (2018): 91–98, https://doi.org/10.1016/j.eatbeh.2018.03.004.

More Like Defeat Days

WHY DO WE have to call it "cheating"? It's such a loaded term. Cheating on a partner is bad. Cheating at Scrabble by subtly attempting to look a word up on Google is bad. Cheating on *The Sims* by typing "Rosebud" to get more money for expansions on a house . . . well, that one isn't so bad, but the point remains—we shouldn't think of our relationship to food in terms of cheating or not cheating. This mentality is toxic.

Many diets incorporate cheat days to prevent loss of motivation and to overcome plateaus in weight loss. It is believed that cheat days improve adherence and maintain metabolic rate. Few things cause a craving more than knowing you can't have a certain food. Diets tend to cause a preoccupation with and increased cravings for foods viewed as "bad." While the rules of a "cheat day" vary from diet to diet, the general concept remains the same: You are allowed forbidden foods when your diet god determines it is appropriate. If your cheat day is Friday and today is Thursday, too bad. It doesn't matter if your family is gathering around pastrami sandwiches or if your menstrual cycle arrives and you need chocolate: Rules are rules, buttercup; stay strong so you can reach that goal you are focused on.

Research regarding cheat days is mixed because of the variation in personalities, relationship with food, and past dieting success. One theory holds that during initial weight loss, cheat days should be avoided. After two or three months of successful dieting and weight loss, one cheat day per week is acceptable. The cheat day might help the person feel less drawn to desirable foods and therefore maintain their motivation to stay on diet. The theory supporting cheating, which is a reward-based strategy, is that allowing moments of indulgence supports increased longevity of a diet.[1]

Here are two perspectives on cheat days:

THE BIOLOGICAL PERSPECTIVE: Incorporating a cheat meal increases metabolism, which causes calories to be burned quicker. Calories burn quicker because of increased levels of leptin, the main hormone responsible for maintaining energy balance in the body, which is secreted by fat cells. When a body usually limits its caloric intake and then one day significantly increases it, leptin is produced at a higher rate, which results in hunger suppression. When we eat less, we lose more. This is extremely appealing to people who want to lose weight. Supporters of the cheat-meal strategy believe that intermittent times of higher caloric intake will trick the hormone cycle into producing more leptin and reduce overconsumption of food. However, as Ian wondered, is this theory or reality?

THE MENTAL PERSPECTIVE: Allowing people to cheat serves as motivation to stick to diet foods throughout the week. It's the psychology of food: the theory that food viewed as a temptation loses its pull because it can be enjoyed on a cheat day. When food loses its power, the likelihood of binge behavior is reduced. Further, when

1. N. Byrne, et al., "Intermittent Energy Restriction Improves Weight Loss Efficiency in Obese Men: The MATADOR Study," *International Journal of Obesity* 42 (2018): 129–38, https://doi.org/10.1038/ijo.2017.206.

people diet, they often feel the need to avoid social gatherings altogether because of the difficulty of saying no when surrounded by everyone else saying yes. Cheat days can allow for more social flexibility.

Ian uses this system and has successfully maintained his weight loss. He acknowledges the possibility that he might be reinforcing the toxic relationship with food that he's sustained for so many years. He recognizes that a "proper" model for healthy eating is to activate mindful food engagements all the time. He knows this and believes that it is too difficult to be mindful with every meal all the time. Considering his personality and his past (unsuccessful) attempts at all-or-nothing dieting, cheat days might be the best solution for him. It might be the lesser of two evils. This approach may support him in controlling his dietary consumption 144 hours of his week and allow for free-for-all eating 24 hours of his week while maintaining the weight that's important to him.

In contrast, every time I tried to incorporate a cheat day during a diet, it became exponentially harder to return to the script the next day. I experienced sugar cravings, headaches, stomachaches, irritation, and FOMO watching my husband enjoy the leftover pad see ew while I ate my prescribed meal. Cheat meals always added 1 to 3 pounds on the scale that resulted in self-hatred and disappointment. The more cheat foods I ate, the more cheat foods I would think of, only realizing it was too late, and I would have to wait until the next cheat day. Cheat days were especially hard for me because of my tendency to engage in emotion-based eating. When I had a stressful, joyous, or intense moment, food wasn't an option, unless it was a cheat day.

With more of my patients asking about the effectiveness of a cheat day, I have learned that my opinions about it must be more flexible. We have normalized cheat days in our diets and even brag about them. People proudly show evidence of their cheat days on social media, claiming, "It works for me!" Cheat days are being used to validate restrictive eating as healthy, and I believe that the more we support the concept of cheat days, the longer diet culture will steal our money and minds. Eating healthy regularly is ideal, of course, but it's not the only way to achieve health. When we adopt a cheat meal/day/week/month (Thanksgiving to Christmas, anyone?) and subscribe to dieting for the rest of the time, we are reinforcing our deep co-dependence on diet culture.

Whenever my patients inquire about cheat days, I ask them to consider some questions: What are you skipping on diet days? Good food? Life satisfaction? More important, perhaps, what are you allowing yourself on diet days? These diet days are most of your days, right? Are you yearning for your next cheat meal every moment? Are you taking any time to appreciate the nutrients you are consuming? Limiting oneself to fruits, vegetables, and protein with a sour attitude is no way to live. That diet will certainly support a wedding-ready body, but for many, it's not satisfying enough to remain committed to for life beyond the big day.

Even just thinking about committing to a new lifestyle is a major emotional undertaking. When we select a new diet, and it tells us to only think of "on-diet" foods, our minds naturally drift. Eating healthy food can be addictive because of how good the nutrients make us feel and how smoothly our minds and effortlessly our bodies function. Unfortunately, eating less-healthy foods can be even more addictive because of the way our bodies respond to sugar, fat, and salt.

Categorizing food as good or bad, right or wrong, on-diet or off-diet only feeds diet mentality and drives the desire to go off the rails. When your doctor discourages you from smoking or eating gluten because your health is suffering, even if you agree with them to some extent, you end up wanting more smokes or chasing more breadsticks than before. When something presents as off-limits, we think about it considerably more than we would normally. This is what cheat days do to us.

Ian claims that he needs cheat days. He says when he eats healthy, he does his best to view food as fuel, but sometimes it feels super restrictive. This feeling of restriction is to be expected when dieting. Following a prescribed and rigid diet eliminates the opportunity for a body to have a say in what it's getting. If taste buds are trained to prefer Popeyes on Monday, Subway on Tuesday, Mom's lasagna on Wednesday and Thursday, and Safeway Chinese food on Friday, it's going to take significant adjustment to retrain a palate, but fortunately, it's a realistic possibility. It happens all the time. During that adjustment phase, it might take some willpower and discipline, but it's temporary, not lifelong. Eventually, bodies won't crave or even tolerate excessive amounts of sugar, food coloring, or fried chicken every day. Instead, as Ian reports, bodies will feel like crap following a meal from Jack in the Box.

Today I am a fat and healthy person who eats a balanced diet most days because that's how my body thrives. I didn't pay some company for this diet; my husband and I have curated it over the years. I don't need or benefit from cheat days. I indulge sometimes, but not as often as I used to. The way I eat will never result in having a body that meets the requirements of the thin ideal, but I know what getting thin requires, and that's not a lifestyle I want to obsess over for the rest of my life.

Breaking the dieting cycle requires understanding what caused you to feel dependent on a diet in the first place. What is your dieting cycle? When and how did it start? On the heels of being bummed about pants being too tight? Following a scary doctor's appointment? Do you eat "on diet" six days a week and eat "off diet" one day a week? Are those days set in stone? Or do they vary depending on your birthday, trips home, stand-up tour dates, Thanksgiving, Christmas, New Year's, your wife's birthday, and the anniversary of when Eddie ate spaghetti for the first time? Step back and analyze each of the habits that reinforce one another to create that cycle. They are typically based on rewards and fear. The most effective strategy for weight loss and maintenance is following a sustainable diet with foods that are enjoyable and promote health. In other words, choose a lifestyle that you can commit to so that cheat days aren't even necessary.

The Eyes of the Beholder

WHAT IS HELPFUL for a fat person depends on who is delivering the information and what that information is. Good help should not harm and soothe; it should enlighten and support. As Ian and I have detailed in this book, being a fat person means being constantly on the receiving end of different forms of harm. The only way to escape childhood fat-shaming is to grow up to be an adult who is fat-shamed—or to lose weight. Fat-shaming occurs everywhere and for all time.

Ian and James Corden have both experienced the heartache of being fat for most of their lives. At times they have gotten ahead of the shamers by becoming them. However, they have also used their platform to enlighten and support those who need it most, the fat viewers who can't escape the realities of their bodies. It is assumed that once fat people get help with their diet and lose some weight, all their problems disappear and they become psychologically healthy. This is untrue; good help includes addressing the whole person.

While being "too fat" can be dangerous, prejudice toward fat people and weight stigma can be more harmful than the physical health concerns that are associated with fatness. In recent studies of how to best support people who are fat, the research focus has shifted from *whether* fatness is related to greater psychological distress to *which* fat people are at increased risk for mental health concerns. Further, researchers are starting to explore the question of whether depression causes increased weight or increased weight causes depression, as it remains unclear how they coexist.[1]

What the data tells us is that mental health is on the line, and because of this, the quality of help received is really important. If a fat person feels ready to accept support in their pursuit of health, they must be the one who determines the source of the help. The recommendation is for good help to come from an influential person whom the individual trusts, someone who will understand the implications of any lifestyle changes the individual will need to make. The individual might perceive help from well-intentioned and concerned family members as an unwelcome intervention and shut those people out. Healthcare professionals who have been well-trained in discussing weight-related concerns can be a great source, if the individual is ready, willing, and able to listen.

When Ian was young, he was supported by his family in very subtle ways. Supporting a family member, especially a young person, can do more harm than good because it can be hard to know the correct words to say and how to say them. When he was older and felt ready to address his weight, Ian sought counsel from a doctor.

1. J. Zhang, "The Bidirectional Relationship Between Body Weight and Depression Across Gender: A Simultaneous Equation Approach," *International Journal of Environmental Research and Public Health* 18, no. 14 (2021): 7673, https://doi.org/10.3390/ijerph18147673; C. Ross, "Overweight and Depression," *Journal of Health and Social Behavior* 35 (1994): 63–79, https://doi.org/10.2307/2137335; D. P. Guh, W. Zhang, N. Bansback, et al., "The Incidence of Co-morbidities Related to Obesity and Overweight: A Systematic Review and Meta-Analysis," *BMC Public Health* 9 (2009): 88, https://doi.org/10.1186/1471-2458-9-88.

For many fat people, approaching a doctor about weight is terrifying, but it made a difference for Ian, a life-changing difference. The doctor didn't sugarcoat his recommendations, and when Ian was ready, he made adjustments to his diet and lifestyle. Good help is out there, and it is available in many forms. Determining when, where, and from whom to seek support is entirely in the eyes of the beholder.

ACKNOWLEDGMENTS

When my brother and I initially thought of writing this book together, we were in the trenches of another diet. We lived in separate cities with very different day-to-day lives, and yet our shared mission to be healthier kept us unified. We checked in with each other more often than ever before. During our phone calls, we discussed the hundreds of challenges we faced, overcame, and were often defeated by—offering one another validation and love. I found these sweet phone calls to be incredibly important for my sanity and well-being. They reminded me that I wasn't alone in my fatness despite feeling so isolated. Thank you, Ian. Thank you for invariably having my back, especially when we were young and fat. Thank you for continuing to believe in me while we wrote this important and cathartic book together. We did it!

To my husband, Tyler, thank you. You are the definition of unconditional love. You remained by my side every step of the way, always happy to challenge my doubt with empowering words, provided constant writing and editorial support, and welcomed collaborative brainstorming at every meal and walk. I could not have written this book without your unwavering companionship. Importantly, thanks for keeping me fed throughout this whole process, my husband. And to my daughter, Sophia. Thank you for making me a mom. When I started this book, you were merely a dream. I was told I wouldn't be able to get pregnant because of my weight. And yet, as I write this acknowledgment, you, my healthy little baby, are resting peacefully in my arms. I promise to love you through all your shapes and sizes as you explore your curiosities in the world.

To my mother, Sue Karmel, thank you. You've consistently encouraged me to find my strength and use my voice when something wasn't right. You have never missed a call when I needed support after being fat-shamed. There is no greater love that I feel from anyone else more than you. Your unconditional belief in me, your little-most, has taught me to love and believe in myself. While it might have taken me a while, I finally understand. To my father, Ivan Karmel, thank you. No matter how crazy my ideas have been, you have always reminded me that I am bright and capable, and to never sell myself short. I believe my fearlessness in setting and achieving difficult goals is due to regularly participating in "Daddy's Deadly Adventures," where you taught me to be tough because I'm a Karmel.

Thank you to the rest of my incredible family: Jessica, thank you for educating me so sweetly to love and embrace my body since my beginning. Rob, thank you for being the protector of this family, and Nick, thank you for being the silent strength. And thank you to my siblings' partners, Ty, Meg, and Dana, for believing in me, and for my nieces and my nephews. Thank you to my Nana for teaching me strength and the power of impermanence—always reminding me when things are difficult that "this too shall pass." I love you the most; my aunt Danielle, thank you for checking in with me every week about my writing process. To my cousin Crosby, thank you for sending me supportive texts nearly every day. And thank you Griffey, my dog, who rested with me every time I sat down to write.

To my supervisor, Michael Fulop, thank you. You gave me the courage I needed to apply to advanced education. When I failed and my other professors turned their backs on me, you stood by my side.

You have taught me the most important lesson from all my studies, and that is to build a relationship with each new patient before ever providing an intervention.

A heartfelt thank-you to the wonderful humans who over the years have trusted me with your health journeys. Every one of you has helped me to become the clinician I am today.

—ALISA KARMEL

I'd like to thank my wife, Dana, for her love, support, insight, and motivation, and for her uncanny ability to bring me a cup of tea at the exact moment my eyes started glazing over while I was writing this book. I also want to thank her for reassuring me "this is normal" as I had a panic attack about every single aspect of writing this book. I'm grateful for every moment of my life, whether painful or joyful, because they led me to you. When the noise of the world goes quiet and the only light is the lamp next to my bed, I look at you sleeping and know for certain that I've gotten the best out of this life because I get to spend it with you.

I'd like to thank the friends who were there for me at every stage of my life. I dwell on a lot of agony in this book, but I was laughing through it all, because I've had the funniest, sweetest friends that anyone could ask for—from preschool all the way through to the very moment I'm writing this sentence. I especially have to thank Nic Nanpei and Sean Jordan.

The biggest thank-you that I'm capable of giving goes to Matthew Benjamin, who edited this book. Alisa and I pulled this story out of our souls. It was messy, disorganized, scattered, and twice as long as it was supposed to be. You rolled your sleeves up and showed us how to turn that into a proper book. You're a prince, and I'll miss our phone calls that would always start out about the book and end an hour later, having talked about everything under the sun. Thank you, thank you, thank you, and thank you to everyone at Rodale Books and Penguin Random House. Thank you to the copy editor. Thank you to the cover artist. Thank you.

I'd like to thank Kara Baker and Rachel Rusch, who have been with me since day one. Your advice and advocacy have made a huge difference in my career, but your friendship and kindness have been an even more important part of my life.

Thank you to Anthony Mattero for getting this book off the ground. Thank you to Ari Levin for putting me on the road. Thank you to everyone at CAA and Avalon for all the impossibly hard work you do while people like me get the credit.

Thank you to Chelsea Handler for giving me my first break and being the most generous stand-up comedian I've ever met in my entire life. Thank you, too, for the constant advocacy and inspiration for stand-up comedians who write books.

James Corden. Two funny fat kids making a TV show. You're a friend and a role model and easily the best FIFA player I know.

Thank you to Ben Winston, Rob Crabbe, James Longman, Josie Cliff, Lauren Greenberg, Louis Waymouth, CeCe Pleasants, and so many other people at *The Late Late Show*.

I'd like to thank the Portland Trail Blazers. Please win a championship in my lifetime, but it's okay if you don't. I still love you.

I need to thank my family. Bear, Jess, Nick, Meg, Ty, Tyler, Maya, Jack, Wyatt, Mikey, Maci, Sophia. I love you all so much. See you at karaoke.

I want to thank Nana, my aunts and uncles, my cousins, and everyone I love to see even though I don't see them enough.

Thank you to the Schwartz family for making me feel like one of the gang from the very first time we met. I hope this shout-out catapults me back to the top of the Favorite Son-in-Law rankings. Sorry, Jeff.

A special thank-you to my little sister, Alisa, co-author of this book. You wrote three full books' worth of books while writing this book, in addition to finishing your doctorate and having a baby. You're amazing. I'm lucky I got to write this book with you. I'm even luckier that I get to go through life with you.

Thank you to everyone who has listened to *All Fantasy Every-thing*, everyone who has come to see me do stand-up, everyone who has watched something I helped create, and everyone who reads this book. I get to make my living making people laugh. I will never get over that.

Thank you to the *Portland Mercury* for giving me my first writing gig. Thank you to Portland State University for giving me a chance to learn. Thank you to Portland for being the greatest city in the world.

Thank you to Tom Johnson and Scott Parker, my comedy fathers.

Thank you to Roxane Gay, Lindy West, Aubrey Gordon, and everyone else who has written about being fat in a way that demands our humanity.

Thank you to apples for being delicious, even though they're good for you. What else? Oh . . .

Thank you to my mom and dad. You gave me life and then you made sure that life was a good one. Your love, hard work, sacrifice, and wisdom are the foundation of everything in me that is worth a damn. I struggled with loving myself. I still do. Through all of that I never felt unloved, because I had you. There isn't a greater gift you can give someone, and I don't take it for granted for a second.

Mom, you taught me that love is presence. You showed me the importance of showing up. Your support and unwavering belief in me gave me the courage to pursue outlandish dreams. If I had become a bank robber, you'd be bragging to your friends about my lavish collection of small unmarked bills and unexploded dye packs. You're a confidante and a counselor, and don't tell Dad, but you're the reason I'm funny.

Dad, I couldn't ask for a better father. You showed me basketball, books about the Civil War, and the Firesign Theatre, and now that's pretty much my entire personality. You taught me how to be tough, you showed me the importance of hard work, you inspired me to grow a mustache. Your absurd sense of humor and impeccable sense of style are traits I can only hope that I inherited. Don't tell Mom, but you're the reason I'm funny.

—IAN KARMEL

ABOUT THE AUTHORS

IAN KARMEL is an Emmy-winning comedian, television writer, podcaster, newspaper columnist, and television personality. He was the co–head writer of *The Late Late Show with James Corden* and has worked on *Chelsea Lately*, the Grammys, the Tonys, and *Who Is America?* with Sacha Baron Cohen.

ALISA KARMEL holds a doctorate in clinical psychology and a master's in nutrition. She provides counseling for weight-centric concerns, including issues related to fatness, obesity, and overweight, such as body acceptance; health behavior improvement; and depression, anxiety, trauma, and other mood disorders.

ABOUT THE TYPE

This book was set in Garamond, a typeface originally designed by the Parisian type cutter Claude Garamond (c. 1500–61). This version of Garamond was modeled on a 1592 specimen sheet from the Egenolff-Berner foundry, which was produced from types assumed to have been brought to Frankfurt by the punch cutter Jacques Sabon (c. 1520–80).

Claude Garamond's distinguished romans and italics first appeared in *Opera Ciceronis* in 1543–44. The Garamond types are clear, open, and elegant.

A portion of this book was set in Optima, a sans serif typeface with a neoclassical flavor. It was designed in 1952–55 by Hermann Zapf (b. 1918) and issued by both Stempel and Linotype in 1958.